Thriving on the Front Lines

Youth and Family Services (YFS) are part of residential and group homes, schools, social service organizations, hospitals, and family court systems. YFS include prevention, education, positive youth development, foster care, child welfare, and treatment. As YFS has evolved advances in research have brought forth a host of promising new ideas that both complement and expand on the original underpinnings of strengths-based practice. *Thriving on the Front Lines* represents an articulation of these advancements.

Thriving on the Front Lines explores the use of strengths-based practices with those who are "in the trenches," youth care workers (YCWs). Commonly referred to as resident counselors, youth counselors, psychiatric technicians (psych techs), caseworkers, case managers, and house parents or managers, YCWs are on the "front lines," often providing services 24 hours a day. *Thriving on the Front Lines* is an up-to-date treatise on the pivotal role of YCWs and those who work day in and day out with youth to improve their well-being, relationships, and overall quality of life.

Unique aspects of the strengths-based framework provided in *Thriving on the Front Lines* include:

- strengths-based principles informed by five decades of research
- discussion of the importance of using real-time feedback to improve service outcomes and "how to" implement an outcome-orientation
- exploration of positive youth development
- two chapters devoted entirely to strengths-based interventions
- an in-depth discussion of how to improve effectiveness through deliberate practice
- how to develop a strengths-based organizational climate.

Bob Bertolino, PhD, is Associate Professor of Rehabilitation Counseling at Maryville University, Missouri, USA, and Senior Clinical Advisor at Youth in Need, Inc. He is also Senior Associate for the International Center for Clinical Excellence (ICCE), and he maintains a private practice and provides consultation and training.

Thriving on the Front Lines

A Guide to Strengths-Based
Youth Care Work

BOB BERTOLINO

Routledge
Taylor & Francis Group

NEW YORK AND LONDON

First published 2014
by Routledge
711 Third Avenue, New York, NY 10017

and by Routledge
27 Church Road, Hove, East Sussex BN3 2FA

Routledge is an imprint of the Taylor & Francis Group,
an informa business

Library of Congress Cataloging-in-Publication Data
Bertolino, Bob, 1965–
Thriving on the front lines : a guide to strengths-based youth care
  work / Bob Bertolino.— 1st Edition.
    pages cm
  Includes bibliographical references and index.
  1. Youth—Counseling of.   2. Adolescent psychotherapy.
3. Solution-focused therapy.   I. Title.
  HV1421.B47 2013
  362.7083—dc23
  2013037214

ISBN: 978-0-415-89521-7 (pbk)
ISBN: 978-1-315-79712-0 (ebk)

Typeset in Minion
by Apex CoVantage, LLC

Printed and bound in the United States of America by Sheridan Books, Inc. (a Sheridan Group Company).

EAst Hampton Continuum

Dedication

To Jim Braun: A world-class leader, champion for children, youth, and families, and extraordinary man. Thank you for showing me the way.

Contents

Preface

Only a life lived for others is a life worthwhile.

—Albert Einstein

In 1989 I was hired on as a residential counselor at an emergency crisis shelter for runaway and homeless youth. The "shelter," as it is known, is part of Youth In Need (YIN), Inc., a nonprofit community-based organization in the Midwest. At the time of my hire, YIN was a small agency with fewer than 30 employees and had an annual budget of about $500,000. In the decade that followed I continued my education and advanced through the ranks of YIN. In addition to resident counselor, I held positions as a drug and alcohol prevention case manager, Shelter youth and family therapist, and Shelter Director. As YIN grew into a nationally renowned organization I was afforded opportunities to develop both personally and professionally.

I began to write about my experiences at YIN and in the field of youth and family services (YFS) in the late 1990s. My aim was to contribute to the limited pool of resources available to those who worked "in the trenches" in YFS. I wanted to further the existing body of literature in three specific ways. The first was to formally introduce the term "youth care worker" (YCW) to capture and define the multiple roles of staff who work with youth and families, particularly in residential settings. A second way I hoped to expand on the available literature was to describe a *competency* or *strengths-based* approach within the field of YFS. Last was the identification of specific strengths-based practices that YCWs could employ on an interaction by interaction, shift-by-shift basis in areas such as assessment, crisis, and staff meetings.

I have now been at YIN for over two decades, working in programs ranging from prevention to treatment to administration in the roles of supervisor, director, vice-president, consultant, and advisor. Experiencing YFS in these different roles has taught me more about successful programs and organizations. What I am most proud of is that strengths-based practice has become the standard in organizations from coast to coast. At YIN, for example, which now boasts over 350 employees and an annual budget of around $18,000,000, a commitment to strengths-based practice can be found in its initial job training curriculum. *Every* YIN employee completes the training, "Strengths-Based 101," on his or her hire (Bertolino, 2011). Throughout this book, we will learn about agencies and programs whose foundations are built on strengths-based ideas and practices.

As YFS has evolved advances in research have brought forth a host of promising new ideas that both complement and expand on the original underpinnings of strengths-based practice (see Bertolino, 2003, 2010; Bertolino & O'Hanlon, 2002). This book represents an articulation of these advancements. In addition, it extends the use of strengths-based ideas beyond traditional residential settings to the numerous others that rely on the contributions of front line staff (who we will refer to as "YCWs") for delivery of successful services. This book is for those persons who work day in and day out with youth to improve their well-being, relationships, and overall quality of life.

How This Book is Arranged

Thriving on the Front Lines delves into issues YCWs face on the front lines and, more importantly, what can be done to meet the challenges of those issues. This book is organized into eight chapters, each with a distinct focus on an area essential to YFS and the role of the YCW. What follows is an overview of the chapters.

Chapter 1 is *Fingerprints: Becoming a Difference-Maker.* Research makes it clear that effective YCWs share several common characteristics. It is equally clear that no amount of training in method or technique will make one a better YCW if his or her worldview is closed down to the idea of change, the importance of hope, the promise of possibility, and the role of strengths. Chapter 1 is dedicated to the personal exploration of worldview and the influence that our "personal philosophies" have on what we do and how we do it as YCWs.

Chapter 2 is *Foundations: Principles of Strengths-Based Youth Care Work.* In this chapter, we will learn about the core principles of a strengths-based approach. Of particular importance is the empirical evidence that informs these principles. Readers will learn how multiple research perspectives contribute to and support strengths-based ideas and how YCWs can import these ideas into everyday practice.

Chapter 3 is *Engagement: Creating and Strengthening Relationships.* In this chapter, we will explore, in detail, numerous ways of engaging youth and families from the outset of services and how to strengthen those partnerships as services continue. Included in this chapter are sections on factors that enhance engagement, the role of collaboration, how to foster cooperation, language as a vehicle for change, and ways to respond to relationships ruptures.

In Chapter 4, *Directions: Information-Gathering and Planning*, we will learn specific ways to collaborate with youth and families to gather important information, assess both risks and strengths, set goals, and create service plans. This chapter includes a wealth of information that can be used at different points of service.

Chapter 5 is *Possibilities, Part 1: Strategies for Changing Views*. Because there are no one-size-fits-all methods, it is important to have a range of intervention strategies to draw on. In this chapter, YCWs will learn about various strengths-based affective, cognitive, behavioral, and relational techniques that can be used to facilitate change and growth in YFS. A crucial aspect of this chapter is discussion about how to select methods and ensure they are a good fit for YCWs, youth, and the context.

Possibilities, Part 2: Strategies for Changing Actions and Interactions follows. This companion chapter to Chapter 5 includes two sections of methods for helping youth and supportive others involved to change patterns of behavior. The first section offers ideas to engage youth in activities aimed at boosting well-being. The second section involves strategies to alter or modify problem patterns or import solution sequences that have been used successfully in the past.

Chapter 7, *Exchanges: Progress and Transitions*, delves into two major areas of YFS. The chapter begins with discussion about the role of teams in YFS and in particular, how meetings, such as staffings, can be used to create new possibilities in stuck situations and better connect staff to one another. The second part of Chapter 7 explores subsequent interactions and two primary variations of youth responses to services: "No improvement/deterioration" and "improvement." Detailed follow-up strategies are offered for each category of response.

The final chapter of the book is *Better: Achieving Excellence in Youth and Family Services*. This chapter explores YCW development and performance. In the first part of the chapter, ideas are offered for how to evaluate the performance of YCWs and increase proficiency through specific steps known as "deliberate practice." Implications for training are also discussed. The chapter concludes with discussion about ways for YCWs to get the most out of their experiences and careers.

To bring the ideas offered in the book alive and connect them to everyday practice, each chapter includes case illustrations, stories, sample dialogues, and discussion questions. Also included are two appendices. Appendix A includes outcome measures discussed in the book and adjoining tools for use with those measures. Appendix B has multiple forms that can be used in different settings in YFS. Examples include intake assessments, service plans, discharge summaries, and a form for service plans and discharge summaries.

A Few Words about Words

In a field as broad as YFS, language and terminology presents a risk of sorts. There is an old Zen tale of a teacher pointing to the sky at an arrangement of stars. As the Zen master tells a story about the stars and constellations, he notices his students staring intensely at the finger he is using to point. When the Zen master realizes what is happening he says, "Look to the sky, not at my finger!" This is an appropriate analogy in YFS. It serves as a reminder that, as we delve into examples and illustrations, we do not lose sight of the human condition and relationships, which cannot be adequately captured by definitions, jargon, or other syntax commonly used in mental health, social services, and educational circles. We want to maintain focus on our primary mission of helping youth and families. This means not getting caught up in semantics.

For the purposes of this book, the term "youth" will be used in reference to the ages eight through 21. Although I've chosen to emphasize this age range, the ideas described throughout have been and can be easily adapted to services offered to younger children and adults. This book is about how we can provide respectful and effective services within any program that serves youth and families.

I will refer to a variety of contexts and situations in which YFS are offered and YCWs practice. In doing so, I will periodically use terms including, but not limited to counseling, therapy, prevention, education, investigation, case management, social services, and so on. These descriptors are meant to highlight specific types of service. I will also use terms such as interactions, meetings, sessions, appointments, and intakes interchangeably. Although the terminology may need to be adjusted given the different environments in which YCWs are working, again, it is the ideas that are paramount. Believe in and live the ideas and the techniques will evolve out those philosophical underpinnings.

It has been said that if you practice something long enough it becomes yours. This is an invitation to take the pages of this book and transform them into something that fits for you and the context within which you work. Please make these ideas and practices yours.

—Bob Bertolino

Acknowledgments

My love, appreciation, and gratitude to my family—Misha, Morgan, and Claire. Thank you for understanding my purpose, for supporting me, and accepting me for who I am. To my mom, dad, stepmom, and brothers and sisters for always being there and showing interest in whatever I'm doing at the moment. You are what matters most to me.

I have spent my entire professional career working in the nonprofit sector. It's where my heart is. During this time I have had the good fortune of working at Youth In Need, Inc. (YIN) for more than two decades. The experience changes my life every day. I feel blessed to say those words because it almost didn't happen.

You see, after 17 years at YIN I accepted a full-time faculty position at Maryville University in St. Louis in 2006. I expected that doing so would reduce my nonprofit work to consulting and workshops. After my decision I asked to meet with our then Senior Vice-President and Chief Operations Officer (COO), Pat Holterman-Hommes, who became President and CEO of YIN in 2013. Before I spoke a word Pat said, "You aren't resigning are you?" I was sad to tell her I was. Pat did not hesitate, "We need you. You are a big part of YIN." I was humbled to the core. She then said something that I will never forget, "You will always have a place here."

We went on to work out an arrangement for me to stay part time at YIN. I am so glad we did. This book is largely about YIN.

I therefore want to express my deep appreciation to my colleagues and mentors at YIN, in particular, members of the Executive Management Team, Pat Holterman-Hommes, Tricia Topalbegovic, Michelle Gorman, Mark Solari, Rob Muschany, April Delehaunty, Amy Putzler, Keri Young, and Tom Owens. To Amy Brown and

Melanie Rodman who everyday exemplify YIN's strengths-based philosophy and are true ambassadors for children and youth. To Chris Turner and Cara Merritt— no organization can succeed without people like you. Thank you all for your belief in me and each other. You and the hundreds of other past and present staff at YIN show what a group of people with a unified mission and vision can do to change the world.

I would not have accepted a job at Maryville University if it were not for the people there. Maryville is a wonderful place and deserving as U.S. News & World Report's top over-performing university in the country in both 2012 and 2013. In particular I would like to thank Drs. Michael Kiener, Mya Vaughn, and Kate Kline, my colleagues in the Rehabilitation Counseling program, Dr. Chuck Gulas, Dean of the College of Health Professions, and the faculty in the CHP who greatly value interdisciplinary education. And lastly, to my current and former students at MU: Thank you for opening up your minds and hearts and for a willingness to challenge yourself to grow. I continue to learn from you.

A big thank you to colleagues and friends whose camaraderie has helped shape (and warp) me over the years especially Scott Miller, Bill O'Hanlon, Charlie Appelstein, and Calvin Smith of the Vermont Coalition of Runaway and Homeless Youth Programs, and colleagues at the International Center for Clinical Excellence (ICCE).

I end by extending my heartfelt gratitude to the Routledge/Taylor & Francis family. Thank you to George Zimmar, Marta Moldvai, and Elizabeth Graber for your vision, patience, and support. I am grateful to be part of the Routledge family.

one
Fingerprints: Becoming a Difference-Maker

Search and see if there is not some place where you may invest your humanity.

—Albert Schweitzer

Of the many aspirations I had in my formative years, working in youth and family services (YFS) was not one of them. I landed in the field by happenstance when I answered an advertisement for a position with a nonprofit community-based organization. My aim then was simple: Find a job that would allow me the flexibility to continue my undergraduate studies and simultaneously moonlight as a musician. What followed was much more—a journey that changed the course of my life.

My career began as a resident counselor or "RC" (a position that has since been renamed, "youth care worker" or YCW) at an emergency shelter for 10–18-year-olds who were homeless, displaced, and/or in crisis. Youth who came to the "shelter" typically remained for a few days to a month, depending on their situations. Many returned home. Others transitioned to long-term settings such as residential placement, transitional or independent living, or foster care. As with all services, there were also youth who left without achieving the change or improvement we had hoped for. The purpose of this book is to provide front line staff with effective practice strategies to increase the benefit of services to youth and spell a reduction in youth who dropout or leave services prematurely and without measurable, positive improvement.

Given the substantive variation in what constitutes YFS and the capacities in which YCWs serve, we will begin with an exploration of two areas:

1   the scope of youth and family services (YFS)
2   the role of the youth care worker (YCW).

The remainder of this chapter will include the following four sections: Lessons from the Front Lines, Personal Philosophy, and Activating Your *Positive* Deviance, and Pillars of Positive Deviance.

The Scope of Youth and Family Services

Broadly defined, YFS include programs that provide safe and respectful education, prevention, therapeutic (treatment), and support services that foster growth and development. Therapeutic programs are perhaps the most widely utilized form of YFS; however, programs that focus on child abuse and neglect (i.e., child protection), case management, foster care and/or adoption (i.e., child welfare), court-based services, and referral and crisis hotlines, and youth development can be found through the U.S. and most regions of the world. YFS are provided in offices, homes, residential programs, schools, corrections facilities, hospitals, drop-in centers, and other settings that serve youth and families.

YFS can be voluntary (i.e., client initiated, optional) or involuntary (i.e., mandated or court ordered, etc.) with varying eligibility requirements. Some programs base eligibility on factors such as income, age, location of residence (where one lives), and severity of problem. For example, a youth may need to be assigned a psychiatric diagnosis, meet pre-established criteria (e.g., severely emotionally disturbed [SED]; severe and persistent mental illness [SPMI]), or some other form of categorization (e.g., victim of crime, sexual offender/perpetrator, etc.) to qualify for services. Some programs have few or no eligibility requirements, depending on how they are funded. Programs can be financially supported through contracts, grants, foundations, private donations, third-party payers (i.e., insurance, etc.), and may involve out-of-pocket payment by recipients.

Many organizations are multifaceted, offering a combination of the aforementioned services. These are sometimes referred to as "one-stop" organizations. YFS may also be provided through a constituency of agencies or community networks. In these instances, each agency offers a specific type of service that typically falls on a continuum of care. For example, one organization may provide residential care while another fulfills educational needs. The success of YFS is contingent on these collaborative, community-based efforts, which are often referred to as "systems of care." As the African proverb goes, "It takes a village to raise a child." To provide the best possible continuum of care, social service and mental health organizations, educational institutions, court systems, and other providers and support services have to work together, from policy through service provision. When systems and services are inadequate and fail, more youth and families suffer. We must keep in mind, however, that systems are run by people. It has been said that failure in YFS is the result of youth falling through the cracks. Perhaps a more accurate statement is that youth slip through people's fingers, which is an entirely preventable problem.

The Role of the Youth Care Worker

Youth in programs (most commonly out-of-home placements) that employ YCWs are very often from highly vulnerable populations. These youth lack positive support systems, experience isolation, live in fear, and are sometimes resentful (Barford & Whelton, 2010; Frensch & Cameron, 2002). In addition, they often have significant psychological, behavioral, and emotional problems, and may become verbally and/or physically aggressive, engage in self-harming behaviors, and act out sexually.

YCWs play a vital and yet underappreciated role in YFS. It is the job of YCWs to guide youth through their daily routines and for carrying out day-to-day services in runaway and homeless shelters, residential group homes, inpatient psychiatric facilities, correction centers, transitional and independent living programs, foster homes, and alternative schools. Depending on the program and setting, YCWs may also be referred to as resident counselors, youth counselors, psychiatric technicians (psych techs), caseworkers, case managers, and house parents or managers. YCWs can be found in administrative, operations, training, and supervisory capacities, however, their primary role is to provide direct service. General duties of YCWs include:

- Providing safety, care, supervision, discipline, and emotional support to youth.
- Completing and/or overseeing daily program tasks and functions.
- Conducting face-to-face or telephonic screenings and/or intake interviews (assessments).
- Meeting formally or informally with youth.
- Leading educational, support, and/or treatment groups.
- Managing crises with youth and in programs.
- Participating in the physical upkeep of facilities.
- Participating as part of a team that may include other mental health and social service workers, health professionals, and educators.

The responsibilities of YCWs do not end with formal job descriptions. To this end, most YCWs are familiar with the phrase, "other duties as assigned." YCWs are in effect the "go-to" persons—preserving the safety and well-being of youth while juggling multiple on-shift tasks. Any given day a YCW in a residential setting could be supervising a group of youth, working to resolve a conflict between two residents, and answering phone calls at the same time; all the while, paperwork awaits. YCWs not only have numerous responsibilities, they carry out those responsibilities in environments that are fast paced and require conscientious, "on-the-spot" decision-making. The role of the YCW is uniquely multifaceted.

YCWs may also assume dual roles. For example, a YCW may, in one instance, work with a youth who is in crisis, serving in more of a "therapeutic" capacity and then be required to take a position of authority and give the same youth a consequence. This duality can pose a challenge and yet over time YCWs learn how to engage youth and negotiate such situations.

Lessons from the Front Lines

So far we have delineated the primary responsibilities and actions of YCWs. But it is what happens day by day, shift by shift, and interaction by interaction that brings the job of YCW to life. Knowledge gained through experience is an extraordinary asset that grows over time. As expected, many lessons will be learned with some being more difficult than others. I experienced this first-hand in my first few months as a YCW. A few lessons could be considered mere subtext—proverbial "learning experiences." On more than one occasion, however, I considered leaving the field for an occupation with fewer "side effects." The worry, frustration, and guilt were overwhelming. There were times when I would leave shifts feeling sad—like I could have done more—or ill prepared—as if I didn't know what I was doing. Fortunately, the benefits of being in YFS far outweighed the side effects. I came to realize that there are few experiences in life that can surpass that of helping a young person in need to have the future he or she wants and deserves.

Two of the lessons I learned as a YCW remain with me today. One came fairly quickly, the other took longer to fully understand and appreciate. Both continue to serve as part of my philosophical foundation and I believe represent important lessons for YCWs.

Lesson 1: Let Youth Show Who They Are

Matt, a 15-year-old, came to the shelter after three years in residential placement, the second half of which was spent with the Missouri Division of Youth Services (DYS). DYS is a last resort for countless youth. It is prison for juveniles. Despite being separated from his family for three years and residing in settings that were at best, rough, if things went well at the shelter, Matt would return home to his family.

I wasn't on shift when Matt first arrived but I was aware of the chatter among staff. One RC described Matt as "super quiet" and "spooky." Another commented that he looked "suspicious." There was more. I heard that Matt's psychiatric diagnoses outnumbered his tattoos, which was quite remarkable since, from what I understood, he had four "colorful" tattoos on his left arm alone. The more I heard the more I wondered: What do I do with this information? Should I be cautious? Afraid? The stories of Matt told of violence and unpredictability. Even a seasoned YCW could be a little unnerved. And I was both unseasoned and unsure. Still, I was cautiously curious about Matt and what difference we, as a program, might make for him.

Aside from the stories being circulated about Matt there was his actual case file. I had grown accustomed to reading dense files and had learned that reports and assessments often provided narrow and negative descriptions of the youth we served. I wondered how labels and diagnoses could be considered science and witnessed how in worst cases they could stigmatize and demean youth. Matt had experienced this very thing when a psychologist labeled him as having a "pathological personality." He earned this label for such frightening behaviors as laughing at things that others might not consider funny, making crude jokes, a fondness for gory horror films, and a "dislike of mornings." The psychologist's description of Matt wasn't out of the ordinary for youth who came to the shelter. In much of the documentation that accompanied youth, it was hard to find anything positive. In Matt's case, his file read like a criminal rap sheet.

To be clear, it wasn't meeting a new youth that made me uneasy—and I was uneasy. I had met many youth. It was what I had heard and read about Matt that had me on edge. I had yet to even talk with the 15-year-old and my confidence had been undermined. I was, admittedly, "under the influence" of a perception.

Then I met Matt. Not the Matt characterized through stories. Not the Matt described on paper. I met the Matt who was nothing like what I had read or heard about. There was a quiet intensity about him that could be, and apparently had been, understood as threatening. He was a young man of few words, which again, led some persons to wonder about what kind of person he was. In a couple of shifts, I witnessed Matt's contagious laughter and ability to engage others through his infectious stories. As we got to know each other better, Matt opened up. He talked about his hopes and dreams. He was aware of his past mistakes and owned up to them. He made no excuses for the behavior that led to his out-of-home placement. What Matt sought was an opportunity to show others the kind of person he really was. That was the very reason the shelter program existed, to help youth like Matt to show who they were and make the most out of new opportunities.

Because Matt had been in out-of-home placements for an extensive period of time, and to create as smooth a transition as possible back home, his stay at the shelter was extended to 10 weeks. This was atypical since youth rarely stayed beyond 30 days. Matt made the most of his time in the program. He excelled through the shelter's level system to the point that a new level had to be created to accommodate his growth. He mentored other residents, helping them to learn about and adjust to the shelter program. Over the course of his stay Matt talked increasingly about his future plans and his actions revealed his growth. He completed work toward his GED (general educational development) and began to explore job options. Matt and I chatted about topics that ranged from cars to careers to what it's like to be in out-of-home placements. He was candid about where he'd been and where he wanted to go with his life. There was every reason to believe in him.

Matt's reunification with his family was a success. But his involvement with the agency did not end at discharge. A couple of years later Matt returned—this time as a formal youth volunteer. He went on to mentor residents at the shelter and even went to Washington, DC, to advocate for services for homeless and displaced youth.

Prior to Matt, I wondered if I had been *overestimating* the youth who came to the shelter. Perhaps I was too optimistic. A supervisor told me as much. Without knowing, Matt reaffirmed in me the importance of knowing *who* people are and separating that from *what* they are doing or have done. Each of us is responsible for what we do and there are, of course, consequences to actions. To help and support youth, who are among the most marginalized in society, we must focus on their capacities to make better decisions, be responsible, and grow. If we do not believe in youth, who will?

Lesson 2: Face Uncertainty with Genuineness and Sincerity

My second lesson did not come as quickly. Regardless of how may shifts I worked as a YCW, I could not shake the sensation that I did not know enough. I trusted in my ability to connect with youth yet I found myself saying, "There has to me more. I must be missing something." I studied other YCWs intently to learn how they did the job. I paid close attention in staff meetings, trainings, and in supervision. I read voraciously and watched videos created for YCWs. I asked questions of anyone who would lend me their attention—even if it was their partial attention. These efforts did little to boost my confidence. I felt it was a matter of time before others realized I was impersonating a YCW.

I concluded that I needed to ask better questions. Surely better questions would elicit more satisfactory responses. I understood that the answers I was seeking couldn't be found in the shelter's written training materials, so I pressed my peers and supervisors. I asked, "How do you know when a youth is _____ (having a flashback, thinking about running away, etc.)?" and "How can you tell that _____ (abuse, divorce, drinking, etc.) is the *main* issue?" and, "What do you do when a youth _____ (refuses to do what has been asked, threatens you, tries to pit you against another staff member, etc.)?" The responses of my peers fell into two general categories. The first was the "This is what you do" group. For these folks, there were specific answers to most situations. The second type of response fell into the "It depends" category. Responders in this group explained that contextual details (e.g., the personality or history of the youth; the type of problem, etc.) were strong determinants in how youth might react in given situations. In both categories of response, there were broad variations between staff, even though the questions were the same.

After hijacking the minds of numerous YIN staff, I came to realize the questions I was most interested in and that had the most influence on my confidence had no definitive answers. There were only ideas and preferred ways of doing things. I gathered that in most situations there were many possible reactions. It wasn't necessary to know the *right* answer. Instead, YCWs need sound rationale, common sense, and the ability to be creative. There was one other thing that became an important lesson in my development: *Face the prospects of uncertainty with genuineness and sincerity.*

It is okay to not know what lies ahead and to not have all the answers. What is required of each of us in YFS is a willingness to give of ourselves, maintain an open mind, and engage others in what sometimes amounts to walking along rocky terrain without knowing how things will turn out. Poet David Whyte (2011) has spoken of the importance of taking the risk to immerse one's self in the unknown:

> If you are sincere about your vocation you will get to thresholds where you will not know how to proceed . . . and where you will forget yourself . . . and where you will start to imprison yourself with the very endeavor that was first a doorway to freedom. And if you don't become disappointed in yourself you're not trying. There is actually no path a human can take with sincerity, with real courage that doesn't lead to heartbreak. It's astonishing how human beings spend an enormous amount of their energy and time turning away from that possibility; trying to arrange for a life where you won't be touched and where you will be left immune to the great forces and elements of life.

We enter YFS with our hearts wide open and an unwavering oath to do our best. No matter the level of commitment and preparation, there are elements of YFS that are unpredictable. At times things won't go as planned. We may become disappointed with ourselves and perhaps even question our abilities. In the face of such challenges it is important that we maintain our courage and patience and remain unfettered in our mission of promoting well-being, building supportive relationships, and promoting positive change with youth and each other. And we are reminded of Lesson 1—setting aside any preconceived notions so youth can show us who they are as individuals.

Now take a moment to explore your personal journey through YFS including those influences that most affect your development and success. As you reflect on the questions that follow, consider both what you already do to meet the challenges of being a YCW and what you will need in the future to grow as your career evolves.

- What compelled me to start working in YFS?
- What do I now find most compelling about YFS?
- How do I cope with the uncertainties that accompany my role?
- What do I do to embrace the role of YCW, including the ups and downs?
- How do I face the daily challenges of being a YCW?
- What do I do or tell myself when things don't go as planned (e.g., with a particular youth, on a shift or interaction, etc.)?
- What do I need to be a successful YCW?
- What keeps me in YFS (and a YCW)?
- How can I have the greatest impact in my role?
- How can my work be even more meaningful?
- What can I do to continue to challenge myself and improve my skills over the course of my career?

Former president of Apple Computer, John Sculley, once described how Steve Jobs convinced him to leave PepsiCo. to work for the future computer giant. Sculley said, "He looked up at me and just stared at me with the stare that only Steve Jobs has and he said, 'Do you want to sell sugar water for the rest of your life or do you want to come with me and change the world?' and I just gulped because I knew I would wonder for the rest of my life what I would have missed." Whether driven by passion, the need for a job, or other personal reasons, each of us has a story about how we got started in YFS. What compels us to work in YFS is worthy of attention since we must give of ourselves to help others. And in the most challenging of times one of the greatest resources will be the ability to connect with that that is truly meaningful about our work. Therefore, your responses are resources for you.

Once in the field there are ongoing factors that weigh largely on whether or not we persevere through the adversity and appreciate the joy of challenge. Long hours, unrelenting job responsibilities, low salaries, and lack of organizational support are but a few of the variables that eventually take their toll and contribute to YCWs leaving their jobs and sometimes, YFS altogether (Barford & Whelton, 2010; Hwang & Hopkins, 2012). Turnover rates with front line staff remain extraordinarily high, averaging between 22–60% annually, with some agencies having as much as 75% of their staff with less than one year of experience (Proyouthwork America, 2011; Wilson, 2009). Staff will sometimes say they simply "burned out." So, if you are in YFS and are beyond one year of service you have surpassed the odds of attrition. Connect with what inspires you and serves as a preventative to burnout. Inspiration is both healing and contagious.

Personal Philosophy

There are divergent perspectives on the issue of how to best prepare and support front line staff. Throughout this book we will explore varying viewpoints that inform this issue. There is, however, one crucial point to be made before moving forward: The person of the YCW is the most important factor in determining how to improve training, systems of support, job satisfaction, and ultimately, the effectiveness of services. Research on the effectiveness of services is particularly substantive regarding the last point. Despite an ever growing panacea of therapeutic models and specialized techniques, *who* provides the services matters much more than *what* particular model or technique is used. In psychology and psychotherapy, two adjoining fields that provide the greatest preponderance of evidence on this issue, the contribution of the provider to outcome is known as *therapist effects* (Brown, Lambert, Jones, & Minami, 2005; Luborsky et al., 1986; Wampold & Brown, 2005). Briefly, therapist effects refer to those factors and characteristics known to influence the individual effectiveness of service providers. Studies have demonstrated that therapist effects account for up to nine times more to outcome than specific methods and models (Bertolino, Bargmann, & Miller, 2013;

Wampold & Brown, 2005). This issue is especially relevant given the degree of direct contact YCWs have with youth.

At the heart of what we will refer to as "YCW effects" is *personal philosophy* or worldview. Personal philosophies emerge out of beliefs, ideas, and assumptions. On the front lines, personal philosophies are continuously put to the test. Although agency and coworker support, supervision, reasonable job responsibilities, effective training, and flexibility in work schedule are a few examples of activities that help YCWs to face the day-to-day challenges, the greatest resource a YCW will have is his or her personal philosophy. To better understand the role of personal philosophy, on your own or with a group of peers, consider each of the questions that follow. You may want to write down your responses should you choose to reflect further on them at a later time:

- What are my core beliefs, ideas, or assumptions about youth and families?
- How have I come to believe what I believe about youth and families?
- What has most significantly influenced my beliefs, ideas, and assumptions as they relate to youth and families?
- How have my beliefs, ideas, and assumptions affected my work in YFS? With colleagues/peers? With the community at large?
- How do I believe that change occurs? What does change involve?
- Do I believe that some degree of change is possible with every youth? Every family? (If you answered "yes" then end here.) (If you answered "no," proceed to the next question.)
- How do I work with youth and families whom I believe cannot (or do not want to or are resistant to) change? What do I do?
- If I do not believe that every youth and family can experience some degree of change, what keeps me in YFS?

What was the result of asking these questions of yourself (and of your peers, if applicable)? What did you notice about your responses? What new ideas do you have that you could apply to your work in YFS? What is one small way that you could begin to apply one or more of your new ideas today? What difference might that make for youth, peers, your agency, and/or yourself?

To fully appreciate the significance of perspective we have to look beyond ourselves to those most in need of a philosophy that emanates hope—our clients. Evidence of this point is everywhere with people in all walks of life—we need only pay attention. Just a few short years after winning her eighth national championship as head basketball coach of the University of Tennessee Lady Vols, Pat Summitt was diagnosed with early-onset dementia, Alzheimer's type. In shock and vulnerable, Coach Summitt was told by a physician that she should step down immediately from the job she loved and get herself out of the public eye as quickly as possible or it would "embarrass" her and ruin her legacy. Attempting to digest the advice of her doctor, Summitt thought, "Who did he think he was? Even if I had an irreversible brain disease—even if

I did—what right did he have to tell me how to cope with it?" She was clear in her words to her doctor, "Do you have any idea who you are talking with? You don't know me, and you don't know what I am capable of" (Summitt & Jenkins, 2013, pp. 17–18). And that's just it—we must know *who youth are* and *what they are capable of.*

Effective YCWs share a series common threads—the first of which relates to their worldview. They maintain an unwavering belief in the capacities of youth and families. For example, where some see deficits and pathology, others see abilities and challenges. Where some see resistance to change, others see communication. Where some see roadblocks, others see hurdles. And where some see setbacks, others see opportunities. No matter the youth, situation, or setting, the most effective YCWs fall into the "others" group with regard to each of the preceding examples. These YCWs maintain what might best be described as "possibility oriented." The following story further illustrates this point:

> A particular class of students had become unmanageable. Their teacher, who was nearing retirement, decided she had had enough and opted for early retirement rather than spend her last year in a constant battle with the class. The school brought in another teacher to take over the class and usher in a sense of calm. To no avail, the new teacher was similarly overwhelmed and defeated by the class. The second teacher soon resigned. The students seemed to take delight in their ability to send teachers fleeing from something they had done all their lives—teach.
>
> In a quandary and desperate for a replacement, the school contacted a teacher who had recently finished her student teaching and was fresh from her university studies. The teacher had applied for a job but hadn't received one due to positions already being filled at the start of the school year. Because the principal feared that the new teacher might not accept the job, he did not reveal details of the previous problems with the class. The new graduate happily accepted the job offer.
>
> About a month after the new teacher had started at the school, the principal's guilt caught up with him. He decided to visit the class. To his amazement, the students were very well behaved. The principal stayed after the class to convey his excitement about what he had observed. He went on to tell the teacher that he was very impressed with the results she had shown with the class. The teacher was surprised at the principal's remarks. She quickly deflected the accolades and thanked the principal for making her job so easy by giving her such a great group of kids for her first real teaching job. The principal, somewhat bewildered, asked the teacher what had given her the idea that they were a great group. She smiled and told him that she had discovered his "secret" on her first day with the class. As the principal stood by, his bewilderment turning toward curiosity, the teacher opened the desk drawer and pointed to a list for the students in the class, their names followed by numbers from 135–170. She revealed, "I found this list of their IQ scores

the first day. I realized that these were gifted children who really needed to be engaged in a challenging way or else they would be bored and troublesome, so I completely changed my teaching plan with them. They responded very well after a few days of rambunctiousness." The principal stared curiously at the list and responded with responded with astonishment, "But those are their locker numbers, not their IQ scores!" It didn't matter. The teacher had already acted on her perceptions and changed the classroom situation for the better.

Like the teacher in the story, effective YCWs do not view people or situations through a lens of pathology and deficit. They are also less likely to subscribe to descriptions that are closed-down, limit options, and depersonalizing, as is often the case with psychiatric labels. Instead, effective YCWs believe not only in the abilities of others, they maintain a relentless pursuit of client strengths and employ those strengths to create future possibilities.

There is an additional point to be made about the role of YCWs—and a rather significant one. YCWs do the kind of work that most value and yet may shy away from. Because many of the youth we serve are extremely vulnerable and have had their voices muted, they have had little or no say-so in the services they receive. A primary example can be found with the number of youth who have been involuntarily put on psychotropic medications. In fact, youth who on Medicaid are far more likely to be treated with psychotropic meds than behavioral health services, despite the concerns over the use of such medications with children and adolescents (DeChillo, 2009; Wen, 2010; Whitaker, 2010). There have also been cases in which YFS facilities have refused to take youth into their programs unless they are put on psychotropics.

As individuals and as a field we cannot tolerate such practices. We can stand up for youth and for what is right by first adopting a philosophy about how every human being should be treated. Then we can work together to change irresponsible and potentially harmful practices through advocacy and action. Together we can improve the landscape of YFS.

Activating Your *Positive* Deviance

If you are reading this passage, you are a deviant and don't even know it. That's a complement, by the way. There's more good news: you are not alone. We need deviance:

Conceived to reduce global malnutrition, by 1991, the Save the Children program was itself starving—financially. Nowhere was the problem more apparent than in the impoverished Vietnamese villages within which Jerry Sternin and his wife, Monique, had been hard at work. Traditional methods such as bringing in experts to analyze the situation, adopting new agricultural methods, and importing food were not only costly, the benefits were short-lived. As soon as the conventional services were scaled back or withdrawn the gains were lost. Afforded little money and time, and with more than half of Vietnamese children malnourished, the Sternins faced a conundrum. The couple was given just six months to create an effective, large-scale program. They needed a new approach, one that broke with conventional wisdom.

Out of desperation, the Sternins decided to try something different. Working with four poor rural communities and 2,000 children under the age of three, the Sternins invited the community to identify poor families who had managed to avoid malnutrition despite all odds, facing the same challenges and obstacles as their neighbors and without access to any special resources. These families were what in the late 1980s Tufts nutrition professor Marian Zeitlin referred to as "positive deviants." They were "positive" because they were doing things that worked in the face of weighty circumstances and "deviants" because they engaged in behaviors that most others did not (Pascale, Sternin, & Sternin, 2010).

What followed was careful observance of the positive deviants in the Vietnamese villages to identify what they did differently to keep their children better nourished. At first, the Sternins and their colleagues were unable to identify any variations from the overall dominant cultural practices. But over time subtle differences began to emerge with the positive deviants. Through careful observation and discussion it was learned that caregivers in the positive deviant families collected tiny shrimps and crabs from paddy fields, and added those, along with sweet potato greens, to their children's meals. Although they were accessible to everyone, most villagers believed the foods to be low class or inappropriate for young children. The positive deviant families also fed their children small meals three to four times a day, rather than bigger meals twice a day, which was customary in that part of the world. It was these seemingly small deviations that accounted for better nourished children.

Armed with knowledge of the practices used by the positive deviant families, the Sternins took another crucial step. They posted these practices in all of the villages. And then something remarkable happened. The rest of the community changed their behavior to match that of the positive deviants, resulting in a rapid decrease in malnutrition in all four villages. Within two years malnutrition rates had dropped between 65 to 85 percent in the villages the Sternins had visited. But it did not end there. Word spread of the success of this effort and other villages sent representatives to learn the practices of the positive deviants, resulting in further decreases in child malnutrition rates in Vietnam.

Positive deviance focuses on success versus failure. It emphasizes the solving of social or behavioral problems by identifying who in a community is able to manage problems by using existing resources. Positive deviance differs from traditional "needs-based" or problem-solving approaches in that it does not focus primarily on identification of needs and the external inputs necessary to meet those needs or solve problems. Instead, it seeks to identify and optimize existing resources and solutions within the community to solve community problems.

This is where you come in. Like the Sternins and their efforts with Save the Children, by virtue of being in YFS, you are a deviant. You have chosen a field that does not pay well, has long hours, has an element of unpredictability, is crisis laden, and requires your unwavering commitment, determination, and drive. *And, we need more from you.* What is requested now is for you to pursue your personal deviance with even more fervor. There is nothing random about successful YFS agencies. They are successful because of individuals whose exceptional behaviors and practices enable them to get better results than their counterparts with the exact same resources. The challenge is to find the best in you and your organization and use those abilities and resources to make changes that improve the quality of YFS. Then others can learn from your successes to create their own organizations of excellence (Bertolino, 2011).

Pillars of Positive Deviance: YCWs, Teams, and Agencies

A focus of this book is successful YFS. Accordingly, there are three "pillars" of positive deviance that underscore YFS. The first is YCWs—including their skills and unique styles or "fingerprints." Second is teams and their ability to function in cohesive and effective ways. The third pillar is agencies. This book involves detailed exploration of the first two pillars and the role they play in helping youth thrive and flourish. Although outside the scope of this book, the agency pillar in YFS is discussed elsewhere in the literature.

As we transition from this chapter to the next, we delve into the role of the YCW as an agent of change, witnessing the lives of youth as they unfold. Consider that there is an estimated 20,000 moments in a day to positively affect another person's life. For the YCW, each interaction is a chance to create a positive experience for a youth. The more positive experiences youth have, the more opportunities they have for character development, the better defined their strengths and abilities, and the more intense their resolve.

You are a difference-maker. To have the greatest impact possible it is necessary to continue to hone already existing abilities, develop new skills, and use those assets in ways that fit with who you are as a person. This is what makes services work. Interventions that are devoid of compassion and genuineness will fall flat. To this end, this book is an opportunity to discover your "fingerprint"—the uniqueness you have to connect with others, positively influence change, and make the world better.

two
Foundations: Principles of Strengths- Based Youth Care Work

It is not enough to be compassionate. You must act.

—Tenzia Gyatso, 14th Dalai Lama

A few years ago I was teaching the first day of a two-day workshop in Rochester, Minnesota. In a sea of 150 or so attendees, two in particular piqued my curiosity. A man and a woman sat quietly in the front row writing notes. I figured they might be writing about the workshop but then again, I had been to all my lectures and I didn't find them all that riveting.

At the final break of the second day, the two participants introduced themselves as David and Carole from the Minnesota Department of Human Services (MDHS). They explained that they were working on a project designed to strengthen the ways in which child protective services (CPS) and child welfare services (CWS) workers engage their clients. I was immediately captivated by David and Carole because of the way they spoke. It was very unusual. David and Carole were administrators who were using the kind of talk that is routinely absent in YFS. They used words like "hope," "strengths," and "collaboration." I can still recall the excitement in their words.

David and Carole, along with others, had worked tirelessly for a new vision of child and family services in Minnesota. They partnered with legislators and maneuvered their way through the state social service system with an aim to change it. What David and Carole had in mind was both innovative and inspiring. They wanted to teach workers skills that focused on client engagement, identification of strengths, and solution-building. Their strategy was first to train CPS and

CWS workers in a few select counties as part of a pilot project, and then expand to the remainder of the state. Our conversation, although brief, ended with the three of us agreeing to talk again by phone once I returned home.

During our calls it became apparent that we shared a common ideology: The way that clients are engaged greatly impacts the course of services and eventual outcome. We considered empathy, positive regard, and collaboration (i.e., working with clients to determine goals of services and ways to accomplish those goals) as crucial elements of "better" alliances. Better alliances, in turn, increase the likelihood of services follow-through by clients, which create more opportunities to positively impact at-risk families and reduce child abuse and neglect.

David and Carole formally invited me to be part of their project. David explained that they wanted me to train MDHS front line staff in the strategies I described in the two-day training—specifically, how to effectively engage clients and to identify and draw on their capacities. David and Carole wanted me to train workers to be "strengths based." I accepted their offer.

Over the next eight years I visited approximately 20 cities and towns, some more than once, throughout the *very big* state of Minnesota. I met hundreds of front line workers, supervisors, and administrators. In a landscape that included involuntary clients, long hours, travel challenges (i.e., distances, weather, etc.), and marginal pay, the MDHS workers were committed to their clients. They did whatever it took to keep children and youth safe and strengthen families.

As the project unfolded, I heard about the successes of the Minnesota project. I was provided with statistics that revealed a reduction in second and subsequent hotline calls with families in which there had been an initial one. More important were the indications that the rates of child abuse and neglect were lowering. The program appeared to be accomplishing what it was meant to do—better engaging caregivers to promote the safety and well-being of children and youth.

Statistics matter. We have to demonstrate that services work and statistical enumerations offer a common language in mental health and social services. And yet the impact of change cannot be fully understood through numbers alone. This was the case in Minnesota. At each stop in my travels, I heard from workers whose families had used their strengths to face adversity and became stronger. I saw the looks of joy and the sounds of satisfaction in the words of front line staff. Change was happening.

About four years into my involvement with MDHS, I received an email from David. It read, "Bob I have to share this story with you. This work is transforming not only the lives of our clients but our workers too." Attached to David's email was a letter from a CPS worker who told of her recent experience.

The worker, who I will refer to as Emily, was a hotline investigator. Every state in the U.S. has a hotline that may be contacted by mandated reporters or civilians if there is suspicion of child abuse or neglect. Emily's job was to investigate allegations and determine what course of action, if any, was necessary. As with the majority of the calls that go to CPS workers the people she visited did not request her help. For the most part, they wanted Emily to go away and leave them alone. But that was not an option. Her job was to protect children and keep them safe.

On a wintery day, Emily was doing that which she had become accustomed to—following up on a call that had come through the state hotline. She arrived at the home of a husband and wife with two children. Although the couple was expecting the CPS worker, they were understandably guarded—saying very little, other than a cordial, "Hello." Emily understood their apprehension. She talked with the parents about the specifics of the call to the hotline and her role, which was to ensure that their children were safe. Emily listened patiently to the parents' account of the events that preceded the hotline call. She gathered information and discussed with the parents ideas about how future situations such as the one that led to the call could be handled differently. Emily believed the children to be safe and the three adults worked together to create a follow-up plan that included resources to help support the family.

The meeting drew to a close and Emily thanked the couple for welcoming her into their home despite the circumstances. The mother replied, "You know, this is the second time we have been visited by CPS. The first was a few years ago. It didn't go well." The mother further explained that she and her husband felt they had not been listened to by the CPS worker. The experience left them feeling invalidated and with a negative view of MDHS.

The mother continued, "But this time was different. You listened to us. You treated us with respect. You've talked about how you could support us." She expressed her gratitude to Emily for her kindness and willingness to work together. Emily was taken aback by the mother's comments. She had not realized the impact of the meeting. Emily once again thanked the couple and headed out the door.

But there was more. One of the persons present during the visit knew something the others did not. What did that person know? Emily and the CPS worker who had visited the couple several years earlier were *one in the same*. It had been Emily who completed the first *and* second investigations. Now, some years later, it was Emily who remembered the couple. Although the couple vividly recalled the experience, they did not recall Emily.

It was then that something changed for Emily. She had been through the strengths-based training and had been using what she had learned. But it was not until the mother's parting words that Emily truly internalized the very point of the training and what she had been practicing. On that wintery day, in a moment's time, Emily understood the value of client engagement.

In her letter to David, Emily expressed how being strengths based with families changed her perspective on both her work and life. She said, "I now understand that being strengths-based is not just practicing a new model. It's a way of being with others. It's a way of life." Emily had found her positive deviance.

Redefining the Strengths-Based Perspective

In 1862, just prior to signing the Emancipation Proclamation, Abraham Lincoln gave his second annual address to Congress. He urged Congress to use fresh eyes as they considered the situation. Lincoln stated, "The dogmas of the quiet past are inadequate in the stormy present. The occasion is piled high with difficulty. As our case is new, so we must think anew and act anew. We must disenthrall ourselves and then we shall save our country." What did Lincoln mean by disenthrall? He meant that we move through life with ideas that we are captivated with but are no longer relevant or true (Robinson, 2011). There are, of course, occasions in which our ideas matter less and carry fewer consequences. YFS is not one of these. A substantive threat in YFS is one of becoming enthralled with ideas that are not simply outdated, but ones that perpetuate negativity, pathology, and deficit. Collectively they contribute to a climate of impossibility, closing down avenues of change. A response to this risk is a strengths-based perspective.

The idea of focusing on strengths is not the province of any one discipline. Fields such as education, business, organizational leadership, and healthcare all have developed approaches based on some variation of a strengths focus. Arguably, the field of behavioral health (which for the purposes of this book will include mental health and social services) has led the charge with its widespread development and adoption of principles and practices that highlight competencies, possibilities, and solutions with individuals, relationships, and groups (Bertolino, 2010; Bertolino, Kiener, & Patterson, 2010; Madsen, 2007; Rapp & Goscha, 2012; Saleeby, 2012). However descriptions of strengths based may differ, each shares the central tenet of identifying and building on abilities and resources to resolve problems and bring about present and future change. In this book, we remain true to this tradition while re-envisioning a strengths-based ideology in YFS.

There are several reasons why it is important to re-envision and, ultimately, redefine what it means to be strengths based in YFS. First, because much of the interest in strengths-based practice relates to the core idea of focusing on the ability of youth, other evidence-based variables have been underemphasized despite their influence on effective services. The success of any service is reliant on multiple variables, so it is essential that YCWs are abreast of the empirical foundations of YFS. A second and closely related point is the presence of well-defined strengths-based strategies that have gone largely underutilized. There exists a wealth of "road tested" methods that can help YCWs to improve their effectiveness. YCWs with expansive repertoires of strengths-based strategies have more options to draw on, no matter the situation. A third reason to redefine strengths-based practice in YFS is to provide a comprehensive description that is reflective of culture and society. A redefinition of a strengths-based perspective addresses philosophical inconsistencies (McMillen, Morris, & Sherraden, 2004; Staudt, Howard, & Drake, 2001) by incorporating current research findings, and most importantly, what works in YFS.

A new definition of what it means to be strengths based does not imply "out with the old, in with the new." On the contrary, a new definition reflects an evolvement in our thinking and practices, an evolvement that is in response to what we have learned.

A New Definition

> A strengths-based perspective emphasizes the abilities and resources people have within themselves and their support systems to more effectively cope with life challenges. When combined with new experiences, understandings and skills, these abilities and resources contribute to improved well-being, which is comprised of three areas of functioning: individual, interpersonal relationships, and social role. Strengths-based practitioners value relationships and convey this through respectful, culturally-sensitive, collaborative, practices that support, encourage and empower. Routine and ongoing real-time feedback is used to maintain a responsive, consumer-driven climate to ensure the greatest benefit of services.

There are several integral components to this definition. First, and also the cornerstone of a strengths-based perspective, is a focus on abilities (i.e., strengths, competencies). Such a focus involves attention to both prevention and intervention. Former president of the American Psychological Association, Martin Seligman, and coauthor Mihaly Csikszentmihalyi (2000) stated:

> What we have learned over 50 years is that the disease model does not move us closer to the prevention of these serious problems. Indeed the major strides in prevention have largely come from a perspective focused on systematically building competency, not correcting weakness. Prevention researchers have discovered that there are human strengths that act as buffers against mental illness: courage, future-mindedness, optimism, interpersonal skill, faith, work ethic, hope, honesty, perseverance, the capacity for flow and insight, to name several. Much of the task of prevention in this new century will be to create a science of human strength whose mission will be to understand and learn how to foster these virtues in young people. Working exclusively on personal weakness and on the damaged brains, however, has rendered science poorly equipped to do effective prevention. We need now to call for massive research on human strength and virtue. We need to ask practitioners to recognize that much of the best work they already do in the consulting room is to amplify strengths rather than repair the weaknesses of their clients. (pp. 6–7)

Service-wise our aim is to identify and activate the already existing abilities and resources of youth. We also assist youth with expanding their perspectives and in developing new skills and systems of support. A strengths-based perspective is therefore two-pronged, involving both the activation and utilization of latent or underemployed abilities *and* the teaching of new ones.

A second component is *well-being*. Well-being is a construct, meaning that it is comprised of several elements. For example, weather is made up of temperature, barometric pressure, humidity, and the like. Each is important but does not in and of itself define weather. Similarly, well-being in YFS is inclusive of three elements or areas: *Individual, interpersonal,* and *social role functioning. Individual functioning* includes positive emotion, engagement, meaning, and accomplishment (Seligman, 2011). In brief, positive emotion includes but is not limited to happiness and life satisfaction. Engagement relates to subjective absorption through experiences in the present. For example, a youth could become engaged in an activity such as painting, in which he or she experiences pleasure, loses track of time, and feels experientially absorbed. Meaning equates to belonging to and serving something that is believed to be bigger than one's self. Accomplishment or achievement is the pursuit of something for its own sake and is commonly seen in the pursuit of success, competence, or mastery.

Another facet of well-being is *interpersonal functioning,* which refers to close, often intimate, positive interactions with others. Most frequently this category includes caregivers, family, and those who play significant roles in the lives of youth. The final area is *social role functioning,* a category that captures the impact of school, employment, community support, and other more general yet important forms of support. As with the elements of weather, each of the three areas of functioning is crucial but does not by itself define well-being; it is their collective value that forms well-being. Our aim for youth is to have greater degrees of well-being at the end of services. As we will learn in future chapters, *positive youth development* (PYD) provides a central way of helping youth to increase well-being.

The revised definition of strengths-based includes a third component—a focus on relationships. Most important here is the supportive role that YCWs play in the lives of youth. YCWs value relationships with youth and view each interaction as an opportunity to work together toward a hoped-for future. To this end, strategies used to strengthen the alliance and promote change are provided with respect to the culture of the youth. The therapeutic alliance, which will be discussed in detail later in this chapter, is arguably the most robust finding in psychotherapy literature.

The final component in defining strengths based is the role of routine and ongoing real-time feedback in evaluating the impact and benefit of services. Real-time feedback is composed of two forms of measurement: *Outcome* and *alliance.* *Outcome* refers to the impact of services, from the client's perspective, on major areas of functioning: Individual, interpersonal, and social role. *Alliance* or process measurement involves elicitation of the client's perceptions of the therapeutic relationship. Routine (i.e., each session or meeting) and ongoing (i.e., from the start of services to discontinuation) feedback improves the effectiveness of services by allowing the client and his or her experiences to serve as a guide. Studies involving the use of real-time feedback show that it as much as doubles the effect size of services, decreases deterioration and dropout rates, and reduces psychiatric hospitalizations and costs of care (Bertolino et al., 2013). For youth, a feedback focus creates a context in which their voices are not only expressed, but they are heard and responded to.

Five Principles of Strengths-Based Youth Care Work

In Chapter 1, we glimpsed into the wide and varied services commonly associated with YFS. We also learned about the many roles and responsibilities of YCWs. So far in this chapter we have explored a redefinition of the strengths-based perspective including its key components. In this section, we outline a series of research-based principles that form the foundation of a strengths-based perspective. These principles are in accordance with the American Psychological Association's (APA) definition of evidence-based practice (EBP): "The integration of the best available research with clinical expertise in the context of patient characteristics, culture, and preferences" (APA Task Force on Evidence-Based Practice, 2006, p. 273). This definition is characterized by three elements: 1) Best available research, 2) Clinical expertise, and 3) Patient (client) characteristics.

Best available research involves commitment to remaining up to date on empirical studies that pertain to YFS and integrating any relevant findings through policy revisions, training, and practice. *Clinical expertise* refers to the role of YCWs as agents of change. As we will learn, the most effective YCWs maintain self-awareness, value professional development, and employ strategies that benefit youth without holding allegiances to particular methods, approaches, or models. Core to clinical expertise, as described earlier in terms of real-time feedback, is monitoring youth progress while in services and adjusting services as needed. A focus is therefore on creating opportunities for YCWs to develop and grow their clinical expertise. In addition, Table 2.1 provides a further list of essential

TABLE 2.1 Essential characteristics of YCWs

1. The ability to feel at ease and comfortable with other people, especially young people: Someone who is relaxed and not threatened by personal interaction.

2. The ability to put others, especially young people at ease: Someone others just naturally open up to, quickly.

3. The ability to project unconditional regard and acceptance of others: Someone who is genuinely nonjudgmental or who can appear to be so.

4. The ability to convey warmth and empathy: Someone who projects understanding of others' feelings and thoughts.

5. Good verbal and interpersonal skills: Someone who gets along well in many different situations and with many different kinds of people and who can use language to seem like one of the group.

6. Good listening skills: Someone who pays close attention to what others say and does not feel compelled to always inject personal thoughts and comments into the conversation.

7. The ability to project enthusiasm: Someone who seems genuinely interested in others and whose enthusiasm engages the interest of others.

8. An awareness of one's own nonverbal reactions: Someone who is capable of maintaining body language and facial expressions that project the above traits and does not convey annoyance or frustration.

9. Physical characteristics that are nonthreatening, not intimidating, or off-putting to others.

10. The ability to *conceptualize* and to think through complex situations as opposed to thinking literally and in a rote manner.

Source: Brendtro, du Toit, Bath, & Bockern, 2006.

characteristics of YCWs. *Patient characteristics* is the third aspect of EBP, emphasizing the importance of providing services with respect to client culture, including expectations and preferences.

The five principles of strengths-based practice described in the next section are in accord with the APA definition of EBP. Each principle stands on its own in terms of its contribution to successful services; however, each principle is but one pillar. It is the collective tapestry of the principles that creates the foundation of a strengths-based perspective. In the book *The Medici Effect: Breakthrough Insights at the Intersection of Ideas, Concepts and Cultures,* author Frans Johansson (2002) detailed how the intersection of ideas from divergent disciplines provides new frameworks for solving problems that are unlikely to be solved from singular viewpoints alone. Similarly, the landscape of YFS requires a broad range of ideas. A strengths-based perspective involves the intersection of ideas including but not limited to psychology, mental health, social services, and education. These principles serve as a compass, providing guidance and direction to YCWs.

The principles will be introduced using a three-level structure. The first level is a description of the principle itself. Next is the "primary competency" associated with the principle. The primary competency represents the overall skill for YCWs to master. The third level includes key tasks associated with the primary competency. These tasks are listed in tables.

Principle 1: Youth are the Most Significant Contributors to Service Success

Primary Competency (PC): Maximize Youth Contributions to Change

Youth are what make services work. They are the engineers of change. The contributions of youth are referred to as *client factors,* which according to research estimates account for between 80–87% of the variance in outcome, far more than any other factor (Wampold, 2001). Client factors primarily involve the *internal strengths* and *external resources. Internal strengths* include optimism, persistence, resilience, protective factors, coping skills, and abilities utilized in vocational, educational, and social settings. Resilience and protective factors are qualities and actions that allow youth to meet the difficulties and challenges of life. Growth and maturation relate to the ability of youth to move through or mature out of individual and lifecycle developmental phases, manage the trials and tribulations of life, overcome problems, and cope with trauma.

Resilience, protective factors, growth, and maturation are closely tied to one another. A specific area of focus that connects these factors has become known as *posttraumatic growth,* in which researchers systematically study the possibility of something good emerging from the struggle with something very difficult (Calhoun & Tedeschi, 2012; Tedeschi, Calhoun, & Cann, 2007). Studies have demonstrated that adversity, great suffering, or trauma can lead to positive growth across a wide range of experiences. Examples include increased compassion for others, openness, spirituality, and for many, overall life satisfaction (Linley & Joseph, 2004).

What makes the most difference for those who find growth in experiences from those who do not? Of the different mechanisms *mindset* appears as the most influential. It is how people perceive the cards they have been dealt and their subjective experiences rather than the events themselves. Youth will experience ups and downs, transitions, and movement through different phases of life. What is most important is that we learn about the meanings that youth attach to their experiences. We invite them into conversations in which they can explore the relevance of developmental, maturational, and transitional processes and changes. In doing so, we take care not to impose personal beliefs but work to normalize experiences and offer alternative possibilities that may promote positive change.

External resources refer to relationships, social networks, and systems that provide support and opportunities. Examples are family, friends, employment, educational, community, and religious supports. External resources also include affiliation or membership in groups or associations that provide connection and stability. Youth support systems are central in maintaining long-term change; focusing on processes that tap into, develop, and encourage such capacities is central to a strengths-based perspective.

An adjunct to internal strengths and external resources, client contributions also include opportunities for new learning and skill development. Psychoeducational and experiential activities are used to help youth to develop a more encompassing repertoire of skills. A combination of already existing strengths and the addition of new skills is a formidable duo that provides youth with a broader range of options and responses for coping with life challenges.

To make the most of the contributions of youth it is necessary that YCWs become versed in and comfortable with the key tasks listed in Table 2.2. Upcoming chapters will include a multitude of ways of building on youth "factors" to enhance the prospects of present and future change.

TABLE 2.2 Key tasks to maximize youth contributions

- Communicate the belief that youth are competent and capable.
- Identify and build on the qualities and characteristics of youth including resiliency, coping skills, and protective factors.
- Listen for, evoke, and develop traits and abilities.
- Identify abilities and past solutions typically utilized in contexts other than the problem area(s) and link them to present situations.
- Identify and assist youth in developing systems of support, community resources, and social networks (e.g., family, friends, educators, employers, religious/spiritual advisors, groups, and other outside helpers and community members).

(Continued)

TABLE 2.2 Continued

- Learn what youth do to get their everyday needs met (i.e., whom they seek out for support, where they go for support).
- Identify what resources youth *already* have in their lives that may be used actively in the present.
- Identify moments (exceptions) in the past or present—even if fleeting—when youth's problems were less present or absent altogether.
- Explore moments in the past or present when youth have made beneficial decisions.
- Even when external influences factor into change (e.g., psychotherapy, medication, etc.) or youth assign change to influences outside of their control (e.g., luck, chance), attribute the majority of change to their own qualities and actions.
- Create opportunities for youth to acquire and develop new skills.
- When others closely aligned with youth have made positive contributions to their lives, share the credit for change with such persons.
- Assist youth with evaluating the benefits of positive change.
- Identify ways that youth can utilize abilities to face future challenges.
- Explore ways that youth can extend change into other areas of life.
- Encourage personal agency and accountability.

Principle 2: The Therapeutic Alliance Makes Substantial and Consistent Contributions to Outcome

PC: Engage Youth through the Working Alliance

The most researched area in psychology and psychotherapy is the therapeutic relationship and alliance with over 1100 studies to date (Norcross, 2011). Findings from these studies have helped to define the alliance, which is considered an expansion of the therapeutic relationship, comprised of four empirically established components, as outlined in the following sections.

The Client's View of the Relationship (including Perceptions of the Provider as Warm, Empathic, and Genuine)

Client ratings of the therapeutic relationship are significantly related to outcome and are widely considered the best and most consistent process predictors of improvement (Bachelor & Horvath, 1999; Baldwin, Wampold, & Imel, 2007; Horvath & Bedi, 2002; Orlinsky, Grawe, & Parks, 1994; Orlinsky, Rønnestad, & Willutzki, 2004). In fact, client ratings of providers as empathic, trustworthy, and nonjudgmental are better predictors of positive outcome than are provider ratings, diagnosis, approach, or any other variable (Horvath & Symonds, 1991; Lambert & Bergin, 1994). Youth who are engaged and connected with YCWs and those affiliated with services are likely to benefit most.

Agreement on the Goals, Meaning or Purpose of the Treatment

Orlinsky et al. (2004) observe, "The quality of the patient's participation . . . [emerges] as the most important [process] determinant in outcome" (p. 324). Youth who are more engaged and involved in services and treatment processes are likely to receive greater benefit. Involving youth in the purpose of services and goals can affect the degree of engagement and therefore, eventual outcome. Negative outcome is often traced to the exclusion of youth from service decisions. Duncan, Hubble, and Miller (1997) stated, "Impossibility . . . is at least partly a function of leaving clients out of the process, of not listening or of dismissing the importance of their perspective" (p. 30). Because youth, generally, are not the ones who initiate services there is a risk of their voices being muted or left out of discussions to determine direction and focus.

Agreement on the Means and Methods Used

In addition to involving youth in determining the purpose of services and goals is agreement on *how* to improve functioning or well-being. In any given problem situation, there are multiple options available in terms of how to approach it. Essential to the success of techniques, methods, and interventions is the degree to which they *fit* with youth. Effective YCWs stay clear of prescriptive, one-size-fits-all methods, instead involving youth in service-related processes.

Accommodating the Client's Preferences

A growing number of studies have identified the role of client expectations and personal preferences on the alliance (Norcross, 2011). Although moderate and strong preferences differ in terms of their influence on the client–provider connection, what is important is that YCWs attend to the values, beliefs, worldviews, and service expectations of youth. Key areas for youth include but are not limited to who should be involved with services, when and where to meet, the length of sessions, and so on.

Each component plays a role in strengthening relationships not only with youth but those who are involved in the lives of youth, such as caregivers. Because the strength of the alliance is an excellent predictor of eventual outcome it is imperative that YCWs attune themselves to practices that enhance engagement. Although the strength of the therapeutic bond is not highly correlated with the length of treatment (Horvath & Luborsky, 1993), there are threats (e.g., distrust of adults, previous experiences with the "system," expectations) to the bond between YCWs and youth. As we will learn, effective YCWs continuously work on their relationships with youth, understanding the importance of forming stable connections. In fact, the most significant difference between average and above-average YCWs is in their ability to form, nurture, and sustain alliances with diverse youth. Table 2.3 offers an array of tasks for strengthening the therapeutic relationships with youth. These tasks will be expounded on in upcoming chapters.

TABLE 2.3 Key tasks for strengthening the therapeutic alliance

- Use active listening, attending skills to connect with youth while recognizing that caution toward professionals may be an appropriate response based on their past experiences.
- Collaborate with caregivers, family members, outside helpers, and community resources to create strong social networks and systems of support.
- Collaborate with youth in setting goals.
- Incorporate the views of involved helpers (i.e., extended family, social service workers, medical personnel, educators, law enforcement, educators) in setting goals and determining directions.
- Collaborate with youth on tasks to accomplish goals.
- As YCWs, attend to our personal contributions to the alliance including possible negative effects.
- Incorporate an outcome orientation as a means to monitor the benefit of services from the perspective of youth and other stakeholders.
- Use respectful, non-depersonalizing and non-pathologizing language when describing youth and the concerns of youth.
- Learn about the preferences and expectations of youth and as best as possible accommodate services to those preferences and expectations.
- Offer options and choices in services and processes.
- Discuss with youth possible benefits and side effects of services.
- Discuss with youth parameters of confidentiality and informed consent.
- Provide rationale for services.
- Incorporate real-time feedback processes to learn and respond to youth's views of relationships.
- Learn and adapt to the ways in which youth use language.
- Demonstrate concern for the well-being, feelings, and interests of youth.
- Compliment youth for positive intentions and actions.
- Consider youth as experts on their lives, learning about, and respecting their ideas.
- Develop and increase awareness regarding personal biases and viewpoints and how they can affect relationships and services.

Principle 3: Culture Influences and Shapes All Aspects of Youth's Lives

PC: Convey Respect of Youth and their Culture

All youth deserve to be treated with dignity and respect and to be given the opportunity to fully develop their potential (Seita, Mitchell, & Tobin, 1996). In cultures that respect their youth, elders teach these core values to the young (Bolin, 2006; Vilakazi, 1993). For youth growing up in out-of-home care the number of consistent figures from whom to learn may be relatively small. Moved from place to place—also known as the "shelter shuffle"—these youth are afforded fewer opportunities to develop their abilities and have those abilities supported and nurtured. Without consideration of cultural influences, YCWs cannot adequately understand youth, their lives, situations, and problems.

Culture specifically refers to a system of shared beliefs, values, customs, behaviors, and artifacts among various groups within a community, institution, organization, or nation. From generation to generation, members of society use their cultural references to cope with their world and with one another. Hays (2007) suggested the acronym ADDRESSING as a way to identify different aspects of culture: Age, developmental and acquired disability, religion, ethnicity, social class, sexual orientation, indigenous heritage, national origin, and gender/sex. Brown (2008) expanded on Hays' perspective to include factors such as other social locations as vocational and recreational choices, partnership status, parenthood (or not), attractiveness, body size and shape, and state of physical health. Culture is a powerful filter through which behavior can be understood; however, no one aspect provides a comprehensive explanation of it (Sue, Arredondo, & McDavis, 1992). This point is particularly important due to the numerous factors that influence the lives of youth.

Cultural competence is a cornerstone of a strengths-based perspective. As YCWs, we work with youth, family members, coworkers, and others are who culturally differ from ourselves. Such persons come from an array of backgrounds, and their customs, thoughts, ways of communicating, values, traditions, and institutions vary accordingly. In our work with youth, we emphasize awareness and learning, forming new patterns of response and ways to effectively apply those responses to appropriate settings. Further, YCWs with diverse backgrounds can draw on their experiences and their general cultural knowledge to match youth's ideas about problems, possibilities, and potential solutions. Thus, knowledge of different cultures and perspectives is beneficial by allowing YCWs to view situations differently without having to align with any one viewpoint. This knowledge also brings with it an expanded repertoire of methods to use that may be helpful in delivering services. To further this idea, Table 2.4 outlines key tasks for attending to cultural influences.

TABLE 2.4 Key tasks for attending to cultural influences

- Maintain self-awareness and sensitivity to one's own cultural heritage, background, and experiences and their influence on personal attitudes, values, and biases.
- Recognize limits of multicultural competency and expertise.
- Recognize sources of personal discomfort with differences that may exist between ourselves as YCWs and youth in terms of race, ethnicity, culture, gender, and other influences.
- Acknowledge that specific racial and cultural factors influence service-oriented processes—understand and respect youth's cultural heritage and practices.
- Develop a multilevel understanding of youth, family, community, helping systems, and other associated relational or systemic influences.

(Continued)

TABLE 2.4 Continued

- Consult others who share cultural similarities and expertise with youth being served.
- Create safe and nurturing cultural, physical, psychological, and social environments and settings.
- Use assessment processes that identify concerns, risks, and threats to cultural safety and well-being.
- Acknowledge and address risks and issues related to cultural safety.
- Acknowledge caregivers as capable of keeping their children safe.
- Create culturally meaningful experiences in services-based activities.
- Use person-first language.
- Individualize services (avoid "one-size-fits-all" approaches).
- Accommodate services to the expectations of youth and families being served.
- Acknowledge youth as teachers and experts on their own lives and experiences.
- Emphasize capacities of youth to adapt, change, and grow.
- Empower youth and supportive others by using practices that identify and employ their unique capabilities.
- Identify, assess, address, and monitor barriers to services, particularly those cultural barriers associated with accessibility.
- Create plans of action that are culturally sensitive.
- Exercise care in matching methods (i.e., techniques, interventions) with youth.
- Utilize strategies that are respectful and reflective of differences.
- Explore exceptions to risks and incorporate them into action plans.
- Employ proactive (as opposed to reactive) systems of response.
- Use culturally sensitive methods of research and evaluation.
- Conduct ongoing cultural self-assessments.
- Conduct program assessments.
- Manage the dynamics of difference.
- Acquire and institutionalize cultural knowledge.
- Adapt to the diversity and cultural contexts of the individuals, families, and communities served.

Principle 4: Effective Services Promote Growth, Development, and Well-Being

PC: Utilize Strategies that Empower Youth and Improve their Lives

Instead of attempting to provide explanations about the nature of problems or pathology, a strengths-based perspective emphasizes positive change in the form of growth, development, and well-being. Central to this notion is a commitment to the possibility of youth experiencing positive change in the present and future. YCWs concentrate on efforts to identify and mobilize factors responsible for change, focusing more on change as a process and less on providing explanations or theories of causality. YCWs practice in accordance with Miller, Duncan, and Hubble (1997), who described the role of mental health professionals as one of enhancing "the factors responsible for change-in-general rather than on identifying and then changing the factors a theory suggests are responsible or causing problems-in-particular" (p. 127).

YFS begin with the basics—ensuring that, at least minimally, the needs of youth are met (Maslow, 1943). Basic needs include, but are not limited to, food, water, sleep, and safety. It is essential that YCWs assume responsibility for helping youth to have their needs met through direct assistance or by offering indirect pathways. An example of direct assistance would be providing emergency shelter to a homeless youth whereas indirect assistance could be referring a youth to a food pantry. It is important to state at this point that it is not impossible for youth to make changes when their needs are unmet. History gives us example after example of the amazing and heroic acts people undertake in the most terrible of circumstances. And while not impossible, it is certainly unrealistic to expect youth whose basic needs are not being met to focus sufficient attention and energy on making and sustaining change in other areas of life.

As described earlier in this chapter with the new definition of strengths based, an orientation based on growth, development, and well-being correlates with improvement in individual, interpersonal, and social role functioning. To assist with improvement of functioning, we consider *how* youth can flourish in society by concentrating on exceptions to problems—times when things have gone better in relation to challenges—and building on those often subtle differences in the present and future. Focusing on exceptions and the prospects of future change does not mean dismissing past events. Just as some will prefer to search for explanations to problems, some may prefer to study the past and past events. From a strengths-based perspective, YCWs acknowledge the role of the past and other potential influences as much or as little as youth and those associated with youth want while placing attention on the prospects of an improved future.

A focus on improvement necessitates keeping an eye out for positive change from the start of services. Factors such as the severity of symptoms, personality characteristics, and the strength of social systems will influence rates of improvement in services; however, research makes it clear that the process of change begins early in services (Miller, Duncan, & Hubble, 1997). Some youth may respond and make appreciable gains more slowly than others; as a result, the most significant portion of change will be demonstrated over the long term, but this appears to be more the exception than the norm. Research suggests that as treatment progresses, a reliable course of diminishing returns occurs with more and more effort required to obtain barely noticeable differences in improvement (Howard, Kopte, Kraus, & Orlinksy, 1986). Even though the amount of change decreases over time, as long as progress is being made, services can remain beneficial. Furthermore, if youth experience meaningful change early on the probability of positive outcome significantly increases (Haas, Hill, Lambert, & Morrell, 2002; Percevic, Lambert, & Kordy, 2006; Whipple et al., 2003). In contrast, when youth show little or no improvement

TABLE 2.5 Key tasks for promoting growth, development, and well-being

---

- Focus on meeting the basic needs of youth (i.e., food, water, sleep, safety).
- Listen for and honor youth's ideas about directions for services.
- View meaningful change as attainable and problems as barriers to progress, not fixed pathology.
- View growth, development, and maturation as part of the change processes.
- Consider individual, interpersonal, and social role functioning as robust indicators of benefit of services.
- Focus on maximizing the impact of each interaction and/or session.
- Monitor change from the outset of services, recalling that change tends to occur early in services.
- In lieu of positive change, engage youth in conversations earlier rather than later to make adjustments in services.
- Emphasize possibilities for change through a future focus.
- Explore exceptions to problems and how change is already happening with youth.
- Focus on creating small changes, which can lead to bigger ones.
- Scan the lives of youth for spontaneous change and build on those changes.
- Approach assessment processes as opportunities to initiate positive change.
- Allow reentry or easy access to future services as needed.
- Use methods that positively reinforce healthy behaviors and functioning.
- Use methods that contribute to youth's sense of self-esteem, self-efficacy, and self-mastery.

---

or experience a worsening of symptoms early on in treatment, they are at significant risk for negative outcome and dropout (Bertolino et al., 2013; Duncan, Miller, Wampold, & Hubble, 2010; Howard et al., 1986; Howard et al., 1996). As an aside, lack of benefit early in services is likely to contribute to greater frustration and loss of faith in services, for both youth *and* service providers.

YCWs seek to be as effective as possible by learning from youth and supportive others involved what minimally needs to happen in each interaction, shift, meeting, and throughout the course of services to bring about meaningful and noticeable improvement. In addition, Table 2.5 offers tasks for promoting growth, development, and well-being.

Principle 5: Expectancy and Hope are Catalysts of Change

PC: Demonstrate Faith in the Restorative Effects of Services

Of the factors that contribute to eventual outcome, none may be as difficult to grasp as expectancy and hope, which is derived from the expectations of youth *and* caregivers about services, the creation and sustainment of hope, and the credibility placed on the rationale for the use of specific techniques (Duncan, Miller, &

Sparks, 2004). The expectations that accompany YFS regarding its potential to influence positive change are substantial. First, youth expectations that services are, at minimum, safe, and at best, able to change their lives for the better, help to act as a placebo to counteract demoralization, activate hope, and advance improvement (Frank & Frank, 1991; Miller, Duncan, & Hubble, 1997). YCWs and other providers' attitudes can promote or dampen hope. For example, an attitude of pessimism or an emphasis on psychopathology or the long-term process of change can negatively affect hope. In contrast, YCWs who have the attitude that positive change can occur even in difficult situations coupled with an emphasis on possibilities tend to instill and promote hope in every interaction, however small. Processes and practices that are respectful, collaborative, honor youths' ideas about change, and create or rehabilitate hope increase the prospects of change.

All YFS involve the use of "rituals"—techniques taught to YCWs and other direct care providers. Techniques, methods, or interventions come in many forms. They can be behavioral practices, crisis de-escalation methods, level systems, and so on. In most cases, what influences change is the youth's *belief* in the technique or method used and in the provider (the feeling of being in "good hands"), rather than the specific technique or method itself. The role of the provider is particularly important—underscoring the tasks described in Table 2.2, under Principle 2.

Expectancy and hope offer a remedy to impossibility. The greatest risk for YCWs is the loss of hope in themselves and their programs. And yet hope is not about looking at the world through rose-colored glasses but instead recognizing what can be done improve the lives of youth in their care. Table 2.6 provides a list of tasks to help instill hope and increase the expectations of positive change in YFS.

TABLE 2.6 Key tasks for increasing expectancy and hope

- Maintain the belief that positive change is possible in all aspects of YFS.
- Demonstrate faith in youth and their caregivers to achieve positive change.
- Demonstrate faith in the restorative effects of services.
- Build on preservice expectancy (i.e., the expectations youth and supportive others may have at the *start of services*).
- Create expectancy for change by focusing on what is possible and changeable.
- Create expectancy for change by using language that is respectful and emanates hope.
- Believe and demonstrate faith in the procedures and practices utilized.
- Show interest in the results of the therapeutic procedure, orientation, or method.
- Ensure that the procedure or orientation is credible from the youth's or caregiver's frame of reference.
- Ensure that the procedure or orientation is connected with or elicits the youth's previously successful experiences.
- Work in ways that enhance or highlight youth's feelings of personal control.
- View youth as people, not as their problems or difficulties or in ways that depersonalize them.

The principles described can be found, in some form, in an array of disciplines. Each principle is empirically supported and important to human relationships, development, and well-being. But it is the strength of their collective influence that matters most. So a starting point is discussion of these strengths-based principles and consideration of how they translate to different settings. The chapters that follow will explore this point in detail.

Back to the Start: What Strengths Based is and is Not

As with other perspectives a strengths point of view is at risk of being misunderstood. First, being strengths based is not about positive thinking or seeing the proverbial glass as being half full, both of which represent oversimplifications. Instead, being strengths based means looking beyond what is immediately observed or believed to be true and making the investment in youth to know more about them. Madsen (2007) has referred to this through the notion of being "appreciative allies," a concept that translates to first acknowledging the negative emotional reactions we may have to clients (in this case youth) whose actions we find intolerable or offensive. In doing so, we open ourselves up to finding something, however small, that we can appreciate and respect about youth. These granules contribute to the foundation for subsequent work and reflect our faith that positive change and successful outcome are possible even in the most challenging situations. Such a perspective can circumvent services by freeing YCWs from predetermined theoretical restraints that suggest impossibility.

Next, some so-called competency-based and collaborative frameworks focus almost exclusively on strengths. The idea is that youth (and people in general) have all the strengths they need to resolve the problems they encounter. This idea is not only a misrepresentation of what it means to be strengths based, it can also be invalidating to those who desperately need helpers to thoroughly understand the different hardships and risks they are facing. Being strengths based does not mean being "problem phobic," neither does it suggest forcing an agenda that focuses only on solutions or what works. Youth are not bottomless reservoirs of ability who have every answer to every life problem. Overlooking serious threats to the well-being of youth is unrealistic and potentially hazardous. A strengths-based perspective does not involve downplaying or altogether ignoring real-life difficulties, pain, and suffering of youth. Rather, it translates to acknowledging and attending to the hardships that youth face and identifying threats while focusing on both the evocation of strengths and education in the service of change. The last relates to creating situations in which youth can acquire new information and develop new skills, which reflects an emphasis on lifelong learning.

Table 2.7 has been included to elucidate differences between strengths-based and non-strengths-based perspectives (i.e., traditional, pathology or problem focused).

TABLE 2.7 Differences between strengths-based and non-strengths-based perspectives

Strengths based	Non-strengths based
• Recognition of the youth as having abilities and strengths.	• Presumption of the youth as lacking in ability and having deficits.
• Recognition of the youth's caregivers as competent and caring.	• Presumption of incapability by caregivers.
• Appreciation that caution toward professionals, if present, may be an appropriate response to past experience.	• Regarding caution as "resistance," lack of readiness, or character-based hostility.
• Recognition of the primary expertise of caregivers, who are full partners in treatment, in relation to their adolescents.	• Caregivers seen as obstacles to treatment, or as entirely dependent on the expertise of professionals.
• Recognition of youth as resilient, with desire for approval from adults, and capacity to make choices of their own.	• Youth seen as fragile or unreachable and unable to make meaningful personal decisions.
• Mental health, other human service professionals and educators seen as offering essential experience and willingness to collaborate.	• Other professionals seen as part of the problem, or as pursuing own agenda (saving money, avoiding responsibility, etc.).
• Recognition that every youth's community contains valuable resources to be tapped.	• Certain communities seen as entirely negative without countervailing resources.
• Recognition that effective treatment involves intrinsic (non-professional) resources, not just professional services.	• Continuing dependence on services and professionals to produce change.
• Recognition that specific racial and cultural factors influence the treatment process and that the child's cultural heritage and practices need to be understood and respected.	• Belief that "everyone is the same," and that good intentions without awareness of culture is sufficient.
• Commitment to a multilevel understanding of the youth, encompassing the youth, family, community, helping systems, culture.	• Belief that understanding of single dimension(s) is enough (e.g., biological, emotional, family, etc.).
• Commitment to consensus-building among key participants as essential to effective treatment and service determination.	• Belief that experts alone are best equipped to make clinical decisions, and that involvement of others will hinder the process.
• Belief that meaningful change is attainable; problems are barriers to progress, not fixed pathology.	• Problems seen as result of regression, fixation and pathology. Tendency to fix blame.

The YCW as a Conduit

Much of my post-secondary education and early training in YFS was seeped in learning theories that were problem focused and pathology laden. It seemed the point of these theories was to reduce suffering, help people to cope better with life and life circumstances, and to have less troublesome existences. Admirable outcomes, perhaps—but negatively skewed nonetheless. Most of what I learned left me feeling hopeless both in terms of my options for helping others and regarding my ability to actually do something that would improve lives.

On the job, my experience was quite different. My clients—primarily children, youth, and families—would show me time and time again how resilient they were. They would meet the challenges in their lives and more often than not leave services better off than when they began. But I was not using theories I was learning. They simply held too negative and pessimistic a view for me and as I discovered, my clients as well. This had me wondering: How then are my clients actually improving?

One possible answer came through a quote I heard, "Sometimes clients get better despite their therapists." I was concerned that that might be true for my clients. Were the kids I worked with getting better by overcoming my ineptness? I had to consider the idea since I was not using the conventional methods of the time—which I assumed to be reliable and valid given the amount that had been written about them. And because I could not explain my clients' improvement I had a difficult time explaining how I could be contributing to their positive changes.

Then something happened. While in my master's program I came across the work of the late psychiatrist, Dr. Milton H. Erickson. I learned that Dr. Erickson was one of the first mental health practitioners to focus on patients' (Erickson was a physician) abilities and strengths (Haley, 1973). Although there were (and remain today) many interpretations of Erickson's approach, what became clear to me was the vision of possibility he saw in others. Where one might see pathology, Erickson saw possibility. And with his vision of possibility came hope. The more I read the more hopeful I became. What Erickson did therapeutically was familiar, his focus on strengths resonated deeply with me. And for the first time, I thought, maybe some sliver of my efforts to help youth and families actually worked.

As I learned about Erickson and studied his cases, I came across one in particular that changed the way I thought about my work in YFS (Zeig, 1982, 1985a, 1985b). At the heart of the story is what I believe to be one of Erickson's lasting contributions to the field of psychotherapy—the principle of "utilization." We will explore this concept in detail later in this book but for now, let's consider that utilization recognizes both the uniqueness of each individual and the unique features of whatever it is he or she is struggling with. Erickson saw what a person brings to treatment as the raw material with which to construct a solution. A person's mannerisms, language style, behaviors, stories, postures, physical peculiarities and even the presenting problem provide material with which to construct a therapeutic intervention. What a person brings to services and even circumstances during services can be utilized effectively for a resolution of the presenting problem.

Here is the story that profoundly influenced my work in YFS:

A former patient of Dr. Milton Erickson had an aunt living in Milwaukee who had become quite seriously depressed and perhaps suicidal. The man spoke with the psychiatrist and asked if he would stop in and see her when he came to the area to give a lecture. Dr. Erickson agreed.

The woman, who had inherited a fortune from her family, was secure financially. She lived alone in a mansion, had never married, and had lost most of her close friends and relatives. Now in her 60s, she had developed some medical problems that required her to use a wheelchair. This had significantly altered her social activities.

Dr. Erickson arrived at the woman's house following his lecture. She was expecting him as her nephew had told her that he was coming. Upon his arrival, the two met and she began to give him a tour of her home. Although the woman had had some changes made to her home to make it more wheelchair accessible, it appeared to be largely unchanged from its original 1890s structure and décor. The house showed faded glory and the scent of musk. Dr. Erickson was struck by the fact that the curtains were drawn, contributing to an overall feeling of darkness. It was as if the majestic old home was a place of depression instead of happiness.

But the woman saved the best part of the tour for last. She finished by showing Dr. Erickson her pride and joy—a greenhouse nursery that was attached to the house. It was in this greenhouse that the woman had spent many tireless, happy hours working with her plants. As the two admired the flowers and plants, she showed Dr. Erickson her most recent project, which was to take clippings of African violet plants and grow new plants from them.

Following the tour, the two continued to speak. Dr. Erickson learned from the woman that although she was isolated, at one time she had been quite active in her local church. But since she began using a wheelchair, she attended only Sunday services. The woman described how she had hired her handyman to take her to and from church and because the church was not wheelchair accessible, he would lift her in and out of the building. Worried about blocking foot traffic, the woman told Dr. Erickson that she would arrive late and leave early.

After hearing the woman's story, Dr. Erickson told her that her nephew was worried about how depressed she had become. She admitted that the situation had become quite serious. But Dr. Erickson told the woman that he did not think that depression was the problem. Instead, what had become clear to him was that she had not been being a very good Christian. The woman was immediately taken aback by this comment, aghast that he would say such a thing.

Dr. Erickson continued, "Here you are with all this money, time on your hands, and a green thumb. And it's all going to waste. What I recommend is that you get a copy of the church directory and then look in the latest church bulletin. You'll find announcements of births, deaths, graduations, engagements, and marriages in there—all the happy and sad events in the lives of people in your congregation. Make a number of African violet cuttings and get them well-established. Then repot them into gift pots and have your handyman drive you to the homes of people who are affected by these happy or sad events. Bring them a plant and your congratulations or condolences and comfort, whichever is appropriate to the situation." After hearing Dr. Erickson's recommendation, she agreed that perhaps she had fallen down on her Christian duty and agreed to do more.

About 10 years later an article appeared in a local Milwaukee newspaper. It was a feature story with a headline that read, "African Violet Queen of Milwaukee Dies, Mourned by Thousands." The article detailed the life of this incredibly caring woman who had become famous for her trademark flowers and her charitable work with people in the community.

I was moved by the story—the resilience of a woman who touched the lives of so many and how Erickson, through one encounter, was able to help her to jump start her life. I had many "take aways" from the story, the most prominent of which was to use whatever youth brought to the table as fodder for change. And if that's where the story ended that would have been enough. But as they say, there was more to the story.

As I continued to immerse myself in Dr. Erickson's ideas I came across a host of other clinicians who had continued the psychiatrist's legacy. I wrote letters to many of them. I received one response. It was from Bill O'Hanlon, a therapist who had codeveloped a model called *Solution-Oriented Therapy*, which was largely based on his interpretation of Dr. Erickson's work (O'Hanlon, 1987; O'Hanlon & Weiner-Davis, 2003). Bill had studied with Dr. Erickson in the 1970s and that experience had significantly shaped his perspective. I first corresponded with Bill in 1992 and met him in 1994 when I began to study with him.

A short time after I met Bill he recounted how Dr. Erickson had told him the story of the "African Violet Queen." Since I had gained so much from it I told Bill how excited I was to hear the story in person. Bill told it in much the same way as I had read it, with one exception. He recounted that after Dr. Erickson was finished he said, "I don't get it. It's a good story, but that's not how we are trained. As therapists we are trained to focus on depression and problems. Why did you talk about flowers?" Dr. Erickson replied, "As I walked through the house the only sign of life I saw was the African violet plants and the nursery. I thought it would be much easier to grow the African violet part of her life than to weed out the depression."

That, in one sentence, describes what it means to be strengths based. We acknowledge that there are physical, cognitive, emotional, developmental, and other hurdles and/or limitations that must be taken into consideration and addressed in any form of human, social, educational, or mental health services. There are, however, in every situation exceptions, opportunities, and solutions that can be drawn on to facilitate growth, development, and well-being. Dr. Erickson had a perspective that emphasized strengths. He followed that perspective with suggestions for developing the woman's abilities and reconnecting her with resources. As YCWs our job is to take strengths-based ideas and go from "bench to trench" by applying them to real-world situations.

All for One and One for All

We have explored how the role of the YCW is reliant on a personal philosophy that reflects elements such as competency, well-being, resilience, and hope. For youth, the absence of hope is one of the most devastating experiences they can have. Its presence, by way of contrast, can lead to new possibilities in how youth experience themselves, the world, and in the actions they take. Although hope is just one aspect of the change equation, it is a necessary catalyst in the larger world and without which we have no art, no science, no education, no imagination, and no sense of opportunity. YCWs who maintain their sense of hope are better able to envision possibilities for change and create opportunities in their interactions with others, particularly on the front lines.

As we know, the front lines are comprised of multiple persons who provide an array of services. We quite simply cannot be successful without each other. We must all be on the same page philosophically. How do we get there? Through commitment, practice, and patience. Each of us has to make a personal commitment to work hard, learn, and reflect. We also have a collective responsibility to get better. Better agencies have better teams, stronger administration, and the like. There is no randomness to success in YFS.

As my agency blossomed from a few dozen employees to over 350 we experienced growing pains. To navigate the growth, we developed a strengths-based philosophy training. We began with current employees and then expanded to new hires. Whether on the front lines, maintenance, administration, human services, or any other capacity, if a person works at YIN they are trained in "Strengths-Based 101" (or "Bob's Brainwash 101" as I've been told it is often called). The result has been a stronger, more cohesive agency from program to program (Bertolino, 2011).

three
Engagement: Creating and Strengthening Relationships

If you talk to a man in a language he understands, that goes to his head.
If you talk to him in his language, that goes to his heart.

—Nelson Mandela

A few years back I taught a workshop on brief therapy to first responders who resided in southern California. The first responders included both medical and nonmedical personnel who were preparing to work in crisis situations such as earthquakes, forest fires, hurricanes, and other natural disasters. It was a group of about 300, and the content of the workshop was at the request of the sponsor, a community mental health board.

Early in the morning session I was speaking about the initial contacts we have with those who are in the midst of crisis. I spoke about how people are often in shock and ways that first responders might engage such persons. At one particular point a woman raised her hand. I paused, asked her name, and invited her to comment. Her name was Sarah, and she stated, "You're talking about therapy. We are not therapists." I asked her to expand on her concern so that I could better understand what she meant by her comment. She elaborated, "Well, what you're describing are things that therapists do. We're not trained to do therapy." There seemed to be some kind of misunderstanding between us so I asked her to describe what she would do if she encountered a person who had just lost her home and meaningful possessions in a forest fire. Sarah said, "I would listen to her. I would let her know I was there for her. I would ask her what I could do for her."

I listened as Sarah eloquently described how she would attend to a person in need. I then asked the audience if what they heard from the participant was similar or different than what they would do. The group agreed with what had been said while adding a few other ideas that made good sense. I then said, "What I am hearing all sounds right. And if I am in another context, it sounds like a physician helping a patient to feel comfortable. In another, it's a teacher making a connection with a student. And given my background what I am hearing sounds like what a therapist would do. But, most importantly, it sounds to me like a person who is trying to connect with another human being—in this instance, in a time of profound loss." I finished by saying, "Be sure to abide by the laws of your state and profession in terms of your scope of practice. Know the difference between the kind of boundaries that are there to protect people from harm and the artificial ones we manufacture in our heads, mostly out of fear. Healing arises from compassion and care for others. What matters most is how we respond to others in their time of need."

At the lunch break, Sarah approached me. "I realized as we were talking how we have been trained to death. We have training on everything. It's seems like something new every week. I think that all the training has desensitized me and maybe even made me paranoid. I've become disconnected while trying to help others. I've been so worried about doing something wrong—of hurting someone while trying to help them. But if I'm not connecting with the people I'm trying to help, then what am I really doing?" she said.

I thanked Sarah for her commitment to helping others as a first responder. I then commented on her self-awareness. "Helping others requires humility. We have maps given to us through books and training which provide us with explanations about what we are *supposed* to do, but the map is never the territory. Since every person is different some things will work, some will not. Making mistakes is part of learning. But you will never be wrong if you extend compassion. The fact that you are willing to reflect on your experience shows you care." Sarah smiled.

At the center of each of my trainings, no matter the composition of helping professionals in the audience, is the relationship. As we learned in Chapter 2, over 1100 studies have been completed on the alliance in psychology and psychotherapy alone (Norcross, 2011). Positive relationships are quintessential to effective services. This entire chapter focuses on how to engage youth and supportive others who may be involved in the lives of youth through helping relationships. Because the views that youth have of YFS staff are a strong predictor of eventual outcome, it is critical that substantial efforts are made to form and strengthen relationships throughout the course of services. Given the amount of time front line staff and YCWs, in particular, spend with youth, conversations to build engagement should begin with those in the trenches.

The ideas and associated practices described in this chapter are meant to both identify classic forms of engagement with which many YCWs are familiar and introduce newer forms that have emerged out of a strengths-based perspective (Bertolino, 2010). This chapter is divided into two sections: *Collaboration Keys* and *Active Client Engagement*. Particularly important to the content of this chapter is its application both *prior* to the start of formal face-to-face interactions and throughout the course of services. The better we engage youth the more they are likely to benefit from services.

The ideas and practices in this chapter are also *isomorphic*. That is, the engagement processes we use in direct services parallel those used in supervision, team meetings, and so on (which will be discussed in upcoming chapters). So, as you proceed through this chapter, please consider how the ideas and practices relate to other contexts and situations.

Collaboration Keys

There are a variety of ways that youth become involved with YFS—through caregivers, social services, court systems, and so on. Most often someone other than the youth initiates services, doing so primarily due to a problem or concern. The idea of "problems" as a gateway to services is not unique. People who see physicians do so because they are ill or not feeling well; however, many also do so as a preventative measures—to ensure their health. In YFS, a paradigm based on pathology perpetuates the field. Emphasis is largely on identifying and explaining problems in terms of pathology, and delivering interventions by experts. There are at least two "problems" with this perspective. First, there is no evidence that focusing on pathology actually improves the lives of youth and leads to better outcomes. Second, a pathology focus de-emphasizes the contributions of youth—their strengths and resources including coping skills, resiliencies, and motivations.

From a strengths-based perspective, we seek to set a different tone in first contacts, knowing this will affect services that follow. Our primary consideration in taking a crisis call, scheduling a face-to-face appointment, completing an investigation, or with any situation that involves meeting youth or supportive others involved with youth for the first time is with making a connection that will create an opportunity for positive change. By forming strong connections, we can help youth to experience a positive bond which as we learned in the previous chapter is part of the alliance, and comprised of elements such as compassion, warmth, empathy, and genuineness.

A strong YCW–youth (or caregiver) bond also improves opportunities to gather information related to the situation and to determine next steps. For example, in a crisis call, it is imperative to collect information about the seriousness of a situation, including any potential safety concerns or risks. First contacts can largely influence what happens next. YCWs who are genuine and warm increase the likelihood of forming respectful bonds with youth and caregivers. Because research indicates that better alliances yield better outcomes YCWs attend to the nuances involved with building safe and secure relationships. Next we delve into areas that YCWs can explore with youth to determine the best possible "fit" for services that follow. We'll refer to these areas as collaboration keys (CKs). The purpose of the CKs is to create and enhance connections that are enduring and beneficial to youth and those who are involved with the care of youth.

Collaboration Key 1: Create Listening Space

Engagement involves careful listening and attention to youth and those involved with services for youth. Of the keys to collaboration, none is more important than creating listening space—room for clients to share stories through their experiences, points of view, concerns, and hopes for change. For some, sharing their stories will be the most important part of services. This is because many youth and caregivers have heard the voices of blame, marginalization, and negativity in previous experiences with YFS.

YCWs begin interactions by asking general questions. Examples of possible opening questions include:

- Where would you like to start?
- What would you like to talk about?
- What is most important for me to know about you and/or your situation/concern?
- Are there certain things that you want to be sure we talk about?
- What is your understanding of our services and how we help supportive others?
- What ideas do you have about how our services and/or coming to see me might be helpful?
- In what ways do you see me as helping you with your situation?
- What do you feel/think you need from me right now?

Not all YFS are initiated by youth or caregivers. There will be instances when youth are mandated or sent involuntarily or caregivers will be required to attend services. In these instances, it remains important to ask questions such as those just listed. We want to invite youth and supportive others to tell us about themselves and their situations—including any dissatisfaction they may have about the choice of involvement with services. The more they are left out of conversations the more service-oriented relationships are likely to suffer. At the same time, YCWs will seek moments to explain, as needed, the purpose of services, their role, and so on. As we will learn in the next chapter, there will be ample time for more direct questions.

YCWs pay especially close attention to youth and supportive others' statements and responses, taking care not to dismiss their internal experience(s) by pushing for change, trying to get them to move on, being too positive, or using other methods that they may experience as being insensitive or disrespectful. YCWs remain aware of the inherent cultural biases that may exist toward redemptive stories. We try not to change, reframe, or invalidate youth or supportive others' nonredemptive, unhappy-ending stories too quickly and without properly attending to their emotional experience. Doing so means avoiding the use of glib explanations (e.g., "I wonder what you are meant to learn from this?" or "What part of you needs or benefits from this pain?") and platitudes (e.g., "Everything will work out"; "God doesn't give you more than you can handle"; and "You are going to be all right"). The use of explanations, interpretations, and metaphors based on YCWs' personal assumptions and biases can alienate and close avenues to change.

To address our personal biases as helping professionals, we adopt a position of cultural curiosity by asking youth and supportive others about their cultures, contributing to a cross-cultural interaction in a mutually influencing relationship (Madsen, 2007). Cultural curiosity involves elicitation, instead of assignment of meaning. YCWs evoke from youth and supportive others the meanings they have attached to events, situations, and relationships as opposed to ascribing some professional explanation or meaning.

To prepare for engaging youth in conversations, psychologist Julie Tilsen (2013) has proposed a set of questions to consider as service providers. These questions can help us to clarify where we stand, what we believe and think, and how we feel before stepping into relational territory. They are meant to shine light on how we position ourselves in our relationships with youth:

- *How do you think of yourself in relationship to youth, and youth in relationship to you?*
  This central question focuses on how we position ourselves with youth regarding cultural and ethical matters. We explore: How do we view the role of authority, professional power and influence? What is your perspective on self-disclosure? We also reflect further on philosophical issues as to how we expect change to occur, whether we (as YCWs to other professional) think that we also learn and change as we work with others,
- *How do you think about the purpose of your relationship?*
  We clarify: What is our role in YFS? What is the role of youth? How do we define what we are doing in our work with youth? What are the results, outcomes, and by-products of this relationship? And what are the implications— meaning and effects—of thinking this way?
- *How do you think about your relationship with external institutions of authority (e.g., licensing boards, professional guilds, third-party payers, corrections/law enforcement, social service systems, medical authorities, education systems, etc.)?*
  This question spawns others that reveal our position on external entities that may be involved with the care, oversight, and treatment of youth. Whom do you work for and account to? What authorities or institutions do you turn to for information and direction? How do you use that information? How do you feel about and use diagnosis and/or labels? How do you communicate with and share information with collateral service providers? How do you talk with youth about this process? How do you manage multiple perspectives?
- *How do you think of yourself in relationship to prevailing cultural discourses?*
  In what ways do you consider the impact of your social location on your identity as a YCW (or other professional in YFS), and in relationship to the social location of youth? How do you think services are influenced by social

discourses and local politics? In what ways do you explore prevailing discourses and their effects on you, youth, and your work?

- *How do you decide to communicate (or not communicate) to youth the ways in which you view all of these relationships?*
  What are your thoughts on transparency? How is transparency different than self-disclosure? What are ethical implications of your stance on transparency? (pp. 3–4)

These questions are intended to encourage reflection. Lack of thought about issues pertinent to relationships can contribute to relationship problems, which, in turn, can affect eventual outcome. In addition, because such questions draw attention to ethics and accountability, there is an increased risk of misunderstanding when these things have not been thought out. One way to reflect on these questions is by talking about them in small groups. Doing so will provide an opportunity to flesh out thoughts and feelings and to hear multiple, and often very different, points of view.

Collaboration Key 2: Address Expectations

Youth and those involved in the lives of youth both seek and begin services with ideas shaped by multiple influences. Media (television, film, radio, magazines), social relationships (family, friends), previous service experiences, and interactions with professionals such as juvenile officers, social workers, teachers, and so on all represent possible sources of information that can at best educate and at worst produce paralyzing fears. Some will express apprehension or fear, others will not. Regardless of whether services are by choice or not, it is critical that YCWs invite youth and those involved to ask questions and share their thoughts in terms of expectations. This can include what might help them to feel more comfortable, what could contribute to a positive experience, what they hope to accomplish, and any ideas as to what might help to get the services or program off to a good start. Youth expectations of services can affect how services progress and the degree to which they can be beneficial (Frank & Frank, 1991). Beyond asking straightforward questions about the expectations of youth, we can strengthen the alliance through active listening, exploring beliefs, and being transparent in answering questions.

A major step for caregivers, and even more so for youth, is just asking for help. Whether through phone calls, walk-ins, expected or unexpected visits, a host of feelings and worries about seeking assistance can come to the forefront. These feelings may be intensified and contribute to a sense of being "one-down" in relation to the provider, potentially contributing to distrust and suspicion. One way to neutralize any ill feelings as well as myths about how things will unfold is to ensure that those involved are able to ask questions *prior to the start of services.*

When services are sought or initiated by someone other than the youth we want to be thorough in answering questions and removing any barriers about what services are or are not. For example, in residential programs it is not uncommon for caregivers to want us to "fix" their kids. It is not necessarily that they are exonerating themselves from the issues at hand, it is merely a perception they carry. If the youth is not the one requesting services an option is to suggest that the caller/contact person (i.e., caregiver) have youth call to do a pre-interview (Bertolino, 2010). Doing so provides an opportunity for youth, who are typically not involved in the decision to initiate services, to ask questions about what to expect. The aim of these conversations is not to get another side of the story or engage in "problem talk" but to answer questions about services. Especially with regard to emergency shelters, and transitional and independent living programs, pre-interviews provide an early opportunity to answer general questions and alleviate anxiety (Bertolino, 2003).

It is worth mentioning that the word "interviewing" may seem antithetical to a collaborative stance, suggesting an asymmetrical relationship. Interviewing in this sense refers to YCWs being open, flexible, and genuine. It also describes a posture of encouraging youth to take the lead and become involved early in decisions. The following examples offer ideas about how to approach pre-interviews.

Case Example 3.1

Caller: I'm calling about my 15-year-old son who has run away several times.

YCW: I'm glad you called. How did you hope we might help with your situation?

Caller: I'm just not sure what you do. Do you take kids like my son?

YCW: Yes. Some of the youth who come here have run away. Others are coping with different problems. We understand that each situation is different. It sounds like you are going through a rough time with your son.

Caller: Without a doubt. I'm trying to figure out what to do. I saw a program on tv—something called "Scared Straight." Do you do that?

YCW: I'm sorry we don't. We have a different approach. The kids who come here stay anywhere from 24 hours to two weeks. During that time we work with them and their families to get things back on track.

Caller: So the kids stay there?

YCW: Yes. The kids who come to our emergency stay here. We also have other programs such as outclient counseling. The youth we see in that program do not stay. They come in by themselves or whenever possible, with those who support them, and see a therapist face to face.

Caller: Oh, I see. Things are pretty bad here. I think we need a break from each other.

YCW: Ok. I want to make sure that I connect you with a program that fits for you.

Caller: If my son came there what would it involve?

YCW: I'd be happy to tell you about the program. I'd also like to gather some information from you to make sure we can provide what you need and if not, steer you in the right direction. Would that be okay?

Caller: That sounds good.

Case Example 3.2

Youth (young adult): I'm calling because I need a place to stay.

YCW: Thanks for calling. Are you some place safe?

Youth: Yeah. But I can't stay here much longer. I've been on my own since I was 17.

YCW: And now you are . . .?

Youth: 18.

YCW: Are you looking for a place to stay until you find another option or something longer term?

Youth: Both, I guess. I heard you guys have apartments if you are homeless.

YCW: That's true. That's one of several programs we have for young people like yourself.

Youth: How do I get in?

YCW: Do you have a few minutes to answer some questions so I can help you with that?

Youth: Yeah.

YCW: Great. First, you said you are in a safe place but can't stay there much longer. Is that right?

Youth: Uh huh. I'm at a friend's.

YCW: How much longer would you say you can stay there?

Youth: Well, my buddy said if I have a for-sure place to go I can stay a week more.

YCW: Okay. If that changes let us know. In the meantime, I'll give you some information about our long-term programs and you can decide if what we have to offer is something you want to pursue.

Youth: Sounds good.

YCW: We have a transitional living program (TLP) and independent living program (ILP). TLP is a house where we start most people in and ILP is the apartments you heard about. What we do is gather some basic information then set up a face-to-face interview. At the interview we do a brief assessment, tell you about the programs, and then consider which of our programs seems to be the best fit. If we don't see a fit we connect you with other resources in the community. Okay so far?

Youth: Yeah.

YCW: If we find a fit we offer you a spot and move forward to have you enter our program. The thing is, and this is really important, only on rare occasions do youth go straight into ILP. Nearly all start in TLP.

Youth: Why? I've been living on my own. I can handle it.

YCW: I can hear the confidence in your voice. That's wonderful. What we have found is that those who are most successful start in TLP. This is because they learn about our program expectations, have a job, and are on a clear path to the futures they want. Does that make sense?

Youth: It does. But I think I am ready for an apartment.

YCW: What do you think about telling us more about your point of view, and your strengths in particular, in an interview?

Youth: Okay. What do we need to do to get going on that?

YCW: Let me get some information and I'll help you get squared away with an interview.

Pre-interviews are an opportunity to flesh out the expectations of all involved. There are types of service in which pre-interviews may not be possible (i.e., child abuse investigations, etc.) in the form described. But there almost always is room for youth and caregivers, in particular, to ask clarifying questions. What is clear is that the more comfortable our youth are the more likely they are to follow through with and benefit from services.

A final area of service expectations is the pre-existing beliefs have about our programs and/or the contexts. The past experiences of youth and caregivers can influence the effectiveness of services rendered. Said differently, reputation matters. One way to address this issue is to directly ask youth and supportive others involved what they know about the organization or agency, program, setting, and so on. Another is to ask about any previous experiences with services. Answers to these questions offer YCWs the opportunity to dispel any myths and clarify what actually happens during service delivery. The following case example illustrates this point.

Case Example 3.3

Anne, an 18-year-old female, came to see me due to problems with substance abuse. During our initial appointment she stated that she had recently seen a social worker at a local community mental health center. When I asked what her experience had been like Anne stated, "The social worker I saw was very nice. She listened really well." When I asked Anne how she knew the social worker had been listening to her she responded, "She would say 'uh huh' and nod her head." I followed, "Is that what you feel you need?" To this Anne replied, "That's not all I need. I didn't go back after a few sessions because I didn't think we were getting anywhere. I need someone to help me come up with some answers." I said, "Let me see if I follow you. Are you saying that what you need is someone who listens really well and also works with you to come up with answers?" "That's right. I need both," Anne replied. Although I had a good idea what would indicate to her that I was listening well, following her response, I spent time learning more from the young woman about how she thought I might help her in coming up with answers. Through the remainder of our time together I continued to check in with Anne to ensure that she was getting what she needed, to determine if any changes or modifications were necessary, and if the ways in which we were approaching her situation were right for her.

It is important to bear in mind that the pre-existing beliefs of youth can affect the entire course of services. Youth whose experiences with a particular organization, program, or provider have been positive are more likely to be involved with and benefit from services. Conversely, negative experiences (e.g., feeling devalued, invalidated, being left out of discussions about services) can affect the degree to which youth benefit from current and future services (both within a practice/

organization and with current or future outside helpers). The questions that follow can help YCWs learn about the expectations of those seeking services:

- Do you have any questions about what our services are or are not?
- Do you have any questions about how we work with persons such as yourself?
- Do you have any questions about what we do here?
- What do you know about our agency/program?
- Do you have any concerns about our agency/program?
- Is there anything you would like to know about our services or what we do here and the possible benefits or drawbacks?
- Is there anything I can do to help you feel more comfortable in starting services?
- (If youth have received services previously) What has been your experience with services in the past?
- (If youth experienced previous services as negative) What can we do differently here to ensure that things go better for you this time? (Bertolino, 2010)

Introducing other factors that may influence how youth expect services to proceed can also prove helpful. These can include but are not limited to intake processes, paperwork and documentation, payment processes, phone calls after hours, crises and emergencies, referrals, clinical supervision, staff meetings, and so on. Youth may have more or fewer questions about specific procedures and processes, but providing information in written form that can be followed up on during meetings is generally good practice. Informational materials should reflect the philosophy and language of the staff and the overall organization or practice and include how those who seek services will be referred to (i.e., "clients," "patients," "residents," etc.), how staff refer to themselves (by name, "Mr. or Ms.," "staff," etc.), and the general language that will be used with youth and those involved with youth, in conversations with staff and other professionals outside the setting, in reports and publications, and in community relations (e.g., fundraisers and interviews).

Collaboration Key 3: Attend to Preferences

As discussed in the previous chapter, one of the four empirically supported components of the alliance is *accommodating the client's preferences*. Programs will vary in practices and youth and caregivers who seek services will often have preferences making it is important that YCWs attend to such nuances. Positive change can be inhibited when program rules or a staff person's practice preferences run counter to or do not match those of youth. There are several ways of tuning into preferences. Examples include asking questions about who should be involved with services, the format of meetings/sessions (i.e., individual or joint meetings, length of meetings, etc.), and physical space and setting of meetings/sessions.

Involvement in meetings can be especially sensitive when it comes to youth. This is because caregivers, court officials and the like may identify youth as "the problem" and expect that them to be seen separately. It is imperative that YCWs proceed carefully, acknowledging different perspectives while maintaining an open mind. However, YCWs who attain multiple viewpoints are likely to have a more encompassing view of the concern(s) at hand. Therefore YCWs should not hesitate to firmly encourage participation, doing so in a respectful manner.

The following examples offer possibilities for attending to the preferences of youth and supportive others involved.

Case Example 3.4

Caller: My daughter is tearing our house apart. She needs to get her act together fast. I need an appointment so someone can talk some sense into her.

YCW: It sounds like things are tense with your daughter.

Caller: Very tense. Can you get her in so someone can get her straightened out?

YCW: One of the things we want to be sure of is that we are getting the information we need to be helpful. To do this I'd like to ask that we not only meet with your daughter but also you and others who you think might be helpful with your situation.

Caller: I can tell you what you need to know over the phone.

YCW: That will be helpful and I do have some questions for you. And we'd also like you to come to the first meeting so we can meet face to face. From there we can decide how to continue.

Caller: I guess that will be fine.

Case Example 3.5

Caller: I'm calling because I have an appointment to bring my son in tomorrow. My worry is that we tried this once before and he refused to talk. Would it be possible for him to talk with someone by himself for just a few minutes? I don't think he'll talk if I'm in the room.

YCW: Thank you taking the time to call and let us know about your concern and how we might help. I will make a note here that you would like us to meet with your son individually for part of the session. Is there anything else we ought to consider for your meeting?

Caller: No, that's it. It's a relief knowing that we can be flexible about this.

YCW: Absolutely. We work as a team so I will make sure that no matter who meets with you in aware of our conversation. And if anything changes you can let us know by calling ahead of time or at the time of the meeting.

Making adjustments to what may seem small aspects can make large differences. Because preferences are subject to change, ongoing dialogue is necessary. The following example illustrates how YCWs can open up dialogue to determine if adjustments are in order in a first contact.

Case Example 3.6

(Family Meeting at an Emergency Shelter.)

YCW: There aren't any right or wrong ways about how we work together. We could keep everyone together or I could spend some individual time with each of you, or we could do a combination of both. Whatever we decide, we can also change. Does anyone here have an opinion about how we should start?

Parent: Well, we tried meeting together in therapy and it didn't work. I think it's because we argued so much and talked over each other that we really couldn't get anywhere. So my vote is that we do something else.

YCW: What might be a good way start?

Parent: I think we should try meeting like this, but if we start arguing, maybe we should talk with you separately. That might be a good idea anyway— to talk to us separately once in a while.

YCW: Okay. Who else agrees or has another idea?

(Two of the family members agree, and one does not give a verbal response.)

YCW: Okay, so two of you agree. Luke, you didn't say anything, but I saw your shoulders drop. What do you think?

Luke: I don't care. This is stupid. I don't have anything to say anyway.

YCW: That's fine. I just want to be sure that if you have an opinion you are able to share it. Will it be okay with you if you and I spend a few minutes together once in a while?

Luke: I guess.

There are, of course, extenuating circumstances that require YCWs to take more directive routes. For example, if a youth uses verbally abusive statements about another and the YCW's immediate efforts do not end such behavior, it may be necessary to dismiss one or more persons from the group. In such cases, those dismissed may be brought back together when they agree to treat others more respectfully. Another situation would be prior knowledge of potential aggressive behavior or when meeting with certain combinations of people could increase risk of harm. Then, the YCW must respond accordingly. Safety and well-being are always a primary consideration.

Safety is also expressed in terms of physical space and settings within which YFS are provided. Physical space includes the design, setup, and accessibility of areas that youth and supportive others may utilize (e.g., reception areas, hallways, stairs, ramps, elevators, waiting rooms, therapy offices, restrooms, parking). Setting also involves pictures and wall fixtures, reading materials (both leisure and educational), toys, and other physical elements that reflect respect for culture, ethnicity, and family background.

Case Example 3.7

I met with a mother and son for an intake assessment. Within the first few minutes it became evident that Miles, the son, was very uncomfortable. I asked him if he was okay but he did not reply verbally. Instead he scanned the room, nervously. His mom then inquired, "Would it be possible to meet in a room where it isn't too loud? I don't mean loud with sound. I mean a room where there aren't many things on the walls . . . that's not as cluttered. Rooms like this make Miles nervous. It's like there's too much going on. Is that possible?" "Sure," I replied. "We have an office that has a couch and two chairs, a bookcase, and a desk, but there are very few other things in it—just one picture. I can show it to the two of you. Miles, if you don't find it comfortable, I have another in mind as well. How does that sound, Miles?" Miles shook his head "yes" and we moved to an adjacent office.

As discussed in Chapter 2, cultural competence is a cornerstone of a strengths-based perspective. Addressing physical environment is one of the more visible ways of conveying cultural safety. It also conveys to our clients that we are listening and concerned about their preferences. Although space restrictions, the timing of meetings and so on can provide barriers to some setting options, oftentimes acknowledging a preference and then making more subtle changes will help. For example, with the situation previously described we would start by asking what we could do with the room to make it more comfortable. This could translate to taking down a few pictures or rearranging some items.

There are of course benefits and drawbacks when it comes to choices about settings. One benefit is that choices will help some youth to feel more comfortable. It can also provide YCWs the opportunity to observe and learn about youth in different settings, such as an office, car or van, park bench, basketball court, and so on. A drawback to different settings—particularly outside a residential building or office is safety. YCWs are always to be aware of their settings and safety issues can arise in any setting; however, the risks are without doubt greater in external environments. Ensuring safety and monitoring variables in external environments is much more difficult. All YCWs should be trained in measures that ensure safety and have support systems in place to respond to potential dangers.

Case Example 3.8

YCW: Our program is set up so that we have a few choices of where we can meet—in one of two upstairs offices, a basement office, or . . .
Youth (Looking downward): Ok.
YCW: Would you rather sit outside? We have a picnic table. Or we could go for a walk.
Youth: Really? A walk would be cool.
YCW: Great. Let's do that.

Case Example 3.9

YCW: We have a few choices in terms of offices where we can meet. We could meet at the main office, which is in the county. I'm there on Mondays and Wednesdays. A second possibility would be to meet at one of our two satellite offices. I'm at the south office on Tuesdays, and we have another YCW who works out of the north office. She's there Tuesday through Friday.

Parent: Wow. I had no idea that I would have a choice. Let's try for a Monday appointment at your county office. My work is nearby and I can come straight over if we can find a time between 4:30 pm and 7:00 pm.

YCW: Great. I've got a 5:00 pm available next Monday. Will that work?

Parent: Yes, that's fine.

Studies suggest that setting variables, often referred to as an aspect of "site" effects, influence the variance in youth and supportive others outcomes (Greenberg, 1999). Said differently, attending to the preferences of youth and supportive others lets them know we care. Although further research is needed to better understand how setting variables truly affect services, most of us can understand the point of feeling more or less comfortable in some settings versus others. Choices offer flexibility, which can strengthen the alliance thereby increasing the likelihood of follow-through. At the same time, we want to hold those with whom we work, accountable for their choices and actions (i.e., missing or being late for appointments, etc.). We maintain a flexible posture whenever possible and yet we fully expect youth and caregivers to follow-through with what has been agreed on.

Collaboration Key 4: Introduce Real-Time Feedback

Cincinnati Children's Hospital (CCH) was considered one of the foremost treatment centers for patients with cystic fibrosis (CF). Patients sought medical treatment with belief that the outcomes at CCH were better than that of other hospitals. There was one problem: It wasn't true. In fact, CCH was average; its patients were living to be about 30 years old. At the best treatment centers, however, the numbers were much more promising with patients living to around 46 years old.

Surgeon Atul Gawande wrote about CCH's conundrum in his 2004 article, *The Bell Curve: What Happens When Patients Find out How Good Their Doctors Really Are?* Dr. Gawande explained that CCH was faced with the issue of what to do about the knowledge they had about their outcomes with CF patients. Hospital administrators made the decision to be transparent. First, they informed their patients of how the hospital's outcomes compared to national norms. Second, and more important, they vowed to do something about their average performance.

So how did CCH go about improving? They consulted with Don Berwick, then CEO of the Institute for Healthcare Improvement (IHI), a small organization with the mission of transforming healthcare. Hospital physicians also studied those centers with the best outcomes with CF. Along these lines, CCH staff narrowed its focus to those factors linked to longevity with CF, namely lung functioning. This concept has been called the 80/20 rule—80% of the results or value comes from 20% of the source or focus. We'll return to this concept in Chapter 4. CCH followed the best treatment centers, emphasizing subtle differences that account for the majority of outcome with CF patients. For example, a decrease in just 0.05% in lung functioning can over time compound and be the difference between life and death (Gawande, 2004). CCH knew that "average" with CF patients meant shorter life span. So they committed themselves to doing what it took to improve and extend the lives of their patients.

A few years ago I was invited to speak on how to improve mental health outcomes at CCH. It was clear by the focus of the conference that CCH's march toward excellence was not limited to CF. The institution was targeting *better* services across the board, an idea that should be on the collective conscience of every organization that provides YFS. And there is good news on this front. We have learned a few things about how improve outcomes with youth and families.

In the revised definition of a strengths-based perspective offered in Chapter 2 the final sentence reads, "Routine and ongoing real-time feedback is used to maintain a responsive, consumer-driven climate to ensure the greatest benefit of services." This statement stands as one of the most important developments in YFS. For decades programs have asked funders to continue to support "good work for good causes." It is understood that most programs do just that. But just as CCH has had to provide data related to its outcomes, how do we really know if a YFS agency, program, or service is truly effective? This very point requires all who work in YFS to more clearly delineate outcomes and *how* those outcomes are measured.

Behavioral health studies conducted over the last 50 years have found that a combination of a client's rating of the therapeutic alliance with the experience of meaningful change in the initial stages of services is a highly reliable predictor of eventual treatment outcome (Duncan et al., 2004). Further, best available research reveals that the use of routine and ongoing feedback provides a meaningful method for documenting the benefit of services. Seeking and obtaining valid, reliable, and feasible feedback from consumers regarding the therapeutic alliance and outcome as much as doubles the effect size of treatment, cuts dropout rates in half, and decreases the risk of deterioration. As the APA Task Force on Evidence-Based Practice (2006) concludes, "Providing clinicians with real-time patient feedback to benchmark progress in treatment and clinical support tools to adjust treatment as needed" is one of the "most pressing research needs" (p. 278).

Available research suggests that two points gain further attention. First, as discussed with the first principle of strengths-based youth care work, youth are the most significant contributors to service success. Next, as stated with the second principle, the therapeutic relationship makes substantial and consistent contributions to outcome. In fact, clients' (in this case, youth and others involved with youth) ratings of the therapeutic relationship are the best and most consistent process predictor of outcome. These two principles make it imperative that YCWs incorporate methods that encourage youth and supportive others to voice their perceptions, ideas, perspectives, preferences, observations, and/or evaluations.

The aforementioned principles are driven by two forms of measurement, which together form real-time feedback: *Outcome* and *alliance*. As outlined in the new strengths-based definition in Chapter 2, outcomes are comprised of three aspects of functioning: Individual, interpersonal, social role. Outcome measurement involves capturing clients' reports of the subjective benefit of services at the *beginning* of meetings (or sessions or interactions). This includes the idiosyncratic meaning attached by the client. Through ongoing monitoring of outcomes, YFS staff are able to learn from youth and supportive others whether and to what degree services provided are beneficial. Further, discussions about progress, lack thereof, or deterioration will be more data driven as outcomes are graphed and monitored. It should be noted that more so than diagnosis, the severity of the client's distress at intake predicts eventual outcome. Clients with higher levels of distress are more likely to show measured benefit from treatment than those with lower levels or those who present as non-distressed (Duncan et al., 2010). Knowledge about youth distress can inform decisions regarding the dose and intensity of services.

Alliance measurement involves monitoring the four components of the alliance described in Chapter 2: The client's view of the relationship (including perceptions of the provider as warm, empathic, and genuine); agreement on the goals, meaning or purpose of the treatment; agreement on the means and methods used; and the client's preferences. Formal alliance measurement takes place at the *end* of each meeting (or session or interaction) to learn how the youth experienced the conversation. However, alliance monitoring also involves periodically checking in. We want to know: Are youth feeling heard and understood? Are they satisfied with the direction of service? Do they feel the means used to achieve goals are a good fit? As meetings/sessions progress and end, YCWs and/or other YFS staff check with youth to learn their perceptions of interactions, again learning what worked well, what did not, and make any necessary adjustments to accommodate their preferences.

There are many types of outcome and alliance measure, some brief and some long. Selection and implementation of measures should be made with great care and will be discussed in more detail in Chapters 4. For now, consider the significance of a commitment to, as CCH did, measuring the benefit of services in a reliable and valid way. With such a commitment in hand, focus turns to how the role of feedback is introduced to youth and supportive others. An example follows of how the topic of real-time feedback might be introduced either prior to or at the start of services:

Introduction

We are committed to helping you to have the best experience possible and achieve the results you want from our work together. To ensure these things we have a way of working that may be a little different than other agencies.

For example we will check in with you periodically to get a sense of your experience. We might ask about what has been helpful to you, what has not, what is working, and what is not. This feedback will help us to make adjustments as we continue.

Along with checking in with you there are two brief questionnaires that can help us to learn from you how things are going and whether our work together is benefitting you. One is completed at the beginning of our meetings (or sessions or interactions) and the other at the end. The one at the beginning is called the _____ and will let us know whether or not and to what degree things are improving. If our work together is successful you should see some indication of that sooner rather than later. In the event that things are not improving in a way that is acceptable to you then we will discuss options. The second questionnaire, _____, which is completed at the end of our meetings (or sessions or interactions), will let us know more about how the meeting (or session or interaction) went for you and what we can do differently in future sessions should you decide to continue services here. We will discuss the results of each questionnaire together. Is that okay with you?

(Following consent) Thank you for your willingness to help us learn how we can best help you with your concerns. We would like to ask that you please be as open and forthcoming as you are comfortable with when we check in and when you complete the questionnaires. I also welcome any feedback, you might have along the way. It is important that you get the results you want and if not we are able to discuss options that may provide a better fit and outcome for you.

Notice the use of "we" in the examples. This is because in most YFS agencies services are provided by a team. We want to convey that we work together. That said, "I" can be used in place of "we." This may be necessary when interactions are consistently held between a particular staff member and a youth. No matter the number of staff involved, it is essential that information gleaned be responded to in a timely manner. In this way real-time feedback serves at least two purposes: To determine the benefit and fit of services. Based on feedback, decisions about type of service or approach, dosage form (i.e., frequency and length of meetings), and/or referral can be made.

From both a community and organizational standpoint real-time feedback provides data to contribute to more reliable and consistent rationale for service decisions. More specifically, the level of distress reported by youth and/or caregivers can play a vital role in determining what type of service represents the best fit at that moment in time. Measuring distress increases accountability and stewardship because it informs YFS workers of how the youth is functioning. As discussed, the use of real-time feedback can help to select the best available type of service and dosage form, which if provided in a timely and efficient manner can help to get youth back on track in their lives more quickly, thereby proving cost effective (Chiles, Lambert, & Hatch, 1999; Kraft, Puschner, Lambert, & Kordy, 2006).

It is understood that some YCWs and YFS personnel—including administration—will be skeptical about the promise of real-time feedback. There is a longstanding belief of many mental health and social services professionals that they "know real change" when they see it. There is no reliable research to support this claim. In fact, the findings are quite the opposite. Studies show that no matter the discipline (i.e., psychologists, counselors, social workers, marriage and family therapists) professionals:

- routinely fail to address dropout in services—which is arguably the greatest threat to mental health (Swift, Greenberg, Whipple, & Kominiak, 2012; Wierzbicki & Pekarik, 2002)
- routinely fail to identify which clients will not benefit from services and which will deteriorate (Hannan et al., 2005; Hansen, Lambert, & Forman, 2002; Lambert, 2010; Warren et al., 2010)
- tend to overrate their effectiveness (Hansen et al., 2002; Lambert, 2010; Sapyta, Reimer, & Bickman, 2005; Walfish, McAlister, O'Donnnell, & Lambert, 2012)
- vary substantially in terms of effectiveness when compared to others with similar training and experience (Baldwin et al., 2007; Wampold & Brown, 2005) plateau in effectiveness without concerted efforts to improve it (Hubble, Duncan, Miller, & Wampold, 2010).

If the best available research is not enough to influence a feedback-driven shift in YFS, we face the prospect of an uncertain future. Pride is not an effective strategy. Once again, however, the news is rather promising when we choose to accept the challenge of demonstrating through empirically tested, not just anecdotal means, that our services make significant and lasting contributions to individuals, relationships, and society. In the coming chapters, we will learn how to measure outcomes in a reliable, valid, and an *inexpensive* way.

Active Client Engagement (ACE)

Some of my most memorable experiences in YFS were as a residential youth care worker (RYCW) in an emergency shelter. Outside of the hustle and bustle of my shifts, attending staff meetings, doing intake assessments and all the duties of a RYCW, were the moments when I would just sit and talk, mostly impromptu, with youth. There were no agendas, no goals. We just talked. And in those moments when *not much was happening, a lot happened.* It could be just before bedtime or "lights out" as we called it, or after a meal when we were cleaning up, or after a youth hung up the phone from talking to a parent. We just talked.

The youth in our program had plenty of therapy—formal time to talk about their "issues." And it makes good sense to the casual observer that those therapy sessions would serve as the pivot points for positive change. But that notion is more myth than fact. Youth are like anyone else, they are apt to share their lives when they feel safe and comfortable, not because a specific time was set up and someone started asking questions. My job as RYCW was to help youth to not only feel safe, but to actually be safe. They were, after all, in my care.

What surprised me was what youth would share in 10-minute conversations before bedtime that they would never tell their therapists. My coworkers would describe similar experiences. Youth would talk to them—seemingly in passing—and the dominos of positive changes would start to fall. Several years later when I became the director of the same emergency shelter I spent time talking with youth, or "residents" as they were often referred to, about which aspects of our program helped them the most and which did not. Rarely did they mention therapy, case management, or some planned intervention as a game-changer. It's not that they were negative about our services. They just didn't talk about the aspects of the program we expected them to. Instead, time and time again youth would describe moments when staff were there for them.

YCWs are indeed the backbone of YFS, spending more time with youth than all other program staff combined. We therefore must give sufficient attention to those practices that are known to make a difference for youth. We'll refer to practices described in this section as *active client engagement* (ACE) (Bertolino, 2010). More concretely, ACE involves the use of language and interaction to strengthen connections and facilitate change. The result is an increase in overall benefit of services.

The Influence of Language and Interaction

Every encounter is an opportunity to connect and encourage. The main pathways to facilitate change are *language* and *interaction*. *Language* is comprised of two forms of communication. The first is what is said verbally. The second form is what is nonverbally transmitted (e.g., voice tone, rate of speech, intonation of words, posture, etc.). To be effective YCWs have to be attuned to both forms of communication.

Interaction relates to the specific ways that YCWs use themselves to engage youth. For example, YCWs may use humor, storytelling, self-disclosure, and so on to strengthen connections. YCWs maintain a posture of flexibility in adapting to the relational styles and preferences of youth, making adjustments based on what is communicated. The concept of relational styles is a fertile area of research. Evidence to date indicates that the most effective mental health professionals are the ones who are able to manage interpersonally challenging encounters (Anderson et al., 2009). Said differently, regardless of the way youth relate to others (i.e., passive, subdued, aggressive, etc.), YCWs who are able to find ways to connect and build rapport with youth tend to know "what to say, how to say it, and when to say it." Used effectively language provides a direct pathway to positive change.

One of the distinctions between a deficit or problem-focused and a strengths-based perspective is the root language. Table 3.1 provides examples of differences between the two. Distinctions in language reflect a vastly different overall focus and a central principle of a strengths-based perspective—growth, development and

TABLE 3.1 Differences between deficit or problem-focused and strengths-based perspectives

Deficit based	Strengths based	Deficit based	Strengths based
Fix	Empower	Cure	Growth
Weakness	Strength	Stuck	Change
Limitation	Possibility	Missing	Latent
Pathology	Health	Resist	Utilize
Problem	Solution	Past	Future
Insist	Invite	Hierarchical	Horizontal
Closed	Open	Diagnose	Appreciate
Shrink	Expand	Treat	Facilitate
Defense	Access	End	Beginning
Expert	Partner	Judge	Respect
Control	Nurture	Never	Not yet
Backward	Forward	Limit	Expand
Manipulate	Collaborate	Defect	Asset
Fear	Hope	Rule	Exception

well-being. Use of language can also affect physiological states. Some words can bring about negative physical experiences, such as heaviness in the body, tiredness, and even somatic sensations (for example, upset stomach, body tension). Others can lead to feeling physically stronger and having an increase in energy. But this is just the beginning. Research suggests that under certain conditions (e.g., stress, threats, catastrophic events), the frontal cortex of the brain, which is responsible for thinking, speech, and language, becomes inhibited, thereby limiting one's ability to reason and articulate thoughts (Gottman, 1999; van der Kolk, 1994; van der Kolk, McFarlane, & Weisaeth, 1996). Concurrently, portions of the area around the brain stem, including the amygdala and hypothalamus that are responsible for physiological reactions, become increasingly active. This combination contributes to hyperarousal, affecting one's ability to regulate emotion and think clearly. One implication of this research is the notion that under perceived stress youth may experience both physiological arousal and psychological shutdown. The result is that youth may experience difficulty to self-soothe, regulate emotion, and respond in calm ways when under distress.

YCWs can respond to the physiological arousal–psychological shutdown with youth in several ways. The first is by paying close attention to their own verbal and nonverbal communication such as voice tone, volume, pitch, rate of speech, and body posture. A second way is to use the strengths-based language offered in Table 3.1. A third way, which will discussed further in the next chapter, is by avoiding unnecessary labels that can minimally upset youth and at worst depersonalize, stigmatize, and harm. Youth are people, not disabilities. Our language needs to reflect this fact. A disability may be an aspect of a youth's life but does not identify who he or she is as a person. Lastly, we can practice to develop good attending and listening skills.

Acknowledgment and Validation

The most effective YCWs keep things simple. They steadily focus on the healing effects of secure, safe relationships. Study after study has pointed to *empathy, positive regard,* and *congruence* as valuable components of therapeutic relationships. Although much has been written about each of these concepts, there is little agreement as to their meanings (Norcross, 2011). In general terms, *empathy* is a person's ability to understand another's perspective or way to experience the world. *Positive regard* is usually described as a person's warmth and acceptance toward the self or another. *Congruence,* sometimes referred to as genuineness, has been characterized by the helper's personal involvement in a relationship and willingness to share this awareness through open and honest communication.

Empathy, positive regard, and congruence can sound mysterious, perhaps because they exist in the experience of those we endeavor to help, which underscores the importance feedback, which we will revisit shortly. Let's first be sure to keep it simple through use of *acknowledgment* and *validation. Acknowledgment* involves attending to what youth have communicated both verbally and nonverbally. It lets them know that their experience, points of view, and actions have been heard and noted. It also serves as a prompt by encouraging youth to continue communicating. A basic way to acknowledging is to say, "Uh huh" or "I see." Another way is to reflect back, without interpretation, what was said. For example, a YCW might say, "You're sad" or "I heard you say you're angry." This can also be conveyed by attending to nonverbal behaviors. For example, a YCW might say, "I noticed you shivered as you talked about your dad" or "I can see the tears."

Validation is an extension of and is most often used in conjunction with acknowledgment. It involves letting youth know that whatever they are experiencing is valid. We want to communicate that youth are not bad, crazy, sick, or weird for being who they are and experiencing whatever goes on inside them. YCWs can use validation to normalize or convey that others have experienced the same or similar things. Validation is commonly expressed through statements such as, "It's/That's okay" or "It's/That's all right." To combine acknowledgment with validation, add words or statements such as "It's/That's okay" or "It's all right" to what is being acknowledged. A YCW using acknowledgment and validation might say, "It's okay to be angry," or "It's all right if you're angry," or "I heard you say that you're sad, and you can just let that be there." Acknowledgment and validation are responses that should be used in all interactions.

Paraphrasing and Summarizing

Acknowledgment and validation are synonymous and can be part of brief interactions (e.g., a YCW might say, "I see" or "Uh huh" to acknowledge another person in a short exchange). However, both are more commonly conveyed throughout lengthier conversations as part of paraphrasing, summarizing, and highlighting. Let's explore each of these concepts through examples.

Paraphrasing can be used as a way to confirm what has been said by using a condensed, nonjudgmental version of what the youth or other involved has said.

Example 3.10

Youth: My dad thinks his way is the only way. "Do this, do that." "Look at me when I'm talking." He's like a drill sergeant. He never lets up. I'm sick of it.

YCW: Your dad's way of approaching you seems relentless to you—you wish he would cut you some slack.

Example 3.11

Parent: I'm really feeling pressure with how to deal with Joe. I mean, it's just one thing after another with him at home.

YCW: It sounds like you're feeling a lot of pressure about how to deal with what's going on at home with Joe.

Summarizing offers a way to check out what has been said by pulling together what a youth or other has said over a period of time (i.e., a few minutes of conversation or different segments from different points of a conversation). Summarizing provides a brief synopsis to acknowledge, clarify, and gain focus.

Example 3.12

Youth (End of a lengthy statement): . . . that's about it. That's what's going on.

YCW: Let me see if I follow you. You mentioned several things that seem to be on your mind. One is the arguing between you and Melissa (roommate in residential program). Another is that it seems to you that things aren't really panning out so far in terms of finding a place to live long term. Is that right?

Example 3.13

Youth: . . . I feel like I could just keep talking about it but it wouldn't get me anywhere. My life is going down the drain and there isn't anything I can do about it.

YCW: It certainly seems like you've been through a lot in a short period of time. First, you thought you were doing better in school than you were. And when you got your grades you were shocked. And on top of that what I'm hearing is that two people who you've been close to and have supported you moved away.

Possibility Language

Part of my first job in YFS as a residential counselor (later renamed residential youth care worker or RYCW) was to answer a 24-hour crisis line. It was essential that we made a connection with callers and developed an immediate plan or they might hang up and perhaps hurt themselves or children. Acknowledgment and validation through paraphrasing and summarizing were helpful in conveying understanding to callers in crisis. There were, however, instances when this kind of active listening was not enough. The conversations would stall. I would acknowledge a caller's frustration by saying, "I understand." The caller would feel heard but follow with statements that suggested "impossibility"—that the situation at hand was unresolvable. The dilemma with these crisis calls was to find a way to balance acknowledgment while simultaneously opening up future possibilities. Not so ironically, the same stuck points were happening in face-to-face interactions (i.e., spontaneous conversations, intake assessments, etc.) with youth. Whether in a brief, spontaneous conversation or an intake assessment, opportunity after opportunity occurred to stimulate change. And yet, they were missed opportunities.

As we will soon learn, the way to introduce possibility in conversation turned out to be simple. It was a matter of making subtle yet influential changes through language. The addition of subtle changes in language seemed to provide the internal validation that youth or caregivers were seeking while creating opportunities to alleviate the crisis. In this section, we will explore a series of ways of making such changes.

Before learning about the first method of introducing possibility, consider that effective helpers such as clinicians, physicians, or teachers use language carefully. For example, psychologist Carl Rogers (1951, 1957), perhaps best known for his contributions to the core relationship factors, often made changes in language with his clients. But Rogers said very little about this aspect of his work in his writings or lectures. This is most likely because he was unaware of doing so. Much the same way a professional tennis player hits a backhand volley or an accomplished musician plays a difficult passage—the most effective (or best at what they do) often respond without deliberate thinking. It is automatic.

It is therefore important to be patient in learning something new; automaticity takes time. A tennis player must hit the same shot thousands of times before it becomes automatic. When we learn new things we want to practice them over and over until they become automatic.

Dissolving Impossibility Talk

The following three methods add a twist to pure acknowledgment and validation (Bertolino & O'Hanlon, 2002). Each of them provides a doorway to different or new view of a potentially closed-down account.

Use the Past Tense

Repeat youth or supportive others' statements or problem reports in the past tense to create subtle openings in their perspectives. If only acknowledgment is used, some will remain stuck. If only a search for possibilities occurs, some will feel invalidated. Using the past tense helps youth and supportive others to feel understood while suggesting that things can be different now or in the future.

Examples

Youth: Things aren't getting any better.
YCW: Things haven't gotten any better.

Youth: She says the most hateful things to me.
YCW: She's said some hateful things to you.

Using the past tense to reflect the problem when the youth or other uses the present tense can offer the possibility of a different present or future. This subtle shift in language acknowledges, validates, and introduces possibility. When YCWs only acknowledge and validate, some will move on, but most will not. Youth will continue to describe situations as impossible and/or unchangeable. Alternatively, some may feel that they are being pushed to move on or "get over it," which can be invalidating. The combination of acknowledgment and possibility suggested by using the past tense offers a way to dissolve present tense problem talk by introducing possibilities into otherwise closed-down statements and conversations.

Translate Youth or Supportive Others' Statements into Partial Statements

Translate youth or supportive others statements using words such as everything, everybody, always, and never into qualifiers related to time (for example, some things, somebody, sometimes, and much of the time), intensity (e.g., a lot, a bit less, somewhat more), or partiality (a lot, some, most, many). YCWs should take care not to minimize or invalidate youth or supportive others' experiences.

Examples

Youth: Nothing ever goes right in my life.
YCW: Much of the time things just haven't gone right in your life.

Youth: I'm always in some kind of trouble.
YCW: You've been in trouble a lot.

All-or-nothing statements can impede change, but combining qualifiers with acknowledgment—going from global to partial—can help to introduce the element of possibility into otherwise closed-down statements. This change in language can create little openings in which change is possible. However, if youth or other feel that their experiences are being minimized or they are being pushed to move on, they will likely respond with a statement such as, "Not most of the time—all of the time." If a youth or other reacts in such a manner, the YCW must make sure the youth or other feels heard and understood by validating further while keeping an eye on possibilities. For example, a YCW might respond by saying, "Your sense is that things have been bad all the time."

Translate into Perceptual Statements

Translate youth or supportive others' statements of truth or reality—the way they explain things for themselves—into perceptual statements or subjective realities (for example, in your eyes . . ., your sense is . . ., from where you stand . . ., you've gotten the idea . . .).

Examples

Youth: Things will never change.
YCW: It seems to you that things will never change.

Youth: I'm a terrible parent.
YCW: You've gotten the idea that you've been a terrible parent.

Notice that some of previous examples involve a combination of methods of changing language. For example, "You've been anxious a lot" (past tense/partial statement) and "You've gotten the idea that you've been a terrible parent" (perceptual statement/past tense) include multiple methods. As discussed, practicing with changes in language will increase automaticity. Practice will also contribute to greater comfort and consistency in identifying and attending to words, phrases, and statements that suggest impossibility.

Using Future Talk: Acknowledgment and a Vision for the Future

Youth or supportive others involved occasionally describe their situations in ways that offer little glimpses of the future and what might be possible. In these instances, they use language like the moving walkways in airports: They can maintain their same pace yet reach their destinations a little more quickly. YCWs can use language in a similar way to move youth and supportive others in the direction of possibilities without their actually having to take steps toward those goals and preferred outcomes.

Assume Future Change and/or Solutions

Assume the possibility that youth or supportive others can find solutions by using words such as yet and so far. These words presuppose that even though things feel stuck or unchangeable in the present, they will change sometime in the future.

Examples

Youth: Things will never go right for me.
YCW: So far things haven't gone right for you.

Youth: My life is going downhill.
YCW: You're life hasn't headed in a direction you'd like yet.

By making only small changes in language, therapists are actually introducing the possibility that change can occur in the future. This seemingly simple shift gently challenges closed-down views and can open doorways to other, more significant changes.

Turn Problem Statements into Preferences or Goals

Take youth or supportive others' problem statements or dissatisfaction and change them into statements or questions that reflect an expectation, preference, direction, preferred future, or goal.

Examples

Youth: I'm always in trouble.
YCW: Would you like to work on finding ways to change you relationship with trouble?

Youth: It just seems like we argue all of the time.
YCW: Is finding alternatives to arguing one of the things you'd like to have happen?

In the course of listening to a youth or supportive others' stories, it can become difficult to discern which problem is most concerning. YCWs must routinely make decisions regarding which words, phrases, comments, and remarks should gain more or less attention. By turning problem statements into goals, RYCWs can acknowledge youth or supportive others statements and simultaneously clarify which problems are most important to them.

Presuppose Changes and Progress

Assume changes and progress toward goals and preferred futures by using words such as when and will.

Examples

Youth: I'm always getting angry and saying things I shouldn't say.
YCW: When you're able to express your anger in ways that are better, how do you suppose your life will be different than the way it is now?

Youth: No one wants to hang out or be friends with me.
YCW: When you've started spending time with people you consider your friends, I'm curious about what other kinds of changes you'll notice.

Presupposition offers a way to orient youth and supportive others toward future changes by linking one change with another. Its use helps to shift the attention of youth and supportive others toward change in general and to active a "ripple effect." Like a stone landing in a pool of water, ripples or additional changes can result with the first splash. Adding conjecture to presupposition in the form of wonderment, or speculation, whether in a statement or a question, can spawn further possibilities about how future changes will make a difference for youth. To use conjecture, simply add "I wonder" or "I'm curious."

Employing future-focused language can be especially valuable with youth experiencing hopelessness, pain, and fear because a lack of a vision for the future often exacerbates these forms of emotional reaction. If youth have the sense that the pain or suffering that they are experiencing now will somehow be alleviated or dissipated altogether, they are better able to keep moving. An ever growing body of literature indicates that people who have a sense that their pain will end and that things will improve in the future have a higher incidence of recovery from chronic illness.

Giving Permission

Some youth and supportive others involved with youth have a sense that they are bad or terrible. A response in these instances is to give permission to experience whatever is going on internally. We want youth and others to know that they are not bad, crazy, or weird and that others have felt the same way. Giving permission for internal experience does not mean giving permission for action. Internal experiences are quite different from the actions. YCWs do not give permission for actions or behaviors that are or potentially could pose risk to youth or supportive others but let them know that whatever they are experiencing is acceptable and that they are also responsible for their actions. There are three kinds of permission:

- Permission to: "You can."
- Permission not to have to: "You don't have to."
- Permission to and not to have to: "You can and you don't have to."

Give Permission "to"

Give youth and supportive others permission for experiences, feelings, thoughts, and fantasies.

Examples

Youth: I feel like running away. How could I feel like that? I must be a bad person for feeling that way when so many people want to help me.

YCW: It's okay to feel like running away, and that doesn't make you a bad person.

Youth: Every time I get depressed, I start cutting on my arms with whatever I can get my hands on.

YCW: It's okay to feel so depressed that you feel like cutting on yourself, and it's not okay to cut on yourself.

Give Permission "not to have to"

Give youth and supportive others permission not to have to have experience, think, or do things that do not fit with them.

Examples

Youth: People keep telling me that I need to go through the anger stage of grieving. But I just don't feel angry. Is there something wrong with me?

YCW: Each person goes through grief in his or her own way. Some will experience anger and some won't. You can take your own path to healing.

Parent: In the support group I attend for parents who've lost children, everyone keeps saying that I need to express anger at my loss because that's a stage of grieving. But I've never felt anger. Is something wrong with me?

YCW: Each person goes through grief in his or her own way. It's okay if you don't go through someone else's stages and take your own path to healing.

Give Permission "to" and "not to have to"

Include both permissions at the same time.

Examples

Youth: Sometimes I'm angry and sometimes I'm not. I must be crazy.

YCW: You can be angry and not angry about it, and that doesn't make you crazy.

Youth: I'm really sad sometimes but then it goes away and comes back.

YCW: It's okay to be sad at times and not at other times and for it to cycle.

Although permission is conveyed through validation, some youth will need more direct confirmation that what they are feeling or experiencing is okay. Permission can be tricky, however. This is because of the different forms. YCWs may need to extend more than one type of permission or youth may feel pressured to experience just one side of the equation or may find the other side emerging in a more compelling or disturbing way (O'Hanlon & Bertolino, 1998, 2002). For example, if a YCW says only, "It's okay to be angry," a youth might say, "But I don't want to be angry!" The YCW can counter this response by giving permission "to" and "not to have to: "It's okay to be angry and you don't have to be angry." Finally, as discussed previously, YCWs should exercise caution regarding the actions for which permission is extended. A YCW would not say, "It's okay to cut yourself and you don't have to cut yourself." Do not give permission for harmful, destructive behavior.

Normalizing

One of the most essential yet least recognized ways of acknowledging and advancing possibility is through normalizing. When youth or supportive others involved know that they are not crazy or weird for feeling the way they do, they often experience deeper degrees of empathy and self-acceptance. We want to acknowledge that what the youth or others is going though is within the range of human experience. To normalize experiences, YCWs acknowledge youth and supportive others' experiences and give them permission to feel what they feel. Just knowing that others have had similar experiences can be liberating and open youth to new perspectives.

Use Everyday Examples

Examples

Youth: When I'm depressed, I feel very alone.

YCW: I've heard others say that very thing—that when they've been depressed, they've felt very alone.

Caregiver: How many people would let something like what happened with my son weigh on them the way I am?

YCW: Given what you've been through with your son, especially in recent days, I think most people would expect it to weigh on you.

Use Self-Disclosure

Use personal experience to normalize youth or supportive others' concerns or problems.

Examples

Youth: I hang on to things for a long time before letting them go.

YCW: I've heard others say similar things, and I've had that experience as
well . . . we sometimes hang on to things until we're ready to let them go.

Youth: I really struggle with math. I just don't think that way.

YCW: I struggled with math as well. What specifically have you found challenging about it?

Use Metaphor

Metaphor is an implied comparison between two dissimilar things.

Examples

Youth: I don't like it when people talk about me when I walk by.

YCW: You mentioned that you really love music and sometimes it's a matter of tuning in what you want and tuning out the rest.

Parent: I feel like I'm treading in rough waters and the waves are splashing
in my eyes.

YCW: Sometimes the waves can be rough and choppy. And, if you're able
look just below the surface, you might notice that it's calmer and
easier to see things more clearly.

When asked about their experiences in YFS—no matter the type of program, youth and caregivers routinely report higher levels of connection with providers when they feel acknowledged and accepted. Normalizing provides an effective way to let youth and supportive others know that they are not alone, are respected, and have experiences that are valid and that do not make them crazy, weird, or abnormal.

Utilization

As discussed in Chapter 2, utilization is an effective way of recognizing both the uniqueness of each youth and the unique features of whatever it is he or she is struggling with. Because youth are the ultimate engineers of their destinies, their strengths and resources provide the fodder for change. It is therefore important that YCWs explore ways to use what youth bring to services—no matter how small, strange, or negative the behavior or idea seems—to open possibilities for change. This process directly contrasts with more traditional approaches that view what youth or supportive others bring as symptoms or liabilities.

Use what is Brought to Services as Resources to Initiate Change

No matter how small, strange, or negative an idea or behavior may seem, use it to open possibilities for change.

Examples

Youth: I don't like sports. I'm terrible at them anyway.

YCW: You've ruled out sports, at least for now, so what else might you focus your efforts on?

Parent: He spends hours tinkering with electronic gadgets. I have no idea why he does it.

YCW: It sounds like he's found something that really grabs his attention . . . something that he's interested in.

Utilization allows YCWs to take behaviors and ideas that are typically seen as deficits, inabilities, symptoms, or negative in general and turn them into assets. It can be a helpful way to get youth moving in the direction of the change they are seeking if they are not already doing so. We want to take care to not be dismissive of points of view that might suggest that an idea or behavior is in some way negative. One way to avoid causing youth to feel invalidated is by first acknowledging their perspectives. For example, in the last part of the previous example, the YCW might say, "I can see why his interest in electronics might lead you to wonder what he gets out of it. How do you think we might help him to use that interest in a way that can help with what you're concerned about?" Acknowledgment of one perspective should not dismiss another.

Matching Language

A final area of attending and listening relates to youth and supportive others' ways of communicating. Youth often communicate in patterns that can go unrecognized and unattended. Matching their language through using words and phrases, speed, intonation, and patterns can help youth create inroads to strengthen connection and initiate change.

Match Youth and Supportive Others' Rate and Pace of Speech

When in sync with the youth, the YCW can change the rate and/or pace, if necessary, to promote relaxation, calmness, to neutralize anxiety, and so on. Take care to not come across as mocking or mimicking, which can be invalidating.

Examples

Youth (Quickly): I sometimes struggle to find the words . . . . [pause] like now.
YCW (Mirroring the client's pace): Sometimes it's hard to find the words . . . [pause] and that's okay.

Youth: I don't know . . . [silence] . . . I just don't know why this happened to me.
YCW: Yeah . . . [silence] . . . Sometimes the answers are hard to come by.

Match Youth and Supportive Others' General Use of Language

Listen to the words of youth or supportive others and use aspects of that language to strengthen the therapeutic relationship.

Examples

Youth: I just don't get it, man.
YCW: Yeah, man, it does seem confusing.

Youth: She just needs to chill. It doesn't help when she's all ballistic.
YCW: If she were to chill a bit, what difference would that make for you?

Match Youth and Supportive Others' Use of Sensory-Based Language

Listen for and match youth or supportive others' use of sensory-based (visual, auditory, kinesthetic/tactile, gustatory, olfactory) language.

Examples

Youth: The way I see it, he'll never change.
YCW: I see . . . that's the vision you've had of him.

Youth: No matter where I turn, the message is the same . . . "you'll never amount to anything."
YCW: It seems like you've been hearing the same message from different directions.

In this chapter, we explored two distinct areas core to YCWs, no matter the program or type of service. The first was the use of *collaboration keys*, and how they assist with learning the expectations and preferences of youth and supportive others involved with services. In addition, the concept of real-time feedback processes were discussed and how to introduce these processes to youth, underscoring the importance of determining the effectiveness of YFS. The second part of the chapter offered a series of linguistic methods that also can be used, in most any setting, program, and interaction. These methods focus primarily on the use of language to promote engagement through acknowledgment, validation, and possibility.

The next chapter we will build on the ideas presented here for strengthening engagement. Focus will be on creating directions in services through information-gathering and planning. Information gleaned through practices detailed in Chapter 4 will be used to further promote change and increase the likelihood of benefit of services.

four
Directions: Information-Gathering and Planning

Efforts and courage are not enough without purpose and direction.

—John F. Kennedy

In late 1990s, Dr. Brendan Reilly, chairman of Chicago's Cook County Hospital's Department of Medicine, saw a need for change within the Emergency Department, which was flooded with 250,000 patients annually, many complaining of chest pain. Emergency room doctors were careful about diagnosis and care for these patients for fear of misdiagnosis and malpractice. So Dr. Reilly utilized three levels of care for the cardiac patients. He also turned to the work of Dr. Lee Goldman from the 70s. Dr. Goldman developed an algorithm based on three risk factors: (1) Is the patient's pain stable or unstable? (2) Is there fluid in the patient's lungs? And (3) Is the patient's systolic blood pressure below 100?, plus an electrocardiogram (ECG). This information provided doctors with a more definitive answer in diagnosing a chest pain. He used those risk factors to develop a decision tree.

Dr. Reilly then collected data at Cook County Hospital that compared doctors' own judgment evaluating heart attacks compared to Dr. Goldman's algorithm and decision tree. For two years data were collected, and in the end, the result wasn't even close. Left to their conventional methods—which doctors believed to be accurate despite substantial variability in their ratings of the seriousness of patients presenting with symptoms of heart attack—doctors *guessed* accurately with the most serious cardiac patients between 75 and 89% of the time. The Goldman method produced accuracy rates of 95%—a 70% improvement. Results in hand, Dr. Reilly implemented the Goldman algorithm full time, making Cook County Hospital one of the first in the country to do so.

The results showed that his staff was able to accurately recognize the patients who were not having a heart attack 70% better using the algorithm and decision tree than using their own judgment and previous standards by which to diagnose chest pain. On their own, they were around 75 to 89% accurate. Dr. Goldman's algorithm and decision tree demonstrated that asking more questions, running more tests, and gathering more information may not be an advantage (Gladwell, 2005).

What do emergency rooms and cardiac patients have to do with YFS? Quite a bit as it turns out. YCWs are at the front lines of providing the best possible care to youth. They need to serve those most at risk in a timely manner while managing the resources they have, which have become increasingly scarce. At Cook County Hospital, Dr. Goldman's algorithm helped to more effectively identify patients who were experiencing heart attacks, which saved lives. Next, the efficiency with which cardiac patients were treated improved. There was clarity about what level of care should be provided to whom, under what circumstances. Further, were the cost savings that would have been incurred had patients been unnecessarily admitted. Finally, the guesswork of doctors in the ER was reduced. Less guessing equaled more reliability.

At the heart of this discussion is information. As a society we are infatuated with it. We collect lots of information on just about everything. In YFS, we are inundated with information. Some of it is required for paperwork and reimbursement. Some information is for liability purposes. Some is due to YCWs' and other providers' personal theoretical frameworks and curiosities. Just as the doctors at Cook County Hospital, we have ideas about what kind of information is most important to attain. And there are certainly instances in which more is better. But is the information we spend so much time accumulating really improving quality and care?

Recall the 80/20 rule described in Chapter 3, that 80% of the results or value comes from 20% of the source or focus. Much of the information we collect in YFS has no bearing on services. It goes into a large file or a mainframe computer and sits. And the amount of time YCWs spend gathering unused data is substantial. In some cases, YCWs report that as much as 60% of the jobs are spent doing paperwork. As a helping profession, and one that involves the safety and well-being of youth, the issue of information is critical to YFS. Information collected in YFS influences most every decision. Because some decisions carry greater significance, the quality of information and how it is evaluated is significant. YCWs therefore face the challenge of determining what kind of information to gather and how that information will impact the direction of services.

The focus of this chapter is on the 20% of information that YCWs gather and use that actually improves services. Central to such information-gathering is the strengths-based principles outlined in Chapter 2 and the collaboration keys described in Chapter 3. Consistent with a collaborative stance, the term "information-gathering" is used as opposed to "assessment." The idea is to use language that reflects collaborative partnerships in which youth and supportive others' expectations and preferences are encouraged.

Strengths-Based Information-Gathering

YCWs will be responsible for collecting and interpreting different types of information. Information-gathering could involve phone or face-to-face contacts and require completion of assessments, surveys, service plans, authorization forms, and other paperwork. Information-gathering may be on a one-time basis, periodic, or ongoing. Some information will come from standardized instruments (e.g., inventories and tests) and procedures (e.g., assessment forms required by hospitals, residential facilities, and HMOs) that are given one time or on a periodic basis. Other information, for example that related to goals, will be gathered on an ongoing basis.

To remain purposeful in helping youth we want to know that information is largely useful, understanding that some information will be collected for non-service purposes such as funder requirements. One way to manage paperwork is through periodic review. Reviews help to identify redundancy in information collected. In addition, it can also assist with filtering out forms that are no longer required or could be shortened. Agency personnel are often surprised at the number of forms that are outdated but were never removed from the main client paperwork. Among other things, unnecessary paperwork contributes to inefficiency regarding how time is spent with clients and in the storage of files. Electronic databases and client record systems also need to be updated making it essential to have a process in place to review what information is collected and again, how it is used to improve services and benefit youth and families.

Let's now take a minute to review some crucial points discussed in Chapter 3 and how they relate to information-gathering. Recall the collaboration keys:

1   create listening space
2   address expectations
3   attend to preferences
4   introduce real-time feedback.

The collaboration keys, when used consistently, create empirically based inroads with youth and others involved with services. More importantly, each is an essential contributor to the second principle of a strengths-based perspective: *The therapeutic relationship makes substantial and consistent contributions to outcome.* Relationships and, more specifically, alliances with youth and supportive others are paramount to the success of YFS. Better alliances yield better outcomes. Although the collaboration keys are vital to early contacts they also play a role as services continue. This is because people's ideas, thoughts, expectations, and preferences change over time. Later in the chapter, we will learn how to continuously monitor the alliance over the course of services by using real-time feedback, which was introduced in the last chapter.

A final point to recap is active client engagement (ACE). ACE lends attention to the use of language to acknowledge, validate, facilitate understanding, and open up possibilities. Our aim is to create new opportunities for future change and rehabilitate hope through conversation. A consistent theme throughout this book is *practice*. Learning to use language effectively takes practice. The more YCWs practice the more comfortable and spontaneous they will be with language and ultimately, the more effective they will become.

Introducing Information-Gathering Processes

Information is a primary driver of YFS. How we gather information is important. Some youth and supportive others will be more hesitant to talk about their lives and situations. We can improve on opportunities to learn about youth by listening, attending, and explaining information-gathering processes. Next is an example of how to talk with youth and supportive others about this.

Introduction

I'd like to ask you some questions that we ask of everyone. The information you give will help us to understand how things are going with you including what you're concerned about and how that's affected you, what you'd like to see change, what has and hasn't worked for you in trying to manage your concerns, and how we can be of help to you. And as we proceed, if you feel like or think we've missed something, please be sure to let us know. We want to make sure that we fully understand what you need. How does that sound?

Because some types of information-gathering are more "front loaded" with problem-focused questions, the YCW must find a creative way to intersperse strengths-based questioning. Even the most pathology-oriented procedures offer opportunities for YCWs to explore youth strengths. Talking with youth about how information will be gathered and used lets them know we are interested in two things. The first is that the information will help with better understanding the seriousness of their concerns. Next, information collected will inform the YCW of how youth and supportive others have managed to keep their heads above water to keep things from getting worse. Specifically, what strengths, resiliencies, and/or resources have they used to meet the challenges with their situations? The dichotomy between problems and strengths is one with which YCWs continuously try to strike a balance. This is because many forms of information-gathering are negatively skewed, emphasizing identifying problems, pathology, and deficit. Being strengths-based means attending to the difficulties faced while exploring internal and external resources that may assist in resolving concerns and complaints.

There are two general ways in which YCWs collect information. Each presents an opportunity for YCWs and youth to work together to strengthen their mutual understanding of the purpose of services. The first form of gathering information is through structured processes in which standardized forms and measures (i.e., behavior checklists, personality tests, etc.) are used to identify problems, risks, safety concerns, etc. Many standardized methods are used just once, during an assessment or interview phase or in initial face-to-face contacts. Others are periodic or ongoing, most commonly to monitor improvement or the effects of services (e.g., outcome and alliance measures).

The second way that information is gathered is through open-ended questions. Informal, open-ended questions create space for the expression of client narratives or stories. YCWs invite youth and supportive others involved in service to talk about their situations and any aspects that might increase understanding. Questions typically serve as a guide so there is consistency in information collected; however, unlike standardized methods there is more "room" for conversations to evolve. It is during such conversations that valuable information is gained. Youth and supportive others will often report less pressure to have to come up with "right" answers and speak "off the cuff," with less interruption from YCWs. We keep in mind that occasions are excellent opportunities to learn about expectations and preferences, and to acknowledge, validate, and open up possibilities through subtle changes in language.

Real-Time Feedback in Action: Putting Measures to Work

An essential method for collecting information in YFS is through real-time feedback measurement, which is comprised of outcome and alliance measurement (see Collaboration Key 4). In Chapter 3, we learned how to introduce the idea of monitoring both the impact of services (outcome) and youth and supportive others' experiences of our interactions with them (alliance). In sum, real-time feedback assists with concerns such as reducing negative outcome and dropout, tracking improvement (benefit), and monitoring the fit between the YCW or other provider and clients. These efforts increase quality, stewardship, and accountability. Although more research is needed, Warren, Nelson, Burlingame, and Mondragon (2012) found that failure to monitor progress on a routine basis (ideally meeting by meeting/session by session) to identify those at risk of deterioration in youth services led to substantially more cases of negative outcome. Conversely, ongoing and routine measurement reduced the rate of service failure. Alarmingly, few YFS organizations actually monitor outcome (and even less monitor the alliance) on a routine basis.

There are many measures available to YFS professionals. Examples of outcome measures include the Outcome Questionnaire 45 (OQ-45)(Burlingame et al., 1995; Lambert & Burlingame, 1996; Lambert & Finch, 1999; Lambert et al., 1996), Youth

Outcome Questionnaire (Y-OQ) (Burlingame, Wells, & Lambert, 1996; Burlingame et al., 2001; Burlingame, Wells, Lambert, & Cox, 2004; Dunn et al., 2005), Clinical Outcomes in Routine Management (CORE) (Barkham, Mellor-Clark, Connell, & Cahill, 2006; Evans et al., 2002) and the Outcome Rating Scale (ORS) (Miller & Duncan, 2000; Miller et al., 2003). Examples of alliance measures are the Revised Helping Alliance Questionnaire (HAq-II) (Luborsky et al., 1996), the Working Alliance Inventory (WAI) (Horvath & Greenberg, 1989), and the Session Rating Scale (SRS) (Duncan et al., 2003). Some measures are free or available at a low cost, others are more expensive, involving licensing or per usage fees. Research of the benefits and drawback of measures is essential to any decision to implement instrumentation.

For the purposes of discussion, the ORS and SRS measures will be used as examples throughout the remainder of this book. The breadth and depth of conversation necessary to fully explain the nuances and details around ORS and SRS are beyond the scope of this book; however, the basics of each measure will be described with more information available through other sources (see Bertolino & Miller, 2013). In short, the ORS and SRS are very brief, feasible measures for tracking client well-being and the quality of the therapeutic alliance, taking less than a minute each for clients to complete and for service providers to score and interpret. Individual licenses for the ORS and SRS are available for free at www.scottdmiller.com. The ORS has been shown to be sensitive to change among those receiving services. Numerous studies have documented concurrent, discriminative, criterion-related, and predictive validity, test–retest reliability, and internal-consistency reliability for the ORS and SRS (e.g., Anker et al., 2009; Bringhurst et al., 2006; Campbell & Hemsley, 2009; Duncan et al., 2003; Duncan et al., 2006; Miller et al., 2003; Reese et al., 2009). The significant impact of using these measures on the outcome of services has similarly been well-documented (e.g., Anker et al., 2009; Miller et al., 2006; Reese, Norsworthy, & Rowlands, 2009). The ORS and SRS measures, collectively known as the Partners for Change Outcome Management System (PCOMS), have met the rigorous standards set by the U.S. Substance Abuse Mental Health Services Administration (SAMHSA) and are listed on the National Registry of Evidence-Based Programs and Practices (NREPP) (www.nrepp.samhsa.gov).

There are two vital points before we proceed. First, several of the sections that follow are dense and more technical. Statistical information is not exciting to everyone but by now hopefully your appreciation for the importance of demonstrating the effectiveness of YFS in a consistent and reliable manner has grown. Having a baseline understanding of the functionality of measures, the empirical evidence, and their role in effective services is paramount. A second point is some YCWs will value the role of outcome in services but not see it as their job to monitor progress. It will be considered a "therapist's" job. Routine and ongoing monitoring of services is *everyone's* business. We are all responsible for the effectiveness of our services and capable of monitoring progress and making adjustments as necessary. So please take care in reading the next sections carefully. Then follow up with peers, colleagues, and supervisors and utilize resources that are available through publications, online, and training.

The Outcome Rating Scare (ORS)

The Outcome Rating Scale (ORS) is a brief, client-rated four-item visual analogue scale measuring the client's experience of well-being in their individual, interpersonal and social functioning. The ORS is designed and normed for adults and adolescents (ages 13+). The CORS is a children's version (CORS) that has been normed for ages six to 12. The YCORS is a "clinical engagement" tool for children below six years, which while it is not scored, is used to provide very young children a way of expressing their well-being and satisfaction with a meeting or session along with the older children and/or adults with whom they may be in services. These tools are available in over 20 languages, and there is a script available for the oral administration of the ORS (www.scottdmiller.com). Samples of the ORS, CORS, and YCORS are provided in Appendix A.

Clinical Cutoff for the ORS

Determining the clinical cutoff for an outcome measure accomplishes two related objectives: (1) It defines the boundary between a normal and clinical range of distress; and (2) it provides a reference point for evaluating the severity of distress for a particular client or client sample. Using the method described by Jacobson and Truax (1991), the clinical cutoff for the ORS was determined to be 25 (Miller, Duncan, Brown, Sparks, & Claud, 2003). The sample on which this score is based is quite large (n = 34,790) and comparison with other well-established measures shows it to be a reasonable differentiator between "normal" and "clinical" levels of distress. For example, the clinical cutoff score for the OQ-45 falls at the 83rd percentile of the non-treatment sample, and the clinical cutoff for the ORS falls at the 77th percentile of the non-treatment sample. Miller and colleagues have reported that between 25–33% of people presenting for treatment score above the clinical cutoff at intake (Miller & Duncan, 2000; Miller, Duncan, Sorrell, & Brown, 2005). While the clinical cutoff for adults is 25, younger clients tend to score themselves higher. Therefore, the clinical cutoff for youth (age 13–18) is 28, and for children (age six to 12) the cutoff is 32. The clinical cutoff is an important statistical numeration because it helps providers in YFS to determine a youth or supportive other's level of distress at the start of services, which as discussed in Chapter 3, is considered the most consistent predictor of eventual outcome.

Introducing the ORS

Following the general introduction of real-time feedback described in Chapter 3 (see Collaboration Key 4) is the specific introduction of the ORS and SRS measures. We will return to the latter later in this chapter. The ORS is completed at the beginning of meetings/interactions. This is because we want to capture the degree of distress experienced by youth and supportive others involved. An example of how to introduce the ORS follows.

Introduction

This scale is the ORS. As you can see the scale has four items: Individual, Interpersonal, Social, and Overall. These are the areas of your life that could show improvement if the work we (all of us at the agency) do together is effective. I'd like you to complete this form every time we meet (or when you meet with others here), giving us a sense of how things are progressing in your life. Today, when we are meeting for the first time, we need to get a "start score" that tells us how things have been in your life before we started meeting. I would like you to look back on the last week, including today, and rate how you have been feeling on each of the four items, with low scores to the left and high ones to the right. Does that make sense to you?"

If a youth, caregiver, or supportive other involved asks for clarification of one of the four subscales on the ORS, they can be explained as shown in the following box.

Individually: If the youth asks for clarification, you should say "yourself," "you as an individual," "your personal functioning."

Interpersonally: If the youth asks for clarification, you should say "in your family," "in your close personal relationships."

Socially: If the youth asks for clarification, you should say, "your life outside the home or in your community," "work," "school," "friends and acquaintances," "church."

Overall: "So, given your answers on these specific areas of your life, how would you rate how things are in your life overall?" It can also be helpful to clients to make it clear that they can score the scale to suit their perception of their life, for example by saying:

"For some who we work with school is really important, so if their functioning is really good socially that reflects on their overall sense of well-being. Others may see their individual functioning as the most important area when scoring their overall sense of well-being. I want you to show me how these three areas of your life influence your overall sense of well-being."

Scoring the ORS

The ORS is scored during the meeting or session, right after the youth or supportive other has filled out the form. To score the ORS, determine the distance in centimeters (to the nearest millimeter, e.g., "5.7") between the left pole and the youth or supportive others' hash mark on each individual item. Add all four numbers together to obtain the total score. A metric rule can be used or a downloadable scoring overlay can be copied onto a transparency (available at www.scottdmiller. com). The transparency can be used as a full sheet with all four scales or cut into small "rules" that can be used to score each scale individually. The score can either be plotted on a paper graph (see Appendix A for examples). As a note, before using the ORS (and all the measures that follow) and making copies check to be certain that the lines are 10 centimeters in length (10 cm).

The graph will show how the youth or supportive other's score compares to the clinical cutoff. Low scores on the ORS correspond to low well-being (or high distress). Note that the average ORS intake score in outpatient mental health care treatment settings is between 18 and 19. The first step in interpreting a youth or supportive other's intake score is simply to describe to him or her what the possible range of well-being is, and/or what the clinical cutoff means, and how the youth or supportive other's score relates to these scores. For example, a 16-year-old youth who has a total ORS score of 18.5 at the first session is examined in the following case example.

Case Example 4.1

I've plotted your score on the ORS on this graph, and as you can see there is a dotted line at 28. What we know is that generally people your age who score below the dotted line are more like people who seek services (or are asked to attend services). They are more like people who are saying, "There are things in my life that I would like to change; things that are bothering me"; and generally people who score above the dotted line are more like a broad range of people who have not chosen to be in services. So your score is here, at 18.5, so you are below the dotted line, does that make sense to you? (youth nods) So it seems that coming here to see me . . . that you're feeling pretty bad, pretty distressed. A 18.5 on a scale of 0 to 40. Does that sound right? Does that match how you're feeling?"

Scores above the clinical cutoff are important to discuss because these youth are at higher risk for deterioration. The most common reason for a score above the clinical cutoff is that youth and/or their caregivers are mandated into services. Another common reason for scores falling above the clinical cutoff at intake is that the youth or other wants help with a very specific problem—one that does not impact the overall quality of life or functioning but is troubling nonetheless. Given the heightened risk of deterioration for youth entering treatment above the clinical cutoff, YCWs are advised against "exploratory" and "depth-oriented" work. The best approach, in such instances, is a cautious one, using the least invasive and intensive methods needed to resolve the problem at hand.

Less frequent causes for high initial ORS scores include: (1) High-functioning youth who want services for growth, self-actualization, and optimizing performance; and (2) youth who may have difficulties reading and writing or who have not understood the meaning or purpose of the measure. In the latter instance, time can be taken to explain the measure and build a "culture of feedback" or, in the case of reading or language difficulties, the oral version can be administered. For high-functioning people caution is warranted. A strength-based, coaching-type approach focused on achieving specific, targeted, and measurable goals is likely to be most helpful while simultaneously minimizing risks of deterioration.

The Session Rating Scale (SRS)

The Session Rating Scale (SRS) is a four-item, client-completed alliance measure. Like the ORS, the SRS is a visual analogue scale that takes less than one minute to administer, score, and interpret. Items on the scale reflect the classical definition of the alliance first stated by Bordin (1979). The scale assesses four interacting elements, including the quality of the relational bond, as well as the degree of agreement between the client and therapist on the goals, methods, and overall approach of therapy. The SRS is available in an adult version (ages 13+), a children's version (CSRS) for children ages six to12 and a version for children below six years (YCSRS). It is also available in a group therapy version (GSRS) and has been translated into over 20 languages. As with the ORS, there is a script available for the oral administration of the SRS (www.scottdmiller.com). Samples of the SRS, CSRS, YCSRS, and GSRS are provided in Appendix A.

SRS Cutoff

The cutoff for an alliance measure is the point at which providers should be especially alert to the possibility of a failure of the working relationship. The alliance cutoff enables YCWs and other providers to identify those relationships that are at a statistically greater risk for client dropouts or a negative or null outcome from services. On the SRS, a score of 36 or below is considered cause for concern because fewer than 24% of clients score lower than 36 (Miller & Duncan, 2004)

Introducing the SRS

The way the SRS is introduced plays a major role in the quality of feedback received and in the strength of the alliance. Like the ORS, the SRS is designed not only to measure but to positively impact what it measures through careful use of the information it provides. The SRS is administered just before the end of each meeting or session, and it is important to frame the SRS by emphasizing the importance of the relationship in successful treatment and encouraging negative feedback. Many YCWs and other providers wonder about youth or supportive others who may for cultural reasons find it difficult to give any kind of critical feedback to a professional whom they perceive to be in a position of authority. These YCWs often suggest that youth or supportive others can feel uncomfortable and pressured by an invitation to provide critical feedback to somebody with whom they feel especially humble. A way to address this can be to frame the SRS introduction in a positive light. Instead of the youth or other feeling they are being asked, "What was wrong with the service I received?" we can emphasize that we are asking, "What could have made this service even more helpful to you?" We can describe this process as our standard way of working with people, and such youth or supportive others may then feel they are being more cooperative if they give us the feedback that we say is critical to our doing our job well. The following is one example of how to introduce the SRS to youth or others involved. Please use the example to inspire you to find your own words when introducing the scales to those with whom you work.

Introduction

I'd like to ask you to complete one additional form. This is called the Session Rating Scale. Basically, this is a tool that you and I will use each time we meet to adjust and improve the way we work together. A great deal of research shows that your experience of our work together (or at our agency)—did you feel understood, did we focus on what was important to you, did the approach I'm taking make sense and feel right—is a good predictor of whether we'll be successful. I want to emphasize that I'm not aiming for a perfect score—a 10 out of 10. Life isn't perfect and neither am I. What I'm aiming for is your feedback about even the smallest things— even if it seems unimportant—so we can adjust our work and make sure we don't steer off course. Whatever it might be, I promise I won't take it personally. I (and we as an agency) am always learning, and am curious about what I can learn from getting this feedback from you that will in time help me improve my skills. Does this make sense?

Scoring the SRS

The SRS is scored in the same way as the ORS. The lines are (should be) ten centimeters in length (10 cm), and are scored in centimeters to the nearest millimeter between the left pole and the client's hash mark on each individual item. Add all four numbers together to obtain the total score. The score can be plotted on a paper graph. Both ORS and SRS scores are typically placed on the same graphs (see Appendix A for examples of graphs).

Research to date on the SRS shows that the majority of clients will score nine or higher out of 10 on each line (Miller & Duncan, 2000). If they do this on all four lines, the total score will be 36 or more out of 40. This score is referred to as the cutoff for the SRS and is depicted by the dotted line on the SRS graph (see sample graphs in Appendix A). If a youth or supportive other scores above 36, it is important to keep in mind that this score doesn't confirm a strong alliance. It may indicate a strong alliance or that at this point in services the youth or supportive other does not feel safe enough to give negative feedback. The best response to a score above 36 is to thank the youth or supportive other for their feedback and to add that you would really appreciate if they would let you know if they think of something later on about the meeting or session that they would like for you to change a bit.

Scores that fall at or below 36 are considered "cause for concern" and should be discussed with youth and/or supportive others who complete the measure prior to ending the session. Single-point declines in SRS scores from meeting to meeting have also been found to be associated with poorer outcomes at termination— even when the total score consistently falls above 36—and should therefore be discussed (Duncan et al., 2003). In sum, the SRS helps YCWs and other providers to identify problems in the alliance (e.g., misunderstandings, disagreement about goals and methods) early in services, thereby preventing dropout or deterioration.

Whatever the circumstance, openness and transparency are central to successfully eliciting meaningful feedback on the SRS. When the total score falls below 36, for example, the YCW can encourage discussion by saying something along the lines of the following.

Case Example 4.2

Thanks for the time and care you took in filling out the SRS. Your experience here is important to me and others who you may work with. Filling out the SRS gives me a chance to check in, one last time, before we end today to make sure we are on the same page—that this is working for you. Most of the time, about 75% actually, people score 37 or higher. And today, your score falls at [a number 36 or lower], which can mean we need to consider making some changes in the way we are working together. What thoughts do you have about this?

When a particular item on the SRS is rated lower compared to the other items, the YCW can inquire directly about that item regardless of whether the total score falls below the cutoff.

Case Example 4.3

Thanks for taking this form so seriously. It really helps. I really want to make sure we are on the same page. Looking at the SRS gives me a chance to make sure I'm not missing something big or going in the wrong direction for you. In looking over the scale, I've noticed here [showing the completed form to the youth or other], that your mark on the question about "approach and method" is lower compared to the others. What can you tell me about that?

When seeking feedback via the SRS, it is important to frame questions in as "task specific" a manner as possible. Research shows, for example, that people are more likely to provide feedback when it is not perceived as a criticism of the person of the other but rather about specific behaviors (Ericsson, Charness, Feltovich, & Hoffman, 2006). For example, instead of inquiring generally about how the meeting or session went or how the youth or supportive other felt about the visit, the YCW should ask frame questions in a way that elicits concrete, specific suggestions for altering the type, course, and delivery of services:

- Did we talk about the things that are most important to you today?
- What was the least helpful thing that happened today?
- Did my questions make sense to you?
- Did I fail to ask you about something you consider important or wanted to talk about but didn't?
- Was the meeting or session too (short/long/just right) for you?

- Did my responses make you feel like I understood what you were telling me, or do you need me to respond differently?
- Is there anything that happened (or did not happen) today that would cause you to not want to talk next time?

Further Considerations

Based on level of maturity, cognitive disabilities, or preference it may be necessary to change the type of ORS and SRS measures used. For example, there will be 11- and 12-year-olds who are more comfortable with the adult versions while there may be 13- and 14-year-olds who prefer the child versions. Scoring for all of the measures is the same so they can be switched easily. Along these lines, we want to be sure the language we use to describe the measures is understood by youth. YCWs are encouraged to practice ways of talking with youth in ways that they will more easily understand. The example of how to introduce the CORS that follows can serve as a guide.

Introduction

I'd like to ask you for your help with something. When we work with kids like you we want to make sure that they are feeling helped. So we use two short scales to keep track of things. The first one we use at the beginning each time we talk, and the second one we use at the end after we have talked. So to begin with I need your help showing me how things have been this last week, before you came here [or I/we came to see you]. Will you help me with that? This scale is the one we use to see how you have been feeling. As you can see it has four lines with smiley at each side, happy smileys to the right, sad smileys to the left. And above the lines it says "me," "family," "school," and "everything," Your job is to think about the last week and how things have been in these four areas of your life, and then make a hash mark on the lines to show me how things are going. The closer to the happy smiley, the better things have been, the closer to the sad smiley, the worse things have been. Does that make sense to you?

Another point, as discussed, youth will frequently present for services at the idea of a parent or other adult such as a teacher who believes that they need it. The key is to figure out which ORS score will be the best measure of the progress of services. In some instances, everyone in the family is there because they experience distress, and in this case each family member scores the scale evaluating their own functioning. The ORS and SRS measures can also be used with multiple persons or "collaterals." For example, a youth and caregiver may each complete a measure. Because youth often rate their situations differently than adults having two or more ORSs can provide points of comparison. In such an instance, a YCW might say, "Johnny I noticed that you have rated things currently at about a 31. Your mom rated things as a solid 18. Can you tell me about the difference between you and your mom's scores?" Differences in scores between youth and caregivers (or stakeholders) are very common. Discussion about differences can be invaluable in clarifying how the presenting issue is seen by both or all the involved parties. The progress as reported by both the youth and the collateral rater can be tracked and used as a reference point for the therapy, with the collateral rating being the most reliable indicator of progress. The YCWs' role is to explore those differences and work toward indicators of improvement that are acceptable to all parties involved.

The ORS and SRS measures are dialogue tools that will inform and improve the way the YCWs and other YFS workers focus on the outcome and alliance of the service provided. Having a graph that is available allows for an open and transparent conversation that includes youth and others' perspectives on decisions about the service delivery. This will ensure that the service is adjusted and tailored in response to the child, youth, or supportive other's feedback. The graph of the ORS and SRS scores will result in patterns of the progress and development over time that can stimulate hypothesis and ideas that can be explored to make sure those involved are getting the help they want. Knowledge of specific patterns will also make it possible for YCWs to respond if there are signs of "threats" to service outcome or alliance (and risk for dropout), and can be used to inform the decision to seek consultation on a particular case. In this sense, the ORS and SRS can be viewed as quality assurance instruments. Chapter 7 will detail some of the most common patterns and describe ways of responding to these patterns.

Lastly, scores can be stored on spreadsheets where the data can be accessed easily and statistics can be calculated. Resources such as the *ICCE Manuals on Feedback-Informed Treatment* (Bertolino & Miller, 2013) are available to assist with calculating and interpreting results. There are also network- and web-based systems to run the ORS and SRS measures and other outcome instrumentation used to monitor the effectiveness of services.

Next Steps: Gathering Information through Interviewing

As discussed, YCWs are often responsible for gathering information that will be shared among staff, those who provide services. Through early contacts such as interviewing, information that will be used throughout services is collected and stored in paper and/or electronic files. In this section, we will focus on types of information that can assist YCWs in helping youth and strengths-based practices for eliciting that information.

Before proceeding, it is important to keep in mind the role of personal awareness. Personal expectations can unconsciously and often inadvertently influence youth and supportive others experiences of services. In research, this is known as the observer-expectancy effect, which underscores the notion that mental health professionals' expectancy biases, whether positive or negative, can influence the course and outcome of services. Thus, YCWs can fall prey to biases and unrecognized assumptions can influence the content, process, and direction of services.

Unfolding Narratives through Open-Ended Questioning

With the addition of real-time feedback to the collaboration keys, we now shift to more concentrated efforts to gather information about youth and supportive others' situations—what brought them to services. From a strengths-based perspective, we are considering how to "screen in" as opposed to "screen out." Screening in means that we search for myriad ways in which we can include and help youth and families in our programs. Screening out, which is the antithesis, is a common practice among programs in which certain criteria lead youth to be excluded from services. A screen-in approach does not mean all youth are accepted into services. Instead, we stretch as much as possible to include youth, knowing that they may not be served elsewhere. Children and youth do not fall through the cracks as has been said; they fall through people's fingers.

A collaborative posture is central to gathering information and we extend this posture to those helpers (e.g., family members, social service workers, probation officers, teachers, etc.) who may be involved or have investment in the services. Being collaborative does not mean never being directive. YCWs may need to become more or less directive depending on youth preferences, context, and issues such as safety, particularly when it comes to risk of harm to self or others.

Whether to complete program forms or ask more general questions, at this juncture is often dependent on an agency's protocols. Some agencies will require that specific content be collected—usually drawn from forms (i.e., summaries, assessments)—and information in place before proceeding. Others will want more information about a situation gathered before moving forward to specific content such as historical information. Here we will begin with open-ended, narrative questions and then shift to more formal ones. Both types of questions can serve as a guide for learning more about youth and their situations. A task of the YCW is to blend open-ended and formal questions.

In gathering information, we are again reminded of the 80/20 rule. We ask: What kinds of information will be most beneficial in helping youth to achieve some measurable, beneficial change? To answer this question, from the outset a primary focus is on what needs to change. A lack of focus and structure can bring about not only a negative outcome but also contribute to frustration on the part of both youth and YFS staff. It is also clear that lack of agreement on the focus of services can lead to the selection of methods that are misguided and a poor fit for youth and others involved. It is therefore paramount that YCWs work to clarify and translate general and sometimes ambiguous concerns into specific ones. Lack of clarity about expectations, what is most concerning to youth and others involved, and what they would like to have different can contribute to dialogues that meander and may ultimately not be productive.

One way to begin to gain focus is by summarizing ORS/CORS scores as a lead in. Using an example used earlier in the chapter, we might say something along the lines of the following.

Case Example 4.4

On the scale we did a few minutes ago you scored 18.5. From what you said, that matches how things have been at home. It hasn't been too great. Would it be okay if I asked you some questions to better understand what it going on and how I might help?

If a youth and caregiver are present (and/or supportive others) we include both perspectives. Here is an example of how to do this, again based on an earlier example.

Case Example 4.5

A few moments ago we talked about the differences between the scores each of you gave. Johnny, you scored 31. Your mom rated things as an 18. If it's okay, I'd like to ask a few more questions to help me to better understand the concerns at home. Will that work?

We then proceed to the simultaneous gathering of information and establishing direction through *funneling*. *Funneling* involves moving from broad conversations to focused ones. The following questions may be useful in developing further focus:

- What would you like to see change?
- What would you like to have different with your situation/life?
- What did you hope would be different as a result of coming here?
- How would you know that the problem that brought you here is no longer a problem?
- What would have to be minimally different to consider working with me/us a success?

These questions not only help to develop focus but also begin to point in the direction of youth and supportive others' preferred futures—what they would like to have different. YCWs want to help youth to create well-articulated, preferred futures and then to turn those visions into realities. When youth already have a sense of a possibility-filled future, YCWs help them rehabilitate and begin to move toward those futures. Some youth will need more encouragement to help them to imagine what is possible and how their futures can be different and better than the past.

The result of asking questions that begin to orient youth toward the future and a more concentrated sense of direction will lead most of them to respond in one of two ways. They could describe what they do not want, which is useful information because it can help YCWs to understand more about youth's concerns and problems. The other way youth typically respond is by conveying what they do want. Whether describing what they do or do not want, youth or others involved commonly respond with statements such as, "I want to be happy," "I just want some peace," "I want to get rid of anxiety," "I don't want to be depressed," or "I don't want him to be so impulsive." The problem with these statements is they are vague and nondescript.

Vague words and ambiguous statements can activate YCWs' beliefs, biases, and theoretical opinions and lead them to assume that they know what youth mean. Imagine, for example, that a youth says he is "anxious." By not taking time to find out what he means by this, the YCW is at risk of relying on his or her experience and understandings of anxiety to guide change processes. Although experience working with youth who have reported "anxiety" in the past may be an asset, the problem is ambiguous without a description of the youth's experience and could lead to misguided attempts at problem resolution. To guard against this, it is important for YCWs to elicit clear descriptions of youth's concerns. *Action talk* provides a way of clarifying unclear, vague descriptions.

Action Talk: Clarifying Language

The quest for clarity is contingent on the use of questions that help to translate vague, ambiguous accounts into behaviorally based descriptions. To do this, YCWs use action talk (Bertolino & O'Hanlon, 2002). Action talk involves determining how youth or supportive others "do" their problem concerns and subsequently, what they will be doing when positive change has occurred and/or goals have been met.

To use action talk, when youth or supportive others use vague, non-sensory-based words, phrases, statements, or labels, YCWs follow up with questions to turn those into action- or interaction-based (that is, involving two or more people) descriptions. For example, if a youth says, "I'm depressed," a YCW might first reply with a question most YCWs are trained to ask, "Could you please tell me what you mean by 'depressed'?" Although a useful question, a different kind of questioning is required to understand *how* the youth *does* depression. We ask, "Can you describe for me what you do or don't do when you are depressed?" or "How would I know by watching you each day that you were depressed? What would I see?" Does the youth oversleep? Miss school? Eat too much or not enough? Our aim is to use action talk to clarify—to understand more about the uniqueness of depression in a person's life. The better the description, the more information is available to help the youth make changes. These three questions assist in clarifying understanding:

- When you are experiencing (concern/problem), what specifically is happening or not happening?
- What do you do or are you doing when you are in the throes of (concern/problem)?
- How do you do experience the (concern/problem)?

A variation of action talk is *video talk,* which involves using action talk to describe the problem or goal as if it could be seen or heard on video. We ask, "If I were to watch a video of you being/experiencing (concern/problem) what would I see you doing that would indicate to me that you were being/experiencing (concern/problem)?" Should ambiguity persist, the YCW requests further clarification.

Action talk is important to more than just clarifying problem descriptions. It shifts conversations to what youth and supportive others want different in their lives or situations so we spend less time on ambiguous descriptors (i.e., anxiety, depression) and more on changing actions and behaviors. As an example, a YCW can use action talk to flesh out what will be different with their situations or lives when the problems that lead them to services are no longer of concern. A YCW might say, "Tell me what will be happening when the problem that brought you here is no longer a problem." and "What will you be doing differently?" Questions below can assist with using action talk to gain perspective on the future.

- How will you know when the problem is no longer a problem? What will be different?
- How will your life be different in the future you want and the (concern/problem) has gone away?
- What specifically will be better when you no longer need our help for the problem that brought you in?
- What will you be doing to maintain that kind of life?

When youth get the sense that they are not making progress, they are at higher risk of not just giving up, but for dropping out of services. It is clear, however, that change is relative and will take different lengths of time depending on youth, their problems, and the severity of those problems. Although youth remain focused on the end point of problem resolution, we can orient them to other aspects of movement. This includes identifying indicators or signs that progress is being made toward the established goals. Here are some questions to assist with this process:

- What will be the first sign or indication that things have begun to turn the corner with your problem?
- What will be the first sign or indication that you have taken a solid step on the road to improvement even though you might not yet be out of the woods?
- What will you see happening when things are beginning to go more the way you'd like them to go?
- What would have to happen to indicate to you that things are changing in the direction you'd like them to change?
- What is happening right now with your situation that you would like to have continue?

Diagnostic and Disability-Related Labels: Person-First Language

Of the various forms of nondescript language, some are more influential. Mental health-related diagnostic labels, for example, may be required for youth to receive services and for those services to be funded. Common labels assigned to youth include ADHD (attention-deficit hyperactivity disorder), anxiety, depression, and CD (conduct disorder), sourced from the DSM (*Diagnostic and Statistical Manual of Mental Disorders*) (APA, 2013). Other frequently used categories of mental health labels include SPMI (serious and persistent mental illness) and SED (severely emotionally disturbed). In addition to mental health labels, which largely address emotional disability, are those used for persons with physical, intellectual, learning, speech and language, sensory, or brain-based disabilities.

Some youth and supportive others find diagnostic labels meaningful; they can defuse any blame regarding their conditions/situations that they or others have placed on themselves. For example, I have worked with clients who expressed relief in knowing that others have been through similar situations and that the diagnosis itself explained their concerns. And many diagnoses have also led to research to find effective treatment approaches—perhaps the best result of labeling.

Concerns with diagnosis and the DSM, in particular, are well documented. YFS workers have to consider the labeling, depersonalizing, and stigmatizing effects that the identification of pathology can cause. Each diagnosis concern is linked to others: Diagnosis is based on identifying deficit and pathology; a pathology focus leads to labeling people as having "disorders"; and labeling can objectify people and depersonalize them. This can lead to youth being seen as their diagnoses rather than as people. Unnecessarily assigning labels can stigmatize youth, possibly subjecting them to prejudices, biases, and in extreme cases, ostracizing them from life activities. It is also worth noting that when it comes to youth, diagnostic labels are only part of the landscape. Labels such as "childish," "egocentric," "manipulative," "oppositional," and so on are not simply negative, they are disrespectful (Appelstein, 1998).

YCWs pay close attention to those occurrences in which there is the risk of youth being seen as—or in some cases, becoming—a condition or label. For example, one might say, "Joanne's schizophrenic" or "Jay suffers from ADHD." In other instances, youth may even use depersonalizing language when referring to themselves by saying things such as, "I'm bipolar" or "Didn't you know I'm hyperactive?" What seems to happen in these cases is that youth lose their sense of self and develop identities consistent with the label. In turn, others involved see only the symptoms associated with the label, losing sight of the youth as a person. In such cases, the diagnosis or label often becomes the focal point of services. YCWs and other professionals then try to resolve conduct disorder, for example, instead of concentrating efforts on trying to understand and support the unique individual whose behaviors fit a specific set of diagnostic criteria.

From a strengths-based perspective, our response to labels and depersonalizing language is twofold. It involves the use of person-first language and action talk. First and foremost, youth are people, not disabilities. Our language needs to reflect this fact. A disability may be an aspect of a youth or other's life but certainly does not identify who the youth is. To learn about youth and who they are as people, it is imperative that we attend closely to how we see others and the words we use to describe their situations. Using person-first language first, we take the "ic" out of the person. Rather than saying "Joanne is schizophrenic," we say "Joanne has been diagnosed with schizophrenia." We also eliminate words such as "suffers," "confined" (i.e., "Javier is confined to a wheelchair"), and "requires" (i.e., "Mia requires glasses"). These words are unnecessary. Person-first language is consistent with the view of disability along a continuum of health (Olkin, 1999). Some disabilities interfere with a person's functioning in some but not all circumstances. Other disabilities have few or no effects on general health. This makes it important to look at the effects of each condition on the range of functions faced by persons with disabilities. Brown (2008) developed this point:

> What is true is that people with disabilities have some (or several) aspects of their bodies that function differently than those of a majority of other humans. Frequently, however, the challenges for these individuals lie not in those physical differences but in the barriers created to fullest possible function by cultural institutions and practice. (p. 29)

A second response from a strengths-based perspective is to use action talk—as described in this chapter—to counter the ambiguity of labels. Instead of saying "Eduardo is working on his ADHD," we say, "Eduardo is working on completing his homework correctly, in a timely manner." In this way, the uniqueness of Eduardo's situation becomes the focus of services, not ADHD.

Diagnosis and labels are part of the landscape of YFS. And YFS are merely a reflection of larger society. Because society tends to be steeped in problem-saturated discourses, the tones of language frequently ring of deficit, negativity, marginalization, and depersonalization. A strengths-based perspective provides a respectful response to pathological discourses by emphasizing abilities and capacities.

The Matter of Goals

Clarifying questions also help to outline the *goals* of services. *Goals* are often simply the opposite of problem descriptions, concrete representations of what youth and supportive others would like to see change. Goals are clearly defined, action-based descriptions of their hoped-for futures and differ from *outcomes*, which are clients' perceptions of the impact that services have on the major areas of their lives (i.e., individually, interpersonally, socially). Outcomes equate to functioning, as captured by measures such as the ORS.

The significance of goals increases when it comes to service planning. Service or treatment planning provides an opportunity to clarify goals and objectives (an example of a service plan can be found in Appendix B). Goals are essential to service planning because they are commonly considered benchmarks of success. It is all the more important to collaborate with youth on goals and communicate those goals clearly in paperwork. This is indicative of collaborative service planning.

The formation of goals requires patience on the part of YFS workers. Youth have different motivations. For example, some will be motivated to achieve desired experiences or goals (e.g., money, freedom) and to avoid unpleasant or unwanted experiences (e.g., boredom, restrictions) (Bertolino, 1999). The same can be said for their parents or caregivers. The following case illustrates this point.

Case Example 4.6

With long wavy brown hair, tie-dyed shirt, and mirrored John Lennon glasses, Michael looked as if he had walked straight off Haight-Ashbury in the 1960s and into my office. Respectful and soft spoken, the 16-year-old was not merely disinterested in school; he loathed it. And Michael was unique in every way imaginable, including the manner in which he skipped school.

His approach was original; it reflected his love for the Grateful Dead. If the Dead were in Oakland so was Michael. Atlanta, Seattle—he was there. He would scrounge up enough for a bus ticket or hitch a ride—whatever it took to get to a show. At some point his mom would notice he was gone and call the police. Sometimes they'd find him in a day or two, other times he'd return on his own after a couple weeks. By the time he came to his first therapy appointment with his mother, Michael had seen a great deal of the United States.

When the three of us met together, Michael's mom expressed her concern about his excessive school absences, poor grades, and lack of "motivation" to complete school. The mother made it clear that she wanted Michael to complete high school. He would then be the first to go to college. Michael said little during that time so I asked to speak with him privately. No sooner had his mother left the room did Michael exclaim, "I'm not hurting anyone. I just don't like school. I want to do my own thing . . . you know, be a Deadhead." There was no mistaking the conviction in his voice.

I acknowledged Michael, "That's honest. I appreciate that there is something in your life that matters a lot to you."

"It's the truth."

"I believe you. So you want to be a Deadhead, eh?"

"Yeah. I want to see them on tour and hang out."

"Tell me about what it means to you to be a Deadhead."

I actually knew a lot about the culture from a couple other YCWs at YIN who are full-fledged Deadheads. But I wanted to know about Michael's experience.

"Their music is cool. I get into it. It's got this vibe. And I just want to go where they are playing and have a great time."

"How do you get there?"

"I hitch."

"That's pretty dangerous."

"I can take care of myself."

"I don't doubt that but there are things out of your control like when you get in the car with a stranger. What then do you do for food and where do you sleep?"

"People at the shows help me out. They give me food and a place to sleep."

"Let me make sure I understand. Other Deadheads help you out by giving you what you need?"

"They do for a while."

"What do you mean . . . for a while?"

"Then you give back."

"Oh I see. So you help out. (Michael nods his head in agreement.) If that's the expectation how long before you give back?"

"Well, once I have a job . . ."

"It would have to be a pretty good job, right? To afford to travel around, help others . . ."

"Dude, there are doctors and lawyers who follow the Dead around."

"Really?"

"Yeah, there really are. They have awesome jobs. They make good money and schedule time off when the Dead are touring."

I was aware that the Dead have a massive, loyal following of people from all walks of life. But Michael's enthusiasm was invigorating.

"Wow, that's a great deal!" I say.

"I know. See what I mean?"

"Sure. But I'm confused about something. You mentioned that people who give back have money—or at least some form of financial resources—which mostly comes from having good jobs . . . right?"

"Yeah," Michael says, looking at me quizzically.

"Well, I'm confused because you are almost 17 and are in the ninth grade for the third time with no possibility of passing. School isn't going well for you at the moment. Not that you want to be a doctor or lawyer, but I'm about as sure as I can be that most of the people you are referring to finished high school; especially the ones who are making enough money and have flexibility in their schedules to follow the Dead. So where does that leave you? You must have a plan that I don't know about."

"Yeah . . . I need to do something about school but I hate it. I am going to get a job though."

"I believe you. But from the sound of it you're going to have to do more than talk about it if things are going to change with school and if you're going to get the kind of job that is flexible and pays enough for your road trips."

"Yeah, I know."

"What do you think the first step toward that is?

"I have to do something about school but my mom . . . I mean, she really wants me to graduate from high school."

"Is that bad?"

"No, but school isn't gonna work for me. I'd do the GED if she'd let me."

"You're saying that if your mom were okay with you getting your GED then you would follow through—go to the classes, take the test . . ."

"No doubt. I would do it right away. I know I can pass it."

Michael was right. It was a dream of his mom's that he would graduate high school. Michael dropping out would mean the end of that dream. And yet there are all kinds of dreams and sometimes new roads lead to new dreams.

When the three of us regrouped, Michael's mom immediately spoke of her hope of Michael finishing school. But there was also a twinge of defeat in her voice. She seemed to know that the path Michael had chosen would inevitably lead to a different end. I acknowledged her desire for Michael, her only child, to finish high school. I then asked what she envisioned things might be like a few years from now for Michael. She glanced up and said, "It's his life, really. I want him to have opportunities to do things that make him happy. I don't know how he will do if school doesn't work out. I then asked her if there were other ways that may not be ideal but would still provide opportunities for Michael in the future.

"You mean like the GED?" She inquired.

"Yes. That is what I mean."

"I don't think he ever really gave high school a shot. He didn't apply himself. He could have done it. I never thought it would come to this. I don't know, maybe it's more my dream than his."

Michael chimed in, "Totally. High school is right for others but not for me. I can still go to college if I have my GED."

"What I am hearing is that you are concerned for Michael. You don't want him to just have just any old future; you want it to be one with options, a happy one. And it's difficult to know that the vision of the future you had for him may be different than the one he has for himself," I said.

"Yeah. It's just not what I planned," she replied.

"What would help you to feel more comfortable with this situation and what Michael wants for himself?"

"That we had a plan. How would this work? And I still don't see how following the Grateful Dead around is a career."

"Mom, I can follow the Dead and have a career. Give it a chance."

We developed a plan that had Michael pursuing his GED and getting a job. Michael's mom could keep her dream of her son having a good life; it would just take some getting used to.

Over the next few months Michael followed through with the plan. He studied for and passed his GED. He got a job to earn money so he could follow the Dead around and help others by giving back at shows. Michael then enrolled in junior college to continue his education.

In August of 1995, Jerry Garcia passed away leaving Michael devastated. In one of our last meetings I reminded Michael of his accomplishments. He had completed his GED, started college, and was employed. And, given his devotion, I have no doubt that Jerry would welcome Michael as a full-fledged "Deadhead."

Being a Deadhead may seem an unusual goal. Youth often describe hoped-for situations within which there are goals. In the case of Michael, being a Deadhead translated to completing his education and having a job, both of which are considered goals. YCWs are patient to let the stories of youth unfold, listening closely for opportunities to achieve and accomplish.

Goals should reflect and match the motivational levels of youth and supportive others. We do this by learning how youth and others involved situate themselves (i.e., involved, not involved) in relation to presenting concerns (i.e., their problems, other people's problems) and what they feel needs to happen for their lives or situations to improve (e.g., nothing, new perspectives, new actions, change in interactions). This information assists in matching methods with the youth's levels of motivation as a means to increase the chance of a successful outcome.

Patience on the part of YCWs is also necessary because what youth and supportive others sometimes express as concerns will not represent things they want to change. They are instead requests for acknowledgment, to be heard. In addition, some youth will convey numerous concerns so it may not always be clear which ones take precedence. For this reason, YCWs always check to be sure that they understand what youth and supportive others want to see change. When multiple concerns persist, we summarize and acknowledge them all and seek to learn which are most pressing. If all concerns are of equal weight to those involved, we work to determine which concerns should be addressed first. One way to do this is to say, "It seems that you have several concerns, all of which are important. I want you to know that we'll address them all. To get us started, please tell me which one or two of the concerns you mentioned rise to the top and should be looked at first."

The term "goals" may be off-putting to some. Although common to YFS workers and funders, for some youth the language of "goals" simply will not fit them. The YCW should be sensitive to language preferences, keeping in mind that we seek a sense of direction and clarity regarding how youth want their lives to be in the future. This means using language that makes sense for youth and supportive others.

Next is an illustration of the use of action talk to develop focus in services.

Case Example 4.7

Youth: Things are out of control.

YCW: Can you tell me about that?

Youth: It seems like nothing is going right—it's just one thing after another.

YCW: Things don't seem to be going well and it feels like things just keep happening—one after another.

Youth: . . . right—one thing after another.

YCW: Do you mind if I ask you a little more about that?

Youth: Go ahead.

YCW: OK. If I were to step into your life and really get a glimpse of it, what would I see that would make it clear to me that it was out control?

Youth: You'd see me being mad.

YCW: How would I know you were mad?

Youth: I would be saying sarcastic things because everything would piss me off.

YCW: I'd see you making sarcastic comments . . . and I can guess how that might cause some trouble . . . but how specifically has that been a problem for you?

Youth: Well, I don't really have any friends . . . I'm alone because of it.

YCW: So for you, being mad, and sarcastic as a result, has interfered with your friendships.

Youth: Without a doubt.

YCW: And is that what you mean by being out of control?

Youth: Yeah, because it feels like I just fly off the handle and say things I shouldn't when I get the slightest bit mad.

YCW: OK. So let me see if I can get a different kind of glimpse. Let's say we were able to take your life a few months into the future and you felt like things were going much better—more the way you'd like—and I could see that with you. What would I see happening that would let me know things were better?

Youth: I wouldn't be ruining friendships.

YCW: What would you be doing instead?

Youth: I'd be making friends and not saying stupid stuff when I got mad.

YCW: So you would be making friends and even though you might get upset once in a while, you would respond differently than you have in the past . . .

Youth: . . . definitely.

YCW: What might you do instead of flying off the handle and saying things you later regretted?

Youth: I'm not too sure exactly what I would do, but something better than what I've been doing.

YCW: Do you think that is something you'd like to spend time on in here? Finding ways of making friends and responding differently when you get mad so your relationships grow instead of splitting apart?

Youth: Yeah . . . that's it.

YCW: I see. And how will that help you when it's happening more often?

Youth: I will be much happier?

YCW: How so?

Youth: In many ways. I'll feel better about myself and have a better social life.

YCW: That sounds good.

As we have learned, youth and supportive others frequently give ambiguous descriptions (i.e., "out of control," "fly off the handle"). It is important to ask clarifying questions and persist when answers include other ambiguous responses. Action talk can assist with this. In addition, clients often report what is not wanted (i.e., "ruining friendships"). Action talk conversations can aid in understanding concerns and their effects on youth and in establishing directions for services.

Goals should be realistic, attainable, ethical, and legal. For example, it is reasonable for a youth who has lost someone close to want that person to return. Even though this is not possible, it may be possible for the person to experience a caring relationship with another person. Often what a youth requests is a symbol for something else. By acknowledging youth and supportive others' internal experiences and views, practitioners can cut through many unrealistic expectations and co-create solvable problems. Next is an example of how a YCW might talk with a youth to form realistic expectations.

Case Example 4.8

Youth: My dad died last year. I wish he were still here. I really miss him. That's really what I want . . . him to be back.

YCW: I'm sorry about your loss. What do you miss most about him?

Youth: He used to listen to me . . . really listen to me.

YCW: How did you know when he was really listening to you?
Youth: He would look me in the eyes and not judge me.
YCW: What did he do to let you know that he wasn't judging you?
Youth: Well, he didn't make comments like, "You should have . . ." or "That was stupid to do that."
YCW: I see. And how did that help you?
Youth: I knew he valued me and I haven't had that since.
YCW: Is that something you would like to experience again in a relationship with someone—that sense of being listened to, not judged, and valued?
Youth: I would love to have that again.
YCW: What would be different for you as a result of having that again?
Youth: I'd feel great. I'd feel better about going through each day knowing that I could talk with somebody who understood me.

When youth propose changes that are unrealistic we want to be sure we are listening carefully to what they are expressing. In most situations, we can help youth or supportive others to achieve some variation of goals or what goals symbolize. In other cases, acknowledgment will assist with filling emotional voids, allowing for youth and YCWs to regroup and work together to find something to work toward.

Action talk and video talk provide straightforward ways to learn what youth and others involved would like to have different in their lives. There are times when more creative strategies will be more effective in generating conversations and a future focus; the following are some suggestions. YCWs are also encouraged to develop their own ideas that may provide a better fit.

Some More Creative Strategies

The Miracle Question

Developed by Steve de Shazer (1988) and colleagues at the Brief Family Therapy Center (BFTC), in Milwaukee, Wisconsin, the miracle question has become synonymous with solution-focused therapy. This popular method is used to help clients envision their lives in futures when their problems have been solved. The miracle question is generally set up when the therapist encourages a client to use her imagination, then asking, "Suppose you were to go home tonight, and while you were asleep, a miracle happened and this problem was solved. How will you know the miracle happened? What will be different?" (p. 5). This question is followed up in detail with questions about the miracle scenario given.

A variation for youth is the dream method (Bertolino, 2003). The YCW asks, "Let's suppose that tonight, while you are sleeping, you have a dream. In this dream, the problem you have is resolved. Tell me about what might happen in that dream that would lead to your problem no longer being a problem. What might happen?" Another variation is to speculate about a past dream: "Suppose that you had a wonderful dream last night or sometime in the recent past. Up until now, however, you haven't been able to recall it. In that dream, you were able to see your future without the problem that brought you to me. What happened?" As with other methods in this section, the answer is then followed by asking other questions to further develop the future vision.

The Crystal Ball

Milton Erickson's (1954) "pseudo-orientation in time" is also viewed historically as a precursor to the miracle question. He used this concept hypnotically by having his patients positively hallucinate (i.e., see something that is not really there) three crystal balls—one each for the past, present, and future. He would have his patients peer into the crystal ball that represented the future and suggest that they could see what their lives would be like without the problems that brought them to therapy. Erickson would then have them describe, in detail, how their problems were resolved. Later, he would essentially prescribe the remedies provided by his patients.

YCWs can use a similar process without the hypnosis by having youth envision a crystal ball, look out a window, or look at a blank wall onto which they can imagine ("project") their future when their problems have been resolved (or at least alleviated enough that they no longer need to be in services) and describe it as clearly as possible by using action talk. Questions that follow focus on having youth describe how problems were resolved. Finally, in "real" time, have youth identify steps to make their future visions reality and begin to take them.

The Time Machine

Another method that involves some imagination and can be particularly useful for youth is the time machine (Bertolino, 1999). It is a way to help them to envision a future where things work out. The time machine is introduced in the following example.

Introduction

Let's say there is a time machine sitting here in the office. Let's say that you climb in and it propels you into the future, to a time when things are going the way you want them to go. After arriving at your future destination, the first thing you notice is that the problems that brought you to here have disappeared.

Next the YCW ferrets out the scenario by using follow-up questions such as:

- Where are you?
- Who is with you?
- What is happening?
- What are you doing?

- How is your life different than before?
- Where did your problems go?
- How did they go away?

Other options for creating a future focus include pretending to peer through a View-Master (a child's toy similar to binoculars in which images are on a small reel and can be changed by clicking a switch) (Bertolino, 1999) and "future screening," which asks youth to imagine that they are able to see their future on a movie screen (Bertolino, Kiener, & Patterson, 2009). The methods described can be modified and used with physical props (such as pictures, drawings). For example, a youth could be asked to create an image on paper of the future she would like by drawing a picture or using cutouts from magazines. The idea is to use what fits for the youth. Whether using basic questions or creative methods, YCWs want to help youth to gain clarity and answer the rudimentary question, "How will you know when things are better?" Once what youth or supportive others involved want is clear, practitioners can begin to collaborate with them on steps to make those positive changes occur.

A further consideration with goals is that youth and supportive others involved may experience frustration knowing the gap between where they are at the beginning of services and where they would like things to be at the end. This frustration can mount over time if improvement is considered insufficient. When youth get the sense that they are not making progress, they are at high risk of both giving up and dropping out of services. YCWs can respond to such frustrations by working with youth and supportive others to identify indicators or signs that progress is being made. These questions assist with this process:

- What will be the first sign or indication that things have begun to turn the corner with your problem?
- What will be the first sign or indication to you that you have taken a solid step on the road to improvement even though you might not yet be out of the woods?
- What will you see happening when things are beginning to go more the way you'd like them to go?
- What would have to happen that would indicate to you that things are changing in the direction you'd like them to change?

By focusing on in-between change, YCWs can help youth and supportive others to identify progress toward goals. This can both counter frustration youth feel and help orient them toward exceptions and differences in regard to their described problems.

Scaling Questions

As a framework for determining concerns, goals, and progress, using questions that focus on quantitative change can be helpful. One way to do this is to use scaling questions (de Shazer, 1991). To use scaling questions, the YCW first establishes a continuum using a scale, most commonly from 1 to 10. Each number represents a rating of how the youth views her life at different junctures (e.g., the present and later points). The YCW introduces the idea of scaling by saying, "On a scale of 1 to 10, with 1 being the worst this problem has ever been, and 10 being the best things could be, how would you rate things today?" Once a number has been given, the YCW uses action talk to ensure that what the number represents is clear. For example, if a youth rates the situation at a 3, the YCW asks, "What specifically is happening to indicate to you that it is a 3?"

With a clear starting point, the next step is to ask the youth what number would indicate that the goals of therapy have been met, that services have been successful, or that sufficient improvement has occurred. If the youth described earlier stated that an 8 would indicate sufficient change, the YCW would then ask her to describe what specifically will be happening when she reaches an 8. Again, action talk is used to clarify.

The final part of scaling in this way is for the YCW to explore with the youth what will indicate in-between change and progress. The YCW might ask, "You mentioned that things are at a 3 now and 8 is where you would like to be. What will it take for your situation to edge forward a little, from a 3 to a 3½?" As discussed earlier in this chapter we want to make sure the change we are looking for is not too big a leap. Although it is possible for youth to make large gains very quickly, it is usually a better idea to focus on movement that increases the likelihood of success.

Multiple Family Members and Outside Helpers

When working with multiple family members attending to each person's preferences, and goals, and ideas about progress is important. Despite differing preferences, most often there are common threads among the complaints and identified goals. In searching for commonality, we coordinate complaints and goals by using three processes—acknowledgment, tracking, and linking. The YCW acknowledges and restates each person's perspective in the least inflammatory way possible while acknowledging and imparting the intended feeling and meaning. Statements that do so are linked by the word *and* because doing so builds on a common concern. What follows is a case illustration of how to use acknowledgment, tracking, and linking.

Case Example 4.9

Freda (mother): I just want her to return to school. It's ridiculous for her to be out. And besides, if she doesn't go, she'll never get the kind of job she wants.

YCW: You're concerned because your sense is there's really no reason for a 16-year-old to be out of school and that it could negatively affect her future.

Freda: Right.

Elsie (daughter): What's the point? I can't stand school. Besides, if you're gonna continue to be on my case, then I'll never go back!

Freda: See, that's what I get every day!

YCW: I can see that it's been rough on both of you. And for you Elsie, you haven't found a reason to go to school and to tolerate it yet.

Elsie: Yeah. School is boring and if she doesn't back off . . . then, forget it.

YCW: And what do you mean by your mom being "on your case"?

Elsie: She constantly says, "You better go. You better go. You can't miss another day!" It's like she thinks that I don't have a clue! I know that I need to graduate to get a good job. Duh!

YCW: OK, and the ways that she's tried so far to get you to go haven't worked so well for you?

Elsie: Nope.

YCW: Let me see if I'm following the two of you. Freda, you'd really like Elsie to return to school, finish her education, and have a better chance of reaching her dreams. And Elsie, you seem to have some dreams for yourself, and even though I haven't heard about them yet, perhaps school is a part of that in some way. So you'd like to find a way to tolerate school so that you can graduate and work toward the career you want. And maybe there are other ways that your mom can be helpful to you with that—ways that don't involve her telling you to go, because you already know that—but ways that you see as being supportive with school.

Each part of this three-pronged approach is central to creating consensus among those involved. Acknowledgment assists by letting each person involved know her concern has been heard and is valid. Tracking allows the YCW to log and follow each concern, and linking via the word *and* provides the thread that weaves each together. Whether families or other multiple-client variations, youth and supportive others are free to clarify any misperceptions or areas of discomfort until mutually agreeable descriptions emerge. YCWs can then continue to flesh out the directions and goals of services.

As in working with multiple clients, collaborating with outside helpers (i.e., mental health, health, family court, educational, social service, etc.) can be a challenging task when varying perspectives are represented. Although outside helpers can have different degrees of influence, it remains important to maintain a collaborative stance. This involves having conversations with outside helpers to learn about their expectations and goals. In doing so, the YCW realizes that those who have stakes in the lives of youth often carry some level of responsibility and ability to alter the course of or end services. Collaboration at this juncture precedes the "how" of services in first agreeing on "what" needs to change or be different. The illustration that follows offers one way to work with an outside entity.

Case Example 4.10

YCW: I want to be sure that I'm clear here. Can you tell me what specifically you want to be addressed with Curtis while he's here in services?

Probation Officer (PO):   Curtis' attitude. He seems to think that parole is a joke.

YCW: What has happened that's given you that idea?

PO: He's stolen, and he keeps thinking that the next time he won't get caught even though he has [been caught] many times.

YCW: You're concerned about Curtis' history of stealing and that he might do it again?

PO: Right.

YCW: What would you need to see happening with Curtis to really believe that he had changed his ways?

PO: It's actually pretty simple. He'd have to quit stealing. Curtis would also have to be more respectful to me.

YCW: All right. And how would you know he was being more respectful to you?

PO: He would talk calmly and agree to do what I ask him to do.

YCW: Curtis, how does that sound to you?

Curtis: Same old song and dance.

PO: That's exactly what I'm talking about. He's always sarcastic . . .

YCW: You mean less sarcasm . . . and what would you see as a respectful way to responding to you?

PO: "Yes sir" would be great. Heck, I'd settle for "okay." But the flip attitude has to go before I'll budge.

YCW: Curtis?

Curtis: Fine.

YCW: So the one thing is how Curtis responds to you. The other is for Curtis to make positive choices and not steal anymore.

PO: Yes.

YCW: What do think about that, Curtis?

Curtis: It's fine. I know that's what I'm supposed to do.

YCW: OK, but does it sound reasonable to you?

Curtis: Of course.

PO: There's the sarcasm again.

YCW: How do you differentiate between what's Curtis just being Curtis and what's cutting, unacceptable sarcasm?

PO: I get your point. It just seems unnecessary to act like that.

YCW: Sure. And I'll bet you hear your share of sarcasm.

PO: Yeah, and it wears on you after a while.

YCW: I can see why.

PO: But as long as he doesn't swear at me and acknowledges what I expect of him, I can let the rest slide.

YCW: How does that sound, Curtis?

Curtis: I can live with that.

YCW (To PO): What, then, might you see Curtis do that would at least make you wonder a little if he's turned the corner with stealing and is ready for a probation-free life?

PO: If he went six months with no further incidents of stealing—well, any violations, other than a parking ticket, for that matter. But I can't see that happening. He's never gone more than a month before.

YCW: So you would be surprised?

PO: That's putting it mildly. I'd be shocked.

Curtis: Now *that's* sarcastic.

YCW: From what I can tell, you both have a flair for sarcasm!

PO: That's for sure.

YCW: OK, well for the sake of clarity, when Curtis has gone six months without any major violations, what will that mean?

PO: I'll advocate for his release from probation.

YCW: What do you think of that, Curtis?

Curtis: Wow. I didn't expect to hear that. That's great.

Involuntary services that involve power differentials need to be acknowledged. Collaboration does not mean that everything is equal, but it speaks to the process of negotiating realistic and attainable change with all involved. YCWs therefore collaborate with outside helpers and incorporate their feedback into sessions.

Because YCWs do not always have direct access, an indirect way for involving outside helpers is to ask youth, "Did [name of outside helper] tell you what [he or she] expects us to focus on here?" If the youth can answer this question (and it sounds reasonable), the YCW proceeds by incorporating those goals or directions into the services. If the youth does not know, speculation can be helpful: "What do you think [he/she] will say when I talk with [him/her]?" YCWs should invite all parties involved to share their perceptions and understandings of what may have been conveyed to them (Bertolino, 2003).

In the event that youth truly do not know what outside helpers' concerns are or what is expected of them or when the perceptions they identify are inconsistent with what the YCW has been told, the YCW gently introduces understanding by saying, for example, "My understanding after talking with [person's name] is that [he/she] will have the sense that you're moving in the right direction when you're [name of action(s)]." This is followed with, "How does that sound to you?" As with working with multiple clients, YCW acknowledges each perspective and searches for continuity between the respective goals.

The involvement of outside helpers represents collaboration at its best. Welcoming multiple perspectives and expanding the system can generate new possibilities and potential solutions. When outside helpers join meetings or sessions, it is important to remember that there are multiple ways to view situations with no one view being more correct than another. At the same time, perspectives that close down possibilities should be challenged and any that can facilitate change in directions and goals promoted.

Structured Processes: Using Forms to Gather Specific Information

In addition to open-ended questions as a means for gathering information is the use of structured-content processes that involve specific questions from pre-established forms. A primary driver for gathering information in YFS is, in fact, the forms required. At the start of the chapter, the issue of collecting useful information was discussed. We maintain cultural sensitivity as information-gathering becomes increasingly structured. Youth and supportive others' experiences, preferences, and abilities determine whether a particular approach is a good fit. Not all forms of information-gathering have been used consistently with culturally diverse populations. In addition, intellectual capacities and other influences in youth backgrounds will affect how and to what degree they will be able or willing to answer questions.

Most YFS agencies have their own forms and paperwork. Appendix B includes two examples of assessment forms. The first example is from Youth In Need, Inc. (YIN). The second example is the Plan of Care Template from the Vermont Coalition of Runaway and Homeless Youth Programs (VCRHYP). Each form has specific content areas with questions to guide conversations. An online search will produce many other examples and structural variations.

A characteristic of some agency paperwork is the tendency to be negatively skewed with focus on problems and pathology. Latitude with preset forms depends largely on program and YCW philosophies. Such latitude is crucial in achieving a balance between problem-focused and strengths-based questions. Although forms may be narrow in scope, there is most always room—and if not YCWs should create room—to ask questions to learn about strengths and *exceptions* to problems while identifying mitigating factors that could put both youth and institutions at risk for unnecessary hospitalizations, increased length of stay, and ineffective services. *Exceptions* relate to times when things are different or have gone differently in regard to problems (de Shazer, 1988, 1991; O'Hanlon & Weiner-Davis, 2003). Exception-oriented questions ask for information about when the concern or problem was less dominating, occurred less frequently, or was absent altogether. Essential to this process is to identify what youth or others involved did differently in such instances. Just by paying attention to differences, some youth and others involved will make small shifts in their views, moving from "it's always that way" to "sometimes it's a little better" or "it's not always as bad as it seems." These shifts, however subtle, can lead youth to doubt their own perspectives, thus opening doorways to view their problems and situations differently.

There are many possible areas to explore exceptions during structured information-gathering. Primary areas include but are not limited to education/school, work/employment, family/social relationships, hobbies/interests, and previous therapy experiences (Bertolino, 2003). Information about exceptions and differences serve as places to not only intervene in the present but also act as building blocks for future change.

Through specific questions about school, for example, YCWs can learn from youth what has worked in the past (to any degree), what worked more recently, and what might work in the future. Efforts can then be made to apply or replicate what has worked at other times with current concerns. It is also important to find out about what has not worked so that YCWs do not unknowingly use methods that youth or supportive others have found either unhelpful or disrespectful in the past. Although it is possible that a youth could still benefit from something that was not previously helpful, it is best to begin with feedback and then search for specific methods to provide a better fit.

Specific questions also help to identify social support systems, which are integral in providing stability and connection. A way to identify these resources and other strengths and supports is through three different tools, "My Strengths" (a strengths-based inventory), "Spokes of Life," and "VCRHYP Resiliency Assessment," all of which can be found in Appendix B. The Spokes of Life, in particular, is a visual schematic that provides a way to help youth identify list persons who make up their support systems and might be helpful in the present or future. The Spokes of Life can also be useful with identifying new social supports.

Are We on the Right Track? Checking in throughout Services

It's called "bedside manner" in healthcare. Physicians, nurses, dentists, and physical therapists are trained more extensively in building relationships with patients than at any other time in history. But healthcare providers know that good patient care involves more than asking if patients have questions. There has to be ongoing attention to patient experiences. For example, during procedures physicians and nurses will say, "Let me know if you have any discomfort or feel any pain." They do this because they want their patients to be as comfortable as possible. Ascertaining the degree of comfort another person is experiencing is difficult—if not impossible—without patient feedback. In addition, patients who are more comfortable (in other words, experience lower levels of pain) typically recover faster. This idea applies fully to YFS.

In each of the last three chapters, we have explored the role of alliance feedback. Earlier in this chapter, we specifically learned how to use the SRS to monitor youth and supportive others' ratings of the alliance. In this last section, we take a page from health professionals through the use of "check-ins." Although instrumentation is important for obtaining feedback, YCWs also want to check in periodically in meetings and sessions to gauge their experiences of helping relationships. Check-ins can and should occur any time YCWs want to better gauge a conversation, if there is a change in the way a youth or supportive other is relating (e.g., becomes very quiet after talking freely) or if a reaction of a youth or other suggests something may be "off." The following questions can be used during meetings/sessions to check in:

- Have you felt heard and understood?
- Do you feel/think we're talking about what you want to talk about?
- Have we been working on what you want to work on?
- How has the session been for you so far?

- Are we moving in a direction that seems right for you?
- What has the conversation we've been having been like for you?
- What has been helpful or not helpful?
- Are there other things that you feel/think we should be discussing instead?
- Is there anything I should have asked that I haven't asked?
- How satisfied are you with how things are going so far on a scale from 1 to 10, 10 meaning you are completely satisfied with things?
- Are there any changes we should make at this point?
- To what degree has what we've been doing met your expectations so far?

Feedback from these questions allows YCWs to learn whether services are on track or adjustments need to be made. YCWs also need to keep in mind that even in strong alliances trouble spots and strains can occur. In fact, evidence suggests that alliances with "tears and repairs" can be better predictors of subsequent improvement than those alliances that are stable and grew linearly (Kivlighan, 2001). The point is that YCWs must respond to feedback and continue this practice through the end of services. In accordance, is a series of questions for use at the end of sessions:

- How was the session/meeting for you?
- How was the pace of our conversation/session/meeting?
- Was there anything missing from our session?
- Is the way we approached your concern/situation fitting with the way you expect change to occur?
- Are there any changes you would recommend if we were to meet again?
- Is there anything you would need me to do differently if/when we meet again?
- How would explain your experience today to others who may be curious?

We are reminded of cultural differences that could influence how youth and supportive others might respond to these types of question. If a feedback-oriented approach is inconsistent with youths' cultural backgrounds, then we respond accordingly. An additional point is the argument that youth may be dishonest when asked questions such as those listed. Our aim is to invite youth to share their experiences so we can be as helpful as possible, not to judge youth's motives or the quality of feedback. It is clear that when youth are not asked for feedback they typically do not volunteer it. And poor alliances are a primary reason for youth or supportive others to end services. Simply, eliciting and responding to feedback reduces the risk of premature dropout, help to get relationships back on track, and increases the likelihood of positive outcome.

This chapter included detailed discussion of information-gathering processes used in YFS. Because of the many settings and roles that YCWs serve in, the application of the ideas presented will differ. A challenge of YCWs is to determine how to implement strengths-based information-gathering processes in ways that most benefit those served. In the next two chapters, we will explore a wide range of strategies for stimulating change in our interactions with youth.

five
Possibilities, Part 1: Strategies for Changing Views

I don't believe in taking foolish chances, but nothing can be accomplished without taking any chance at all.

—Charles Lindbergh

In 1990 at the second Evolution of Psychotherapy conference in Anaheim, California, Dr. Viktor Frankl (1905–1997) gave a keynote address in which he told a compelling story of his life. The Viennese psychiatrist, known worldwide for his book, *Man's Search for Meaning*, described how he was physically and psychologically abused and tortured and nearly died several times while imprisoned in three Nazi concentration camps. During his address, he detailed a wintry day in Poland in which he was marched through a field with a number of other prisoners. He was wearing thin clothing, with no socks, and holes in his shoes. Very ill from malnutrition and mistreatment, he began to cough. The cough was so severe that he fell to his knees. A guard came over and told him to get moving. He could not even answer because his cough was so intense and debilitating. The guard began to beat him with a club and told him that he would be left to die if he did not get up. Dr. Frankl knew this was true because he had witnessed it before. Sick, in pain, and being hit, he thought, "This is it for me." He did not have the wherewithal to get up.

Suddenly, he was no longer there. Instead, Viktor Frankl found himself standing at a lectern in postwar Vienna giving a lecture on the "Psychology of Death Camps." He had an audience of 200 rapt with attention. The lecture was one that Dr. Frankl had worked on the whole time he was in the death camp. He talked about the psychological factors behind dehumanization. He then described why, in his view, some people seem to survive the experience psychologically and emotionally better than others.

It was a brilliant lecture, all in his mind's eye. He was no longer in the field—he was dissociated—but vividly involved in the lecture. He told the imaginary audience about the day Viktor Frankl was in that field being beaten and was certain he did not have the strength to get up and keep walking. Then, exactly at the moment he was describing to his imaginary audience finally being able to stand up and start walking, his body stood up in the field. The guard stopped beating him and he began to walk; haltingly at first, then with more strength. He continued to imagine this lecture all the while he was doing the work detail and through the cold march back to the death camp. When there, he collapsed into his bunk, imagining this brilliantly clear speech with an ending that received a standing ovation. Many years later and thousands of miles away in Anaheim, California, this vision became a reality when Dr. Frankl received a standing ovation from 7,000 conference attendees.

In his writing and lecturing, Viktor Frankl conveyed the importance of a vision of the future, which people who are experiencing pain, suffering, and difficulty often lack. He believed that out of vision emanates meaning, hope, and possibilities. Central to this idea is envisioning a future that differs from the past, one in which things work out for the better—a preferred future. That future vision was a starting point for Frankl's personal journey; it was so compelling he had to get up and walk. Had he not, he never would have given that brilliant speech. His vision led him to take action in the present to make it reality in the future. To do this, the first order of business was getting up off the ground and starting to walk.

Youth frequently experience a diminished or absent vision of the future. As YCWs, we play a pivotal role first in helping these youth to envision futures with hope and possibilities. Next, we assist them in making plans to achieve that future. And last, we work with youth to take steps to make that future a reality. To aid youth in achieving their preferred futures we refer to our own philosophies about the future to maintain a sense of hope and possibility while fending off pessimism and negativity.

This chapter and the next are straightforward in terms of providing "interventions" that can be used to "jump-start" change. In this chapter, we will learn about methods for changing views. Chapter 6 offers ideas for changing actions and interactions. Both chapters involve two variations to promote change with youth and others involved in their lives. The first relates to what YCWs can do to intervene. The second concerns what actions youth and supportive others can do to stimulate change. We are reminded that while some methods appear to be more concrete than others all are forms of intervention. Whether it is developing rapport, attending to expectations, or changing language, we are trying to facilitate change and in doing so positively affect the present and the future. With this in mind, methods described in this chapter are used to facilitate growth, development, well-being, or some hoped-for goal or outcome (see Principle 4 in Chapter 2). We work *toward* some form of change rather than trying to move away from or escape something (e.g., shifting attention to what has worked rather than what has not). In other words, we seek the presence rather than the absence of things.

We also keep in mind that to increase the probability that the methods described in this chapter will work they have to fit with youth and the context or situation. There are many choices in terms of methods and techniques but the research is clear that the most effective YCWs follow the principles in Chapter 2 as the foundation for any intervention. So while there may be an inclination to skip ahead to the techniques and methods—"what to do"—doing so undermines the very factors most responsible for change and growth.

Better than Zero: Positive Youth Development

Viktor Frankl taught us the value of focusing on future change. Research validates this point, demonstrating the benefits of a focus on change in general (as opposed to an explanatory focus) with youth. As discussed in Chapters 2 and 3, a change focus and in particular, emphasis on early change, is crucial to growth and development. A change focus is also consistent with improved well-being, which as discussed in earlier chapters, is indicated by individual, interpersonal, and social role functioning. To wit, functioning with regard to youth is underscored by the following constructs of positive youth development (PYD):

1 rewarding bonding
2 fostering resilience
3 promoting social, emotional, cognitive, behavioral, and moral competence
4 fostering self-determination
5 fostering spirituality
6 fostering clear and positive identity
7 building belief in the future
8 providing recognition for positive behavior
9 providing opportunities for prosocial development
10 fostering prosocial norms. (Catalano et al., 2004)

PYD is seen as an ongoing process of engaging youth in safe, secure environments through activities, interventions, and programs that promote growth, development, and overall well-being. Success in YFS is defined largely by the degree to which youth achieve improved functioning as evidenced by the nine outcomes of PYD. This point represents an evolvement from a traditional perspective in YFS. The traditional view in YFS has been to focus on eliminating symptoms and problems—getting youth back to "zero"—the point at which things aren't particularly bad or good. We now aspire to much more. Our aim with the interventions in this and the next chapter is to work with youth to develop skills they need to flourish by reducing negative symptoms *and* by building positive emotions, purpose or meaning, positive relationships, and positive accomplishments. We believe youth can do better than zero. To ensure that interventions help youth to flourish we ask: *How can this intervention benefit the youth in relation to PYD?*

To increase the likelihood of positive outcome we collaborate with youth and supportive others and utilize action talk to maintain clarity about goals and the focus of services. As always, ongoing and routine real-time feedback serves as a compass for determining the strength of the alliance and progress, lack of progress, and deterioration. A strengths-based culture is a responsive culture.

In Chapter 2, a list of essential characteristics of YCWs was provided. Please revisit this list before proceeding with the sections that follow. YCWs who practice in accordance with the essential characteristics increase the likelihood of success with interventions, and overall positive change.

Matching through Fit and Effect

In choosing from interventions in Chapters 5 and 6, we consider two things: *Fit* and *effect*. By *fit* we simply mean, is the chosen intervention appropriate for the youth? Does it fit the youth's worldview, culture, and ideas about change? *Effect* translates to outcome—did the intervention, at minimum, benefit the youth (e.g., keep a situation from getting worse, increase self-worth, etc.), and at best lead to a positive, measurable outcome? Both fit and effect are two ongoing considerations for YCWs in determining how attempts to facilitate change are working.

Let's again revisit the 80/20 rule. Not all information is equal neither is it helpful. We want to be selective and gather information that will assist with resolving problems and moving things forward. In the sections that follow, we will focus on several areas of information that are considered critical to determining how well an intervention might fit with a youth. The point is to learn what we can do to reduce guesswork and provide more of an empirical basis for choosing methods.

We begin this chapter with ideas for increasing the fit of interventions. We then learn about a series of interventions for facilitating positive change with views and perspectives. Chapter 6 will involve strategies for changing actions and interactions. In Chapter 7, we will discuss the role of effect, and how the use of real-time feedback can be used to monitor the benefit of interventions and the overall progress of youth.

Increasing Fit with Interventions

In this section, we consider several variables that can help with choice of intervention. Each is pivotal in increasing the fit between YCWs and youth. Because interventions are delivered through relationships the ideas described in the preceding chapters continue to serve as the threads that inspire and support change.

It is worth noting that YCWs will not always have time to explore each of the variables that follow, particularly when dealing with crises. In Chapter 6, we will learn more about methods that can be used as "on-the-spot" interventions. At the same time, prior knowledge of the variables that follow can better prepare YCWs for problem situations. Thus, YCWs are encouraged to invest in conversations that may set the stage for the future. Once again a challenge to YCWs is determining what information will be useful (the 20% of the 80/20 rule) and what will not. We want to avoid spending time gathering information that will not help with the situation at hand. Next are three areas that can help to bring focus in the selection of interventions.

Relationship to Concerns/Problems

Particularly important is the way in which youth and those involved align themselves with concerns and problems. One of the mistakes of YCWs and mental health providers in general is attempting to intervene without a clear sense of how youth and those closely assigned with youth see themselves in relation to concerns and problems.

Youth and their caregivers will express varying degrees of association with concerns. For example, some youth will declare responsibility for the entirety of problems with statements such as, "I'm the one who got drunk" or "I need to change." Some youth will decline any involvement and perhaps assign responsibility to others for concerns/problems stating, "It's her fault" or "It's got nothing to do with me." Others will align themselves with some portion or aspect of concerns: "We both are responsible for what happened" or "I have been unreasonable at times."

A further way to better understand associations youth may have with concerns can be found with their use of pronouns such as "I," "me," "mine," "my," "we," "us," "our," "you," "he/she," "him/her," and "they/them." When youth use any of the first seven pronouns listed, they are likely accepting some level of involvement with their concerns/problems and perhaps in bringing about change. The absence of self when using pronouns such as you/he/she/they/them can indicate that clients remove or distance themselves from involvement with problems. Because youth self-references are embedded in context, YCWs must remain aware that various pronouns mean different things in different cultures (e.g., the use of "you" by some Hispanic youth may include themselves: "When you get up in the morning, you need to have your homework finished").

Finally, the following questions can assist with exploring how youth situate themselves and supportive others in relationship to presenting concerns:

- Who would you say is involved with this concern/problem?
- What would you say is your part, if any, in all of this?
- What's your role, if any, in what's going on?
- On a scale of 1 to 10, how involved would you say you are with the concern/problem?
- In your estimation, who needs to do what about the concern/problem?

Information gleaned from the answers to these questions helps with choosing interventions. For example, youth (and supportive others involved) who see themselves as having little or no role problems are unlikely to do anything different to change their situations. Interventions should therefore be aimed at helping youth to change their views or perspectives, which is the focus of this chapter. By contrast, youth who more closely align themselves with problems are likely to be more amenable to changing their behavior and how they to relate to others. In these cases, we can employ interventions that emphasize changing views *and/or* those outlined in Chapter 6, which encourage action.

Coping Style and Development

When effective, the answers to these questions not only reveal hints about how youth expect things to change in their lives with current situations but also their coping style. Coping style indicates whether youth tend to be more internalized or externalized both in how they deal with stress and in difficulty with solving problems. Knowing whether a particular youth is more or less introverted or extroverted assists with choice of intervention. For example, youth with internalized coping styles may benefit more from methods that focus on internal experience such as feelings and thoughts whereas youth with externalized coping styles are likely to respond better to methods that focus on behavior or action.

In addition to coping style, YCWs are cognizant that youth will vary in terms of emotional, intellectual, and physical ability. We consider factors that might affect a youth's comprehension and ability to respond to an intervention. To increase the prospects of effectiveness we consider the developmental fit of interventions, steering clear of "one-size-fits-all" all methods.

Preparing for Change

In most cases, information gleaned from methods detailed in previous chapters will provide a sufficient understanding of youth and supportive others with whom we are working. We move to build on this knowledge by asking "orienting" questions, which offer a glimpse of how they have experienced change in their lives in past situations. The following questions can serve as a guide for learning about how youth change:

- How do things usually change in your life?
- What prompts or initiates change in your life?
- What have you done in the past to resolve your concerns/problems?
- What ideas do you have about how change might happen with your concern/ problem/situation?
- If someone you know had this concern/problem/situation, what would you suggest he or she do to resolve it?
- What has to happen before the change you are seeking can occur?
- At what rate (i.e., slow or fast, over days or months, etc.) do you think change will occur?
- Will change likely be in big amounts, small amounts, incrementally, and so on?
- Do you expect change to occur by seeing things differently? By doing something different? By others doing something different?
- What thoughts or ideas have you been considering about how this problem has come about and what might put it to rest?

- Given your ideas about the problem, what do you think would be the first step in addressing it?
- What might you do differently as a result of the thoughts or ideas you've developed?

It is usually not necessary to ask more than a couple of questions to gather information about a particular concern. The point is to do our best to consider those variables that are likely to increase the probability of positive change. To our questions some youth will answer, "I don't know." This kind of response need not be a deterrent. Questions are invitations to share information not inquisitions into the lives of youth—which they are often used to from adults. If no information is gleaned say, "Okay. I just thought I would ask. Please let me know if anything comes to mind." At that point the YCW does the best to select interventions that best fit the youth and the situation.

For YCWs interested in formal frameworks for considering how prepared youth are to make changes in their lives the *stages of change* (SOC) model is an option (Prochaska & DiClemente, 2005; Prochaska et al., 1992; Prochaska & Norcross, 2002). This model explores how individuals tend to move through varying stages (i.e., different levels of concern about ongoing and situational problems) and corresponding degrees of motivation and willingness to respond. For example, early SOC suggest an emphasis on interventions that promote changes in views whereas later SOC open up further possibilities through actions and interactions. The SOC have been found to be a good predictor of outcome and according to the American Psychological Association (APA) a promising means for enhancing factor of fit (Steering Committee, 2001).

Pathways of Intervention

As discussed, this chapter and the next are companions, highlighting two essential pathways to initiate positive change with youth: *Changing views* and *changing actions and interactions.* Views include cognitions, thoughts, ideas, perceptions, beliefs, evaluations, interpretations, attention, and identity stories. *Actions and interactions* refer to patterns of behavior and patterns of interaction. Interventions aimed at changing views can be used with most youth whereas those that target behavior and interactions are typically contingent on how youth see themselves in relation to concerns. As we know, youth who do not agree that there are problems, or who acknowledge the presence of problems but do not align themselves with those problems, are less likely to respond to efforts to change their behavior. YCWs therefore proceed with caution in requesting that youth *do something* to change things.

Both primary pathways contain sub-paths, within which are multiple forms of intervention. The interventions detailed can be used independently or they can be combined together. In choosing interventions, YCWs are encouraged to consider those factors that are likely to increase the fit.

Creativity is also important to success. Picasso once said that all children are born artists; the problem is how to remain an artist as we grow up. YFS settings are not unlike some educational settings in which creativity is considered more of a byproduct than a necessity to the task at hand. In YFS, interventions are often formulaic or "canned." The idea is that by following a series of steps a predictable outcome will occur. Anyone who has worked with youth has found this to be a false pretense. What is needed is creativity. Although examples will be provided for many of the interventions listed, it is the creativity of YCWs—derived from knowledge of the youth, experience, and curiosity—that improves the likelihood of success.

All attempts to promote change should also involve feedback. We want to know: What were the results? What was the youth's experience in the situation in which the intervention was used? And finally, don't be afraid to fail. If something doesn't work, *learn from it.*

Changing Views, Pathway 1: Identify and Build on Exceptions

Any time we can help youth and others involved with youth to change their views by altering, shifting, or broadening their perspectives we increase opportunities for change. New perspectives mean new possibilities. In the next few sections, we investigate several ways of changing views through *exceptions*. After that we will learn about a second way of changing views, through *attention*.

Search for Exceptions

One of the most important things for YCWs to remember, particularly when things are not going well, is that problems will vary in intensity. There will be times when the problems youth experience will be dominating and times when youth will have more of an upper hand. YCWs extenuate the latter, searching for small openings known as *exceptions*. Exceptions are moments at which problems are less influential, more manageable, or absent altogether. Exceptions also include times when problems were expected to occur or get worse and did not. The significance of exceptions cannot be overstated. By identifying moments at which youth and supportive others have more influence over problems we are highlighting ability and coping skills, and promoting resilience.

In searching for exceptions, we are not trying to convince youth of their strengths. We do not say, "Look at how smart you are. Now go use your smarts." Instead, let youth convince us through their actions. To do so we identify instances in which things went differently and we ask questions about those situations. For example, a YCW might say to a youth who is experiencing anxiety about taking a test, "You've mentioned how this test has really raised your anxiety level and yet you've described how you managed to keep your focus and maintain a 3.4 GPA in school. How have you done that?" To a parent who has described his son as being "out of control," "You have said that he's out of control, and yet you mentioned that yesterday his teacher said he kept his cool when another boy taunted him in class. How do you think he was able to do that?" The following is an illustration of how to search for exceptions in an intake assessment with a parent and her daughter.

Case Example 5.1

Mother (referring to her daughter, Nadia): She never goes by the rules. In fact, I don't know why we even have rules. She doesn't think they apply to her.

YCW: It seems to you that Nadia really hasn't been up to par with the rules. Tell me a little about the rules she's broken that have been most bothersome.

Mother: She doesn't do her chores. That's the main problem. I just can't get her to lift a finger.

YCW: You're saying Nadia hasn't helped out as much as maybe she should?

Mother: Not at all. I'd settle for any effort at this point.

YCW: When was the last time you can remember her pitching in?

Mother: I don't know. Maybe a month ago she helped her stepfather with the dishes.

Nadia: A month ago! I did them yesterday! Are you blind?

Mother: Wonders never cease. You should have done them anyway.

YCW (To Nadia): Was that a fluke? Or do you sometimes do other things too and pitch in more?

Nadia: My room is always clean.

YCW: Really? How do you keep it clean?

Nadia: It's easy. I just make sure I have it straight before I go to bed.

YCW: Terrific. What else do you sometimes do?

Nadia: I take out the dog every morning.

YCW   (To her mother): Is that accurate?

Mother: Well, yeah, she does. But she's responsible for doing those things.

YCW: Right. There are some things that she's responsible for and it's been frustrating to you when she hasn't done them all. Is it safe to say that with some rules she shows more responsibility than others?

Mother: Yeah, that's true.

Root questions to explore for exceptions are as follows:

- When is the problem not a problem?
- Think about a time when the problem did not happen. What was different about that time?
- What do you notice about the times when _____ is less of a problem? What is different?

- What is different about the times that _____ is less noticeable?
- How far back would you have to go to find a time that _____ was less dominant in your life? What do you recall about that time?
- Tell me about a time that you expected _____ to happen but it didn't. What happened instead?
- What is different about the times when things go a little better?

We exercise caution with "all or nothing questions" (i.e., the problem happened or it did not happen) as some youth or others involved will have difficulty identifying times when problems were absent. They will respond, "The problem always happens. There aren't any times when it's better." A further consequence is that some clients will experience invalidation, feeling that the YCW is glossing over the severity of the problem or situation. In such cases, we further acknowledge and simultaneously search for smaller exceptions. The following is an example of how to do this.

Case Example 5.2

Youth (Mya): I'm always depressed. I just can't think of times I'm not.
YCW: Let me see if I can better understand. It really seems to you that you've been depressed all the time.
Mya: Yeah.
YCW: What was the most depressing day this past week?
Mya: Thursday.
YCW: What happened on Thursday?
Mya: I didn't get up until about two in the afternoon. Staff tried to get me up but I told them to leave me the hell alone. I blew off work too. I was supposed to be there at five.
YCW: That was a rough day. And what was Friday like? It was a depressing day too but just a little less so than Thursday. What was a little different about Friday?
Mya: I still didn't get up until noon but did go to work.
YCW: How did you get yourself to do that, Mya?
Mya: If you miss two days in a row they fire you. I need the job.
YCW: So how did you get yourself going?
Mya: I got up and took a shower and ate something.
YCW: Taking a shower and eating helped?
Mya: Yeah, I always feel better when I do those things.
YCW: And there are times that don't feel like getting up or going to work and on those days you may or may not take a shower and eat, even though those things make you feel better.
Mya: Yeah.
YCW: How about today? How did you get yourself here to talk with me today so early in the morning?
Mya (Brief pause): I don't know. I guess I just knew it would help.
YCW: How did you go from thinking about coming here to actually doing it?

Mya: I did the same thing. I took a shower and ate . . . but Casey (another YCW) talked with me this morning too. She understands how mornings are for me.

YCW: Casey understands what's happening with you. How does she let you know she understands?

Mya: She cheers me on. She says, "Mya, how can we make this the best day ever?" She encourages me. When she works I get up and get going a lot quicker.

YCW: So in addition to taking a shower and eating another thing that helps is when Casey is on shift. If you're okay with it I'd like to learn more about how Casey supports you and maybe even talk with her. Would that be okay?

YCW: Sure.

By learning about "worst" times we can then inquire about instances that were "a little better" or different. Small differences that build on already existing abilities, resiliencies, and resources that have gone absent due to the distress of the problem can foster positive change. They first need to be identified and discussed. No matter how large or small, exceptions are fodder for present and future change.

We also keep in mind that not all questions will create new leads. As mentioned earlier, a common response of youth to exception-oriented questions is "I don't know." This kind of response need not derail conversations. A side effect of exploring exceptions is that just talking about them can create a shift in perception. Although we will explore this idea in full later in this chapter, for now we consider that exceptions can help youth to "notice the unnoticed." Without having to recount details of situations, by raising consciousness about times when things have gone differently we divert attention toward success. Next, we explore variations on the core idea of exceptions.

Building Accountability through Exceptions

In Chapter 3, we learned of ways to use language to acknowledge, validate, and introduce the element of possibility into otherwise closed-down situations. These methods provide respectful, subtle inroads for promoting new views. Larger changes often emerge through smaller ones that are initiated through language. Here we focus on a series of methods to use acknowledgment to promote personal agency (in other words, responsibility and accountability).

Although these influences can shape behavior, with few exceptions (i.e., certain intellectual and developmental disabilities) they do not cause it. Examples of statements of non-accountability might include: "I have a chemical imbalance. If I don't get my medication, I can't control what I do," or "He's ADD. He can't help it," or "That's what bipolars do."

We acknowledge and validate what youth feel experientially while inviting accountability for their actions. Next are several ways to do this.

Reflect back Non-accountability Statements without
the Non-accountability Part

Take what a youth or supportive other has said and repeat back the portion of
the statement that conveys accountability while leaving out the part that implies
non-accountability.

Examples

Youth: He called me a name so I hit him.
YCW: You hit him.

Youth: I didn't get my medication, so I didn't remember to do my homework.
YCW: You didn't do your homework.

Use the Word "and" to Link Internal Experience and Accountability

When statements of non-accountability are given, reflect back what youth are
experiencing internally and link it to what they are accountable. To do this, YCWs
use the word "and," instead of "but." This does two things. First, through acknowledgment, youth know that the YCW is not trying to change how they feel. Next, it
holds youth accountable for what they do—their actions and behaviors.

Examples

Youth: I get so upset that I just start cutting on my arm.
YCW: It's okay to feel upset and it's not okay to cut on yourself or hurt yourself.

Youth: I can't get my work done when she's on my case.
YCW: You can feel like you can't get your work done and you can get it done.

Identify Counterexamples that Indicate Choice or Accountability

A third way to promote a change in viewing through language and invite accountability is to search for exceptions to the actions or behavior for which youth are not
claiming accountability. Again, aside from certain identified conditions, YCWs can
make generalizations here because it is impossible for people to do negative behaviors 24 hours a day. Once exceptions have been identified, they can be amplified.

Examples

Youth: My mom hit me a lot when I was little—before they put me in foster
care. Some lady staff make me really mad. They remind me of my
mom. I just want to hit them.
YCW: I'm sorry about the way you were treated when you were little. And
it makes me wonder about something that Mary the YCW said

yesterday. She said two days ago when she asked you to do your chore you got as angry as she's ever seen you. But you didn't take it out on her. You did your chore even though you seemed mad. How did you do that? What did you do instead?

Youth: It's in my family. My father and uncles were alcoholics. I can't stop drinking.

YCW: Your sense is that if it runs in your family, then you're predestined to have it run your life as well. And you mentioned last time that there was a period of time earlier this year when you didn't drink for a month. How have you been able to take responsibility for yourself even with a family history?

Suggest Alternative Viewpoints that Fit the Same Evidence

With alternative viewpoints, the YCW gives a more benevolent interpretation of a situation. In psychotherapy, this method is referred to as "reframing." An important distinction is the use of conjecture or curiosity. Conjecture involves phrasing that allows ideas to be offered without imposing them. This is typically done by beginning comments with "I was curious" or "I wonder." By combining conjecture with interpretation, a YCW might say, "You've said that you see your worries about school as a weakness, something that interferes with you taking risks—such as meeting new people. At the same time, I wonder if there are times that your anxiety acts as kind of a safeguard—perhaps protecting you from taking leaps that may be a little too risky in that moment."

The stories YCWs propose are no more valid, correct, or true than those of youth or vice versa; the point is that some stories open up possibilities whereas others close them down. YCWs focus on engaging in meaningful exchanges from which new stories of hope and possibility emerge. A further example of how a YCW might cultivate an alternative story with a parent is by saying, "You get the sense your son just wants to do anything he wants when he wants to do it. And I'm wondering if he's trying to find a way to be independent and make his own decisions. When you come down hard on him, perhaps the only way he can see to show he's independent is to rebel and resist you, even if it gets him in trouble." The following case illustrates the use of this method.

Case Example 5.3

Youth: My mom doesn't have a clue about what's going on, but she thinks she does. What a joke! All she does is ground me and make rules and try to make my life miserable. If she wants me to hate her, she's doing a good job.

YCW: It seems to you that your mother's mission is to put restrictions on you and make your life miserable.

Mother: I've tried to raise him to be respectful of others and look at the result! It's a rare day when he goes by the rules. All he does is fight with me. I'm very bitter about it.

YCW: You've tried hard and it seems that your efforts to teach him so far haven't been as successful as you'd like—things haven't gone the way you'd like yet. I can see how that might make you bitter.
Mother: I am.
YCW (To youth): You know, your mom hasn't raised a 16-year-old boy before, and you haven't been a 16-year-old before. I wonder if your mom is doing what she thinks is best for you, and that maybe she will need some further education about what it's like to be a teenager in this day and age. No matter the age, we keep on learning. (To mother) You mentioned before that you have a 19-year-old daughter who is doing well. Perhaps you're finding out that it can be different to raise daughters and sons. Some of the things you've tried haven't worked and some have—because on those rare days you get through to him. So I'm wondering if you're still making the adjustments in raising a 16-year-old son versus a 16-year-old daughter.

YCWs take care with introducing new interpretations. Youth who get the sense that their experiences or views are being given short shrift or trivialized are more likely to close down. The way interpretations are offered is as important as the interpretations themselves. For this reason, it is important to employ ways to monitor the alliance as a means of gauging how direct or indirect the introduction of an alternative story ought to be. When effective, a new interpretation of the same evidence or facts can lead to a new perspective for youth or others involved. If youth change their frames of reference, their actions are more likely to be in accord with those views. For example, a father who believes that his son's behavior is a result of manipulation will act in one way. However, if the same father sees his son's behavior as an indication that he needs more affection from him, the father is likely respond in a new and, hopefully, more productive way.

Sometimes the stories youth have of themselves become so embedded in their lives it becomes hard for them to see anything but the problems. When people seek or are referred to services, one of the major concerns is that they have started to organize their views of themselves and others' views of them as their illnesses. Pathologized youth behave pathologically. The job of the YCW is to help such youth and those involved with youth to change their views and therefore both see and experience themselves as capable and accountable (Bertolino & O'Hanlon, 2002).

Search for Hidden Strengths

YCWs can also search youths' lives to find out about hidden or nonobvious aspects that do not fit or are incompatible with their disempowered (hopeless, helpless, or stuck) views about themselves or their problems. By tuning their ears to the sounds of hope and possibility, YCWs often hear things during the course of conversations or sessions that contradict the views that youth have of themselves or others have of them, such as being out of control, unable to change, or irresponsible. The process is similar to finding a picture of a polluted urban scene and noticing a pristine mountain lake stuck in the middle or sitting with a youth who is wearing extremely wrinkled clothing but an exceptionally well-ironed tie that was put on perfectly. YCWs need to train themselves to notice what is right with youth.

To a youth who has poor handwriting and says, "I just can't write!" the YCW could search for small indicators in his writing that show a hidden strength: "Take a look at that letter g. And also at that j. They are both well-formed letters and they sit well on the line. How were you able to write those two letters so well?" In searching for hidden strengths, YCWs ask youth or those close to them how they explain the inconsistency between the youth's poor handwriting and the well-formed letters. From there, the YCW can work to amplify and extend those aspects so that the exceptions begin happening more and more often.

Case Example 5.4

Jonah, 16, struggled with his confidence, feeling he wasn't good at anything. The effects of his lack of confidence were evident to others around him. Jonah would decline involvement in activities he really wanted to participate in. In talking with Jonah it was learned that at one time he had been in Boy Scouts, but was forced to dropout when he was placed in foster care due to abuse by his father. Jonah had been very successful in Boy Scouts, earning numerous merit badges. One of those merit badges was in communication. When asked how he was able to meet the requirements for the badge, Jonah's expression began to change. A smile grew across his face as he reflected on his past accomplishments. He then said, "I forgot. I did a lot in Scouts." The discussion then turned to what Jonah had learned about communicating with others. He was able to generate a list of skills important to communication. From there he began to use those once forgotten skills to make new friends and engage in activities.

Foster Resilience

A significant number of youth seen in YFS have been exposed to circumstances that entail adversity or risk. Common risks of youth include lack of economic resources, underprivileged circumstances, high-crime areas, and abusive environments. Despite what sometimes appear as insurmountable circumstances and odds, many youth manage not only to survive but also in many cases thrive later in life. A growing body of research on *resilience* shows how individual differences to stress and adversity can help youth to cope with such odds (Masten, Cutuli, Herbers, & Reed, 2009). Youth, who are among the most marginalized in society, are also among the most resilient. The following offers an example of the resilience of youth.

Case Example 5.5

A 12-year-old boy, Evan, was referred to me for outpatient psychotherapy. Evan had been seen by more than two dozen psychiatrists, psychologists, and therapists over a period of six years prior to seeing me. He had been assigned 11 diagnoses, which appeared to change when a new psychiatrist was assigned; new diagnoses also meant continuous changes to his medications. Evan had also been hospitalized psychiatrically five times. Due to persistent behavioral and emotional problems Evan had been passed along through a mental health system that did not know what to do with him.

Evan faced numerous challenges within his family. His mother was diagnosed with several moderate to severe psychiatric disorders, including psychosis. Her emotional struggles were evident during sessions. In addition, Evan's father battled severe alcoholism and was dealing with an assortment of ongoing health problems. The family also faced housing and financial stressors.

Despite the challenges, Evan demonstrated the ability to care for himself, and, at times, others in the family. He reminded his mother of his appointments at the clinic and coped with her erratic behavior on a daily basis. He helped his father around the house and would care for him even though he was frequently embarrassed by his episodes of drinking. Evan seemed to know how to get the help he needed, routinely seeking out the help of teachers, neighbors, friends, and mental health professionals. Evan became known at the clinic for his resilience. He not only met many of the challenges he faced but also progressed in services, overcoming the behavioral concerns that led to his initial referral. Evan mined his own resourcefulness, and in doing so, taught his parents and others how to do the same.

Resilience is an aspect of youth contributions to change (see Principle 1 in Chapter 2), which is the most significant determinant in eventual outcome. Although influential, resilience is sometimes overlooked or missed due to an emphasis on sweeping moments in which youth overcome extraordinary circumstances. While resilience can reveal itself in many ways, more often it is evident in smaller, less remarkable ways, in specific situations and contexts. The aim of the YCW, therefore, is to explore youths' lives for small, everyday examples of resilience as opposed to more global ones.

Tapping into resilience involves two components: (1) Searching for qualities of resilience and (2) finding out about the actions that resulted from being resilient. Orienting youth and others involved toward these aspects of themselves and associated actions can help them to change their views of themselves and situations. The questions that follow can be used to assist in identifying and developing resilience.

Qualities of Resilience

- What qualities do you have that are helpful to you in times of trouble?
- What allows you to keep going when you're facing everyday challenges?
- What would others say are the qualities that you have that keep you going?

- Who are you that you've been able to face up to the challenges that life has presented you?
- What does it say about you that you are able to face adversity?
- What kind of person are you that you are willing to stand up to life's challenges?

Actions Informed by Qualities of Resilience

- What have the qualities that you possess allowed you to do that you might not have otherwise done?
- Given the type of person that you are, what do you do on a regular basis to manage the challenges that you face?
- How have you managed, in the midst of all that's happened, to keep going? How specifically have you done that?
- Tell me about a time when you were able to deal with something that could have stopped you from moving forward in life. What did you do?

As with all forms of exception, we do not try to convince youth of their resilience, neither are we implying or suggesting that youth and others just take stock of their qualities and all will be well. Doing so would be invalidating to those who are suffering and in pain. Instead, youth convince YCWs of their resilience through their actions, past or present, which are revealed through their answers to questions. Thus the questions just suggested are designed to elicit and evoke from youth their inner qualities and the actions they have taken. Such a focus creates a context for youth to shift views and at the same time attribute change or "control" to their personal qualities, internal abilities and resources, and actions (Bertolino & O'Hanlon, 2002).

Life Witnesses as Supports

The youth's world is a powerful resource. Composed of significant others (i.e., family, partner, friends, spiritual advisors, teachers, coworkers, classmates, Scout leaders, coaches) and community resources, valuing witnesses, as they are sometimes known, are sometimes identified through conversations with youth. At other times, we need to ask about them. The questions can help to find out about such people:

- Whom have you met in your life who knew or knows exactly what you've been going through? How does he/she know that about you? How has knowing that he/she understands been helpful to you?
- Whom do you look up to? In what ways do you look up that person or persons?
- Who has helped you through tough times? How?
- Who knows who you really are as a person?
- When you're struggling, who knows just what to say or do to get you back on track?
- What has this person(s) said to you in the past that was helpful?

If youth have a difficult time identifying supportive others, searching for what they have found helpful rather than the helpful people themselves can be useful. A question to ask about this is, "When things were going better for you, how did others make a difference in your life?" Through this form of inquiry, YCWs can get an idea of what made a difference for youth and then work to establish possibilities in other contexts that could lead to positive connections. For example, YCWs could suggest that youth become involved in activities that they previously enjoyed or might enjoy (e.g., sports, clubs, hobbies, arts, support groups).

In some cases, it will be necessary for YCWs to either explore an existing system to see if there may persons who could play a role in the life of a youth or expand the system to recruit new members. The following example illustrates how members of the community can serve as life witnesses, thereby providing care, guidance, and stability.

Case Example 5.6

While doing contract work for a local community mental health agency, I worked with youth who had been labeled severely emotionally disturbed (SED). Many of these children and adolescents had been given up on by other providers. Fourteen-year-old Quinton was referred to me after his family had moved to the area. They had lived in three different states over a period of two years, seeking mental health services (for example, individual and family therapy, psychiatric services) at each new place of residence due to Quinton's behavior. They had been through traditional office-based family therapy, intensive home-based services, and medication management. Not even contacts with local law enforcement and the family (juvenile) court seemed to make a difference.

According to his mother, each time Quinton entered a new school, he would "have enemies within five minutes." He had been in numerous physical fights with classmates and neighborhood youth and had verbal altercations with school staff. He also had mostly failing grades, had been caught stealing, and would frequently come in after curfew. Quinton had been suspended from school 11 times in two years; his parents felt hopeless about the future.

While working with the family, I explored many different avenues. At times, Quinton appeared to have turned the corner and would do better for short periods of time, usually a week or two. However, it appeared to be two steps forward and three steps backward. Just when it seemed that things had improved, Quinton would get into a fight or some other type of serious trouble.

On one spring afternoon, Quinton and I were sitting on the front porch of his home when a purple truck pulled into the driveway across the street. This clearly sparked his attention. As a man stepped out of the truck, Quinton yelled, "Hey Cole, what's up?" The man turned, waved, and replied, "Not much. Come on by later." When I asked Quinton who the man was, he answered, "He's cool. He helps me out sometimes. I just like hanging out at his house."

After talking with Quinton, I asked his mother about Cole. I found out that Cole was in his mid-30s, was married, and had a young child. Quinton's mother said, "He spends a lot of time over there and Cole doesn't seem to mind. It's weird, but Quinton really listens to him and respects him." I then asked the mother if I could have permission to talk with Cole. I made it clear that Cole did not have to know the details of Quinton's trouble but suggested that since Quinton seemed to respond well to Cole, he might be someone to talk to. Quinton's mother readily agreed and signed a consent form giving me permission to talk with Cole.

The next day I met Cole after he arrived home from work. I introduced myself and said, "I've been working with Quinton and his family because things haven't been going so well lately. And the reason I've come to you is because I understand that Quinton really looks up to you." Cole smiled and added, "Well, he does spend a lot of time over here, and we like having him here." I followed, "It seems to me that he really gets something from his relationship with you. And what I'd like to know is, would you be willing to continue to be that positive influence in his life and perhaps teach him what you know about dealing with trouble and conflict?" I did not need to be any more specific. Cole knew what I was getting at. He smiled and replied, "I'd be happy to."

Over the next several weeks Quinton's behavior changed dramatically. His fighting stopped completely. He made more of an effort at school as evidenced by the elimination of suspensions and improvement in grades. He began helping out with his younger sister and coming home on time. Within six weeks of my conversation with Cole, Quinton had made a complete turnaround.

At different junctures in this book, we have talked about the importance of support systems in the lives of youth. Many times such persons are easily identified, other times YCWs will need to cast a wider net to identify those who may help. But life witnesses are not merely supportive people; they go through developmental stages and life rituals such as birthdays and graduations with youth. Life witnesses can also be formally brought together as a group with a focus of providing support and guidance. This idea is commonly referred to as "wraparound."

Wraparound

Wraparound represents a team approach to forming systems of support to help youth and families in the environments in which they live versus out-of-home residential and foster care placements, for example. Wraparound is not a specific approach but instead a process of involving trained community personnel for coordinating youth, family, and community collaborations as a means of empowerment (Sparks & Muro, 2009). Our aim with wraparound teams is to gather persons who can serve as support for youth. Better support systems will provide youth with access to persons who not only care, but who also have experience and knowledge about the world. The more "reference points" youth have to draw on the more opportunities they will have to see their lives differently and reimagine the future.

The wraparound process begins with identifying people who have in the past and/or could in the future contribute to the support of a youth. Potential team members are people who are relevant to the well-being of the youth (e.g., family members, other natural supports, service providers, and agency representatives). To assist with this, the "Spokes of Life" form, which is included in Appendix B, can act as a visual guide for this process. Once possible supports are identified those persons, if not already involved, are contacted (following appropriate consent).

After potential team members have been contacted they are brought together to discuss the purpose of the wraparound. This includes determining the role that each person might play to support the youth. The team then collaboratively develops an individualized plan of care, implements this plan, and evaluates success over time. The wraparound plan typically includes formal services and interventions, together with community services and interpersonal support and assistance provided by friends, kin, and other people drawn from the youth and/or family's social networks. The team convenes frequently to measure the plan's components against relevant indicators of success. Plan components and strategies are revised when outcomes are not being achieved.

The overall wraparound process of engaging the youth and/or family, convening the team, developing the plan, implementing the plan, and transitioning the youth out of formal wraparound is typically lead by a YCW or other YFS staff who is considered the "wraparound facilitator." The facilitator is sometimes assisted by a family support worker. The wraparound process, and the plan itself, is designed to be culturally competent, strengths based, and organized around family members' own perceptions of needs, goals, and likelihood of success of specific strategies.

Changing Views, Pathway 2: See Things Anew through Attention

A primary pathway to help youth to change their views is through shifting attention. By diverting attention to aspects of situations that have gone unnoticed or absent we can isolate what has worked in the past and could perhaps work in the future. Interventions that focus on shifting attention are similar to those that involve exceptions because of the emphasis on strengths. A difference is that the interventions described in this section accentuate those elements or aspects of experiences, thoughts, actions, or situations that perhaps have been reduced to the background.

In the 1970s Bandler and Grinder (1975) wrote that people often delete (omit), distort (modify descriptions), or generalize (make general conclusions about) parts of an experience that they remember. To illustrate, if you were asked to sit in a room for 10 minutes then step outside the room and describe what you saw to another person, you would inevitably provide a skewed description. You might, for example, leave out the fact that there were six tables and only recall having seen four (omission). You might also remember the walls as white when they were beige (distortion). And you might describe the chairs as all being covered with fabric when 12 of the 20 were fabric and the other eight were fiberglass (generalization). The consequence of deletions, distortions, and generalizations is that people, in this instance youth and supportive others, typically act in accordance with their views. Our aim is to create opportunities to notice the unnoticed in ways that lead to new ways of seeing the world. Next is a variety of ways to do this.

Broaden Perspectives

Perhaps the most common way that youth and others involved in the lives of youth get stuck is through what they pay attention to. What is noticed, or in other instances, goes unnoticed can increase or reduce distress. What seems to happen in such situations is that youth or others will see only certain aspects of a particular circumstance or situation and develop a perspective based on that narrow view. That view then becomes a driving force behind a problem. The task of the YCW is to help youth and supportive others to broaden their perspectives by orienting them to aspects of situations that are "under the radar." These shifts in attention provide a spark to otherwise closed-down situations.

The following is an illustration of how a case manager in an independent living program might work with an older youth to broaden his perspective with a situation he's experiencing with his boss.

Case Example 5.7

Youth: It doesn't matter what I do, it's never good enough for my boss.

YCW: It sounds like a tough situation. Say more about that.

Youth: I'm on time. I do my work. I do a good job. He doesn't think so. It's not good enough for him and it aggravates me. I don't like the job anyway but I have to work to stay in the program.

YCW: I can see why it would be aggravating. It seems like whatever you've done to this point hasn't been good enough for him. I'm glad you've stuck it out. It sounds like you have your eye on the future.

Youth: I do. I want to quit but I won't. But it doesn't matter how hard I try.

YCW: Tell me more about how your boss not recognizing your hard work has affected you.

Youth: He always finds something wrong with whatever I'm doing on shift.

YCW: For example?

Youth: Yesterday I finished stocking the shelves and he yelled at me because a few of the cans had the labels facing to the side . . . and it was just a little bit.

YCW: I'm sorry that happened. It sounds like a tough situation. [Youth nods in agreement.] And I'm curious, what other kinds of things did you do while on your shift.

Youth: I also swept the floors. I also helped unload a truck of supplies.

YCW: What did your boss say to you about your job of sweeping the floors and helping with unloading the truck?

Youth: He didn't really say anything?

YCW: Did he ask you to redo anything?

Youth (Pondering the question): No. He just stared at the floor. That was it.

YCW: What does that mean to you?

Youth: Well, I guess that's how he says my work is okay.

YCW: It sounds like he's not the kind of person who really gives out praise. He just lets you know that the work is okay by not saying much about it.

Youth: Yep.

YCW: Sometimes he comes down on you and other times when the easy thing would be to say "good job" he just looks at what you've accomplished and says nothing. What do you suppose was different about the jobs you did yesterday? I mean, he commented on the cans but not on the other work you did. He could have found problems with those other things too.

Youth: I guess sometimes he doesn't have anything to say.

YCW: Is it possible that sometimes he approves of your work or maybe it meets his expectations?

Youth: I don't know. Maybe. But why doesn't he tell me when I do a good job?

YCW: That's a great question. You should be told when you have done a good job.

Youth: Thanks. I guess I don't hear him tell others they do a good job either. It's not just me.

YCW: You've seen the same thing with others. And your boss not recognizing what you do well doesn't mean that's as good as it gets—it just helps us both to know that sometimes your work meets with your boss' standards. And it's clear when he's unhappy but not when things are acceptable to him.

Youth: Totally.

YCW: What will help to remind you that you're a hard worker who does a good job?

Youth: I know that more now. I guess I need to look at what I get done each shift.

YCW: What else?

Youth: I can't always please him.

YCW: You can take satisfaction knowing you did your job as best as you can and there still will be times when your boss will make a comment. And it won't always be because you did the job incorrectly but because he will have a preference.

Youth (Laughing): That's for sure.

As with any form of intervention we take care to acknowledge youth by conveying an understanding of the situation. We are not in a race to solve problems. Instead we are working with youth to observe, to notice, or to pay attention to aspects that not only broaden what a situation might look like, but to open up new possibilities for actions. In the next chapter we will explore the point of taking action to bring about change.

Find a Vision for the Future

We began this chapter with a story about Viktor Frankl, who offered us an alternative perspective to Freud's notion that our lives are determined by our pasts. Instead, Dr. Frankl posited that a well-articulated vision of the future could influence one's perceptions of the past, and, most importantly, actions taken in the present. Waters and Lawrence (1993) stated, "One of the great deficits of most therapy is the lack of a proactive vision of what people need to move towards instead of a sense of what they need to move away from" (p. 9). Youth who have a sense of the future can be helped to further develop their visions and map out actions to move them toward those futures. For other youth, the path begins by imagining that it is possible to have a future that is different from or better than the past. As discussed in Chapter 4, a future focus begins with information-gathering processes through which youth gain a sense of direction by knowing what they want different in their lives.

YCWs can help youth with an improved sense of the future to work backward to the present to determine (from that direction) what the next steps might be to make those visions reality. For example, if a youth who is shy envisions a future in which she has more friends, what would be an appropriate step to take when she makes new friends? Perhaps, instead of her usual strategy of looking away and becoming quiet, she might make eye contact and say "Hi" or join a club, or volunteer in the community rather than isolating herself from others. She might talk with a school counselor or be connected to a mentor to help overcome her reluctance to speak in social situations. The point is that if she is beginning to get a new sense of her future, new actions probably would arise from that new sense.

Bringing a preferred future alive has three aspects. The first is to help youth to connect with and articulate their preferred future vision or sense. The second step is to identify possible barriers, either internal (i.e., stories, beliefs, fears, self-imposed limitations, restricted views of one's identity) or external (i.e., lack of money, lack of skills, lack of knowledge, prejudices or biases in the world). To deal with making the preferred future a reality, the third step is to create an action plan to negotiate or overcome the barriers and begin to move toward that future. This overall process is future pull (O'Hanlon & Bertolino, 2002). To assist with each aspect of future pull, some possible questions follow. These questions should be reworded depending on both the youth and his or her use of language and comfort with what is asked.

Identify a Vision for the Future

This first task is to help youth to create a vision of the future based on what they want for themselves and, perhaps, for supportive others around them. The following questions can assist with this:

- What is your purpose in life?
- What is your vision of the future?
- What dreams/goals did you or do you have?

- What are you here on the planet for?
- In what area could you make a contribution?
- What kinds of things inspire you?
- It's two/five/10 years from now and you have made a decision to follow a particular path. What does that path look and feel like?

Identify Barriers to the Preferred Future

A second step involves barriers. Beyond having a sense of where they want to go with their lives, some youth perceive hurdles or barriers in their way. They feel or think that they are inadequate to the task of making their vision happen. Others believe that certain things must happen before they can pursue their preferred futures and dreams. The next questions can assist with identifying and negotiating perceived barriers:

- What, in your view, stops you from realizing your dreams or getting to your dreams/visions/goals?
- What are you afraid of?
- What do you believe must happen before you can realize your dreams/visions/goals?
- What are the actions you haven't taken to make your dreams/visions/goals come true?
- What are the real-world barriers to deal with to realize your dreams/visions/goals?
- What would your models, mentors, or people you admire do to realize this dream/vision/goal? If they were you?

Make an Action Plan to Reach the Preferred Future

The questions in the first two sections will be enough for some youth to trigger a change in their views and help them move forward but not for others who need to do something to make their visions reality. They need to make a plan of action. This final step includes questions to help youth clarify the actions they need to take to make their preferred futures happen:

- What could you do in the near future that would be steps toward realizing your dreams/visions/goals?
- What would you do as soon as you leave here?
- What would you do tonight?
- What would you be thinking that would help you take those steps?
- What images or metaphors are helpful to you in taking these steps?
- Who would be the best person to keep you on track, coach, and monitor you?
- When will you agree to take these steps, and how will the follow-up happen to ensure that you have taken them?

This process can be followed as outlined; however, it is not necessary that the questions be applied systematically or in sequence. An alternative is to intersperse future-focused questions periodically as they fit a particular situation. The intention is to create pathways that provide opportunities for youth to orient their views from the past or present to the future. This can represent a major departure for youth; it can expose them to new possibilities that were not apparent to them previously. It can also clarify directions for services, introduce meaning and purpose, and lead to a restoration of hope.

Encourage Youth to Cast Doubt on Their Thoughts

YCWs are typically the initiators when it comes to helping youth to change their thoughts. A twist is to encourage youth to do the disputing. To do this YCWs suggest to youth that each time they have repeating thoughts or obsessions they think of at least three things they could do in the present or the future that could change their situations for the better. The following case example illustrates how this idea might be used.

Case Example 5.8

An 18-year-old stated that he would never have friends who liked what he liked (i.e., art, reading, board games). The YCW encouraged the young adult to go to a local bookstore during a busy time (after 6:00 pm or on a weekend) and sit in an area where he could see the bookshelves that have books that he enjoys reading. He was asked to sit for no less than one hour and count how many persons in his age range walked through the aisle and showed at least minimal interest in the kind of books he likes. When he returned, he informed the YCW that there had been 26 people stopped to look at the kind of books he enjoys. Of those present, 11 were in his age range. The young man stated, "That's way better than I thought." The youth then paused and with a shy expression reported, "Actually, I met a girl who is reading the same book I am."

Shift between the Past, Present, and Future

There is such a thing as being stuck in the past, too much in the present, or overly daydreaming of the future. For some youth shifting from one realm to another might bring about a change in perspective in relationship to their concerns and problems. To do this, YCWs work with youth to determine which realm they seem to be overly focused on. From there, there are many possible shifts. Youth could shift their attention from the past to the future, the present to the past, the future to the present, and so on. For example, if a youth is analyzing her past to the point of becoming increasingly depressed, a YCW might suggest that she consider what she is aware of and thankful for in the present and how she feels when she connects with that sense of gratitude. The example that follows shows how this method works.

Case Example 5.9

A 17-year-old female youth in an independent living program (i.e., an apartment) was feeling overwhelmed about the prospects of her future. She stated that even though her family did not want her living with them they still expected "great things" from her. Although the young woman enjoyed thinking about the future and what it might bring, she felt like that was all she ever did and had a difficult time appreciating much of anything. Given her affection for nature, it was suggested that she go to a place she found relaxing and stare out into the scenery, focusing only on the sights and sounds of the environment, and appreciate the moment as much as possible. By doing this, she was able to gain relief in the present whenever necessary and appreciate the future in a way that was right for her.

Shift Focus from Internal Experience to the External Environment or other People or Vice Versa

Some youth will spend more time in their inner worlds whereas others focus on what is going on around them. Depending on the context, too much of one or the other can spell trouble. It is not a matter of being introverted or extroverted but where someone places attention. As a means of helping youth to become unstuck, having them shift from focusing internally to externally or vice versa can be useful. The following example illustrates shifting from internal to external.

Case Example 5.10

A youth who had been abused by a caregiver while in foster care was experiencing severe anxiety triggered by flashbacks. Just prior to his flashbacks, he would become very internally focused, stating that he would become "trapped" in a place that was "hard to get out of." He wanted to be able to "feel better" and reduce the intensity of the flashbacks. Through further conversation, it was learned that the flashbacks ranged from high intensity (i.e., he would hyperventilate) to low intensity (i.e., he would experience mild agitation). The youth remarked that the intensity seemed to increase when he was "really trapped, focusing inside." He also stated that the intensity decreased "when I can get out of my mind." A plan was developed to help him shift his attention from internal to external. The first part was to recognize the signs that he was beginning to "go inside," which included becoming very quiet and then breathing more rapidly. He would then look at the things around him (i.e., in the environment) to remind himself that he was in the present, not the past.

Shift Sensory Attention

A final way of shifting attention is to have youth move from one sensory modality to another. This could involve shifting from seeing things to listening, from listening to touching, from touching to smelling, and so on. As with others described earlier, this method can be especially helpful with youth who become fixated in one specific realm. The case that follows illustrates this method.

Case Example 5.11

A youth was experiencing flashbacks associated with years of sexual abuse. Some evenings she would become overwhelmed with vivid memories that had a paralyzing effect on her. It was learned that her deceased mother had been a constant source of support and comfort for her. The youth had kept many gifts from her mother. One that she treasured the most was a bracelet her mother had given to her on her 16th birthday. She began wearing the bracelet every day, and when she would start to have flashbacks, she would physically touch the bracelet. This would shift her attention from the visual to the kinesthetic or tactile (bodily) realm, bringing her out of the flashbacks.

The methods outlined in this chapter offer ideas for helping youth and supportive others to change how they view themselves, situations, and their lives. A change in view can trigger overall change, keeping in mind that in nearly every situation views and action go hand in hand. That is, action must follow to experience the benefits of changes in views. In the next chapter, we will explore myriad possibilities for changing actions and interactions. Through these interventions, youth and those involved in the lives of youth can learn more effective ways to navigate their lives and achieve their visions of the future.

six
Possibilities, Part 2: Strategies for Changing Actions and Interactions

> Most folks are about as happy as they make up their minds to be.
> —Abraham Lincoln

There is a story about a man who was imprisoned for years. One day in the prison shop where he worked, his eyes caught little bits of bright wire amidst shavings on the floor. He began gathering and saving them in a bottle in his room to brighten things up a bit in the cell. After years of confinement, he was finally released from prison and brought the bottle full of wires with him to remind him of his years there. Now an old man and unable to work, he spent days waking at the exact hour the warden had decreed the prisoners should awaken and going to sleep at the usual prison lights out time. He paced back and forth in his rooms in the same patterns he had while confined to his cell, four steps forward and four steps back. After some time of this, he grew frustrated one day and smashed the bottle. He found the mass of rusted wires stuck together in the shape of a bottle (Lord, 1990).

Some of the problems youth face take the form of patterns—routine reactions to other persons or situations that have gone astray. Whether brief or unfolding over time, problematic patterns tend to repeat in the lives of youth. The result is these patterns interfere with youth having the kind of lives they want. The role of the YCW is to assist youth and supportive others who may be involved change problem patterns through strategies that promote personal agency—accountability—and positive coping. Because YCWs work in a wide range of settings and programs, it is necessary to have a toolbox with a variety of tools. This chapter provides multiple tools through three sub-pathways for changing actions and interactions.

The methods detailed in this chapter require youth to change their behavior or *what they do* to improve their life. Viktor Frankl spoke of the importance of having a vision for the future. And yet, if he did not get up and begin walking while being tortured by Nazi guards his future as he envisioned it would not have happened at all. At some point, change necessitates action.

It is clear that tools (i.e., interventions, methods, techniques) alone are not enough. It is the ability of YCWs to connect with youth, draw on strengths, and as illustrated in the opening story, change persistent and disruptive patterns that interfere with the visions youth have for themselves. We are reminded that what matters most in terms of the effectiveness of services is the fit of our interventions with youth.

Changing Actions and Interactions, Pathway 1: Exercises in Happiness and Well-Being

Psychologist Martin Seligman tells a story of how he began his trek into the world of *positive psychology*—the study of how to build thriving individuals, families, and communities (Seligman & Csikszentmihalyi, 2000). Not long after being elected president of the American Psychological Association, Dr. Seligman was pulling weeds in his garden when his five-year-old daughter, Nikki, joined in. Being goal oriented, Seligman was driven to get the task done. Nikki had other plans. She threw weeds into the air and danced around. In his frustration, Seligman yelled at her. She walked away, only to return and say, "Daddy, I want to talk to you." "Yes, Nikki?" replied her father. "Daddy, do you remember before my fifth birthday? From the time I was three to the time I was five, I was a whiner. I whined every day. When I turned five, I decided not to whine anymore. That was the hardest thing I've ever done. And if I can stop whining, you can stop being such a grouch."

Nikki's words stayed with her father. And so began an investigation into how people achieve greater degrees of well-being (i.e., happiness). What Seligman found astonished him. Studies on negative states outnumbered those on positive states 17 to 1 (Myers & Diener, 1995). This fixation on problems, pathology, and deficit had become so ingrained in the fabric of society that the majority of well-intentioned researchers had virtually ignored the possibilities of studying well-being. Seligman set out to change the lopsided focus of psychology. What he and other researchers have found has significant implications for YFS.

A fundamental finding that emerged from the study of well-being is that we are largely mistaken when it comes to beliefs about what will and what will not increase happiness. In brief, bad things don't cause the permanent decrease in happiness we fear they will, while good things don't cause the permanent increase in happiness we think they will. As a society, we are generally poor at predicting what will make us happy. It turns out too much time is spent on things that make little difference in the long run. As discussed in Chapter 2 in "redefining the strengths-based perspective," outdated ideas, in this case those related to well-being, often translate to misguided efforts to bring about change. There is good news, however. Several decades of research has deepened our understanding of what influences happiness and life satisfaction (Peterson, 2006; Seligman, 1991, 2002, 2011).

Researchers suggest that happiness is determined by a combination of a set point (i.e., genetics), life circumstances (with estimated percentage-wise contributions of 50% and 10%, respectively), and intentional activities (Lyubomirksy, 2007). Intentional activities are believed to make up 40% of the variance in happiness, meaning that a change in routines and habits or "mental flossing" can pay huge dividends. Translation: Youth can learn brief exercises that when used routinely can assist in fending off depression, anxiety, and a host of health problems. The key is to start youth early and not wait until they are adults to teach skills associated with self-care and well-being

To be clear, not all issues that youth face are equal. Some are clearly more painful and leave more substantial lasting impressions. But we can help youth to exercise their "muscles of resilience" to better cope with such experiences by encouraging a focus on several key areas including having a wider range of social connections, sense of freedom, and life purpose. By social connections we mean family, friends, community members, and other life witnesses, as detailed in the previous chapter. Freedom relates to making choices and accepting the responsibility that goes along with choice. This is a crucial point because happiness has everything to do with choice. People who are not free are unable make choices because their rights have been taken away or they are being held captive in some way, limiting their opportunities to engage in activities that increase well-being. Related is a final area—life purpose, which equates to meaningful experience and involvement with activities that require giving of self.

There are many methods that can be used to influence happiness (see O'Hanlon & Bertolino, 2012). A few of these will be described shortly. Before using these methods, please consider the following points:

1   Focus on fundamental skills such as listening, attending, and eliciting feedback and respond to that feedback immediately as a means of strengthening the therapeutic relationship.
2   Collaborate with youth on determining which exercises provide the best fit.
3   Encourage youth to use agreed on exercises in a routine and ongoing manner, continue those exercises that have proved beneficial, and experiment with new ones as needed.
4   Package exercises (i.e., use multiple exercises) to increase the likelihood of benefit to youth. (O'Hanlon & Bertolino, 2012)

With these considerations in mind, what follows are a few examples of exercises youth (and YCWs) can use to increase happiness.

Exercises to Increase Happiness

What Went Well

For one week, each night, have youth write down three things that went well during the day. The items should be specific, not general. For example, "I got up in the morning" is too general. "I got up in the morning and applied for three jobs" is specific. Second, for each of the three items have youth write down what contributed to the situation going well. The third and final part of the exercise is to reflect on the collection of good things at the end of the week. As an additive, it is suggested that youth share what they have written with YCWs or supportive others.

Gratitude

The purpose of expressing gratitude is to let the recipient know how much they are appreciated and valued. It is also apparent that gratitude is the gift that gives back. Perhaps the most direct path to increasing one's happiness is by giving to others without the intention of receiving anything back—and yet, more often than not doing so *will give back.*

One exercise is for a period of one week, have youth write down one thing each day that they are grateful for. What is written should be different each day. When possible, at the end of the week, youth are encouraged to share one thing they are grateful for with the person to whom they are grateful.

Conscious Acts of Kindness

Studies show the benefits of expressing kindness to others. Research indicates that people who extend kindness in some deliberate way feel much happier than those in control groups. There's more good news. Feelings of happiness tend to last for a few days—even some time after the exercise is over (Lyubomirsky, 2007). For this exercise have youth complete one conscious act of kindness each day for a week.

Savoring

Have youth think of a positive experience in which they can recount feelings of comfort, joy, or excitement. Suggest that youth focus only that experience, becoming fully immersed in the good feelings. It can also be suggested that youth tune into the sensory aspects—the sights, sounds, tastes, smells, and bodily sensations associated with the experience. Afterwards, have them write down or talk about what they experienced.

Mindset

The research of psychologist Carol Dweck (Blackwell, Trzesnieswki, & Dweck, 2007; Dweck, 2006) has shown that more important than believing in your abilities is believing that you can *improve* those abilities. Central to this idea is the difference between a "fixed mindset" and a "growth mindset." With the former, youth believe that their capabilities are already set while in the latter they believe that qualities such as aptitude and temperament can improve through effort. In the final chapter, the benefits of a "growth mindset" will be discussed as it applies to YCWs. Here we consider a way it can be used with youth.

To do this, have youth brainstorm, for 10–15 minutes, about all the positive qualities they can think of for themselves. YCWs may want to suggest qualities as well with youth having the final say-so as to whether or not they agree. Next, assign a problem for youth to try and solve. Typically, when youth have immersed themselves in a positive mindset they show more creativity and success in problem solving. And personal achievement can increase well-being.

Broaden and Build

Have youth listen to a song, watch a movie, or read a passage from a book. Next, have them identify one of five emotions (i.e., joy, contentment, fear, anger, or neutral) they feel. Then, have youth make a list of everything they would like to do at that moment. Last, have youth review the list to take note of the ideas they developed. This exercise can influence spontaneity, creativity, and positive emotions (Fredrickson, 2009).

Act "As If"

Have youth imagine the future they would like to have. Ask, "What specifically would I like to be happening in my life _____ (e.g., three weeks, six months, one year from now)?" Next, talk about experimenting with the vision created. Encourage but do not push youth. Suggest that for the next few days or week (or until the next session/meeting) youth to "pretend" and act "as if" the part of the vision has already occurred. In follow-up, ask the youth to report on his or her experience with acting "as if." Consider asking what was the most profound aspect of acting "as if" and/or what differences they noticed.

Exercise a Signature Strength

All youth have strengths. A pair of psychologists have identified a series of cross-cultural "signature strengths" that indicate character qualities and virtues (Peterson & Seligman, 2004). For this exercise, first have youth complete the strengths survey (www.viasurvey.org). The survey is free and will take about 30–60 minutes depending on the youth and his or her reading ability. Once completed, the youth's signature strengths will be listed according to value. Review the results with the youth then refer to the top five. Next, create a new way that the youth can use each of those strengths. For example, if a top five strength for a youth is "Fairness, Equity, and Justice," have her choose a new cause (i.e., something she has not spoken up about in any significant way) and determine a way she can advocate for that cause.

Or, with a youth who has a top 5 strength of "Love of Learning," have him strive to learn something that is outside of his typical studies. If the youth loves history, plan a trip to an art museum and learn something new. One way increase follow-through with this exercise is for a YCW to do the exercise at the same time.

Giving Back (Volunteer)

At first glance it may seem counterintuitive to ask youth who have so little to volunteer their time by giving back to others. And yet, the therapeutic value of doing so can be immeasurable. Although money may be an incentive for youth the act of giving to others through volunteer activities boosts happiness more, and for a longer period of time. For this exercise, have youth choose a cause they are interested in and then identify ways to volunteer for that cause. Volunteering can be one-time or ongoing with an organization or group of others who are need. Examples might include volunteering at an animal shelter, walking an elderly person's dog several times a week, or participating in an activity to raise awareness about an issue. YCWs can assist with identifying opportunities to volunteer. It is important to have youth write about their experiences with volunteering and reflect on the meaning of their activities.

Other exercise options include having youth perform *random* acts of kindness, play a leadership role in activities, choose activities rather than just "going along," look for new ways to avoid being bored, join a "movement" (e.g., volunteering for a cause, etc.), and practice self-gratitude. Our aim with these exercises is to build positive experiences through routine—better mental health hygiene. That is why the exercises are brief and can be done at different times, an important consideration with youth. Research indicates that positive experiences such as those brought about through brief exercises can counteract negative experiences. But there is a caveat. The number of positive experiences has to outnumber the negative ones, which is why the use of multiple exercises is recommended. The *positivity ratio* can be used as a point of reference here. The positivity ratio is a term suggesting that experiencing positive emotions in a 3 to 1 ratio with negative ones leads people to a tipping point beyond which they naturally become more resilient to adversity and effortlessly achieve greater degrees of well-being (Fredrickson, 2009).

Changing Actions and Interactions, Pathway 2: Depatterning

A retired man bought a new home near a junior high school. The first few weeks following his move brought peace and contentment. Then the new school year began. The afternoon of the first day of school three boys came walking down the street, beating on every trash can they encountered. The man was unable to move the trash cans elsewhere and the banging continued each day until he decided to take action.

One afternoon, the man walked out and met the young percussionists and said, "You kids are a lot of fun. I like to see you express your exuberance like that. Used to do the same thing when I was your age. I'll give you each a dollar if you promise to come around every day and do your thing." The boys were elated and agreed to continue their drumming. After a few days, the man approached the boys and sadly said, "The recession's really putting a big dent in my income. From now on, I'll only be able to pay you each fifty cents to beat the cans." Although the boys were displeased, they agreed to continue their banging.

A few days later the retiree again approached the boys and said, "I haven't received my Social Security check yet, so I'm not going to be able to give you more than twenty-five cents. Will that be okay?" "A lousy quarter?" the leader drummer exclaimed. "If you think we're going to waste our time beating on these cans for a quarter you're nuts! No way, mister. We quit!" The man went on to enjoy peace again (Gentle Spaces News, 1995).

The preceding story is an example of the second pathway of changing actions and interactions, *depatterning,* which involves altering repetitive patterns by changing one or more aspects of problem sequences. Once again, crucial to methods aimed at changing problem sequences is creativity. Oftentimes impossibility is the product of too narrow a focus. By joining existing patterns and making small changes problem patterns can be altered.

Again, action talk is a necessity of repatterning. Through action talk we move youth and others involved from vague descriptions to clear, observable ones. From these descriptions, we can search for any contextual aspects of problems that repeat. These repeating sequences are related to time and space and represent the patterns that can be altered, modified, or disrupted. To identify problematic patterns, YCWs explore the following areas:

- What is the frequency (rate) of the problem? How often does it typically happen (once an hour, once a day, once a week)?
- What is the typical timing (time of day/week/month/year) of the problem?
- What is the usual duration of the problem? How long does it typically last?
- What is the range of the problem's intensity?
- Where (location and spatial patterns) does the problem typically happen?
- Who else is involved? What do others who are around or involved usually do when the problem is happening?

Because problems do not occur in a vacuum, we are listening for the contextual aspects that help to better understand the circumstances and variables associated with problems. Oftentimes problems will be described metaphorically as "broken records" or the same thing over and over again. By understanding problem sequences, we can choose any number of points to intervene. What follows is a series of ways to depattern problematic patterns to help youth and others to move toward their preferred futures.

Change the Frequency/Rate of the Complaint or the Pattern around It

Change how a particular aspect in a problem sequence occurs by encouraging youth to do the pattern more or less. This method is paradoxical in that we are suggesting that youth or supportive others do the very thing that is the problem. It can be very effective with a host of situations, particularly when YCWs suggest youth continue problems or symptoms so they may be "studied." For example, a youth might be told to "continue _____ (fill in the blank) so we can learn more about it." This method should never be used with behaviors that are harmful to self or others, illegal, or cause unreasonable distress.

Case Example 6.1

A youth who argued about his curfew with his foster parents on weekend nights was told to continue his arguing but to make sure his point was being heard he should argue every night.

Change the Duration of the Complaint or the Pattern around It

Problem patterns often run their course in predictable fashion. A possibility is to either increase or decrease the length of the problem pattern. Similar to changing the frequency/rate of problems, increasing the length may seem illogical (paradoxical) to youth or caregivers. Again, this method should never be used with behaviors that are harmful to self or others, illegal, or cause unreasonable distress.

Case Example 6.2

An 11-year-old, Keith, would scream very loudly when he did not get his way. His mother was at her wits' end. In talking with Keith's mom about the sequence of events around the problem, it was learned that the longest Keith had screamed was about 30 seconds (with short breaks to breathe). The screaming never went on beyond half a minute because his mother would give in each time, stating, "I just can't take it so I give him what he wants."

There were several possibilities for changing the pattern and the mother stated she was "open to any and all suggestions." I encouraged her to consider the possibility of changing the length of the time that Keith spent screaming. I said, "This may sound weird, so please bear with me. You said that the longest Keith has screamed for is about 30 seconds. It becomes too much for you and you give in. What do you think would happen if you encouraged him to scream for a longer period of time?" The mother's first reaction was to say, "I couldn't do that. I couldn't take it." I followed, "I certainly can understand that. But do you really think he would?" The mother smiled, "I see what you're saying. He wouldn't expect me to tell him to scream longer because I always tell him to stop." "That's what I was thinking," I replied.

I reminded the mother that we wanted to think as creatively as we could without trying to find the correct answer. Further, whatever was tried needed to be something she agreed with and would actually follow through on. Finally, if something didn't work, we would modify or abandon it. We came up with a plan where, the next time Keith did not get his way and began to scream, she would wait him out. To do this she would focus on her watch and time the length of his scream. When he quit, she would encourage him to scream longer, for a full minute.

The evening following our meeting Keith was told "no" and he began to scream. At first the mother felt herself drifting back into her old pattern of trying to get him to stop. She quickly caught herself, sat down in a chair, and glanced at her watch to keep time. Surprised by this, Keith looked at his mom, tried to distract her then stopped screaming. The mother responded to the silence, "Twenty seconds of screaming isn't enough. You need to scream for at least one minute to make sure you got it all out. You owe me another forty seconds." Keith was shocked by his mother's reaction. He grunted and left the room. A short while later, the mother told Keith no for something else and as he took a deep breath to scream, she looked down at her watch. Keith stopped and again left the room. The pattern had been disrupted.

In our follow-up meeting, I explained to Keith that it was perfectly fine for him to get upset. However, there were better ways of letting his mom know how he felt. We then proceeded to work on ways that he could let her know how he was feeling and what he needed.

Prescribe the Symptom

A form of paradox is to prescribe the symptom. The central idea is to encourage the continuation of problems that youth or others are complaining about. Sometimes just suggesting that youth do what they do not want to do disrupts problem sequences. The intention behind this method is not to deceive but to change pervasive patterns that have not responded to other methods. As with the first two methods in this section, it should never be used with behaviors that are harmful to self or others, illegal, or cause unreasonable distress.

Case Example 6.3

Nelson, a 12-year-old who resided in a short-term residential program, would hide his books and assignments and refuse to do his homework. When Nelson and I met, I told him that he was predictable and that I knew exactly what he would do. That evening at study time he would hide his books and refuse to do his homework. I added that I was smarter than he was because I was older and had been to college. I then suggested that he continue to hide his books so there would be even more proof about how smart I was and how predictable he was. Nelson was not impressed by my comments. He informed me that he was not predictable and that I had no idea what he was going to do that evening regarding his homework. I told him to continue his "game" and I would continue to be smarter than him.

The next day I arrived for appointments. I was told that Nelson had been eagerly awaiting my arrival. Nelson raced through the door after school and blurted, "Ha! I'm smarter than you! I'm smarter than you!" "How's that?" I asked. "I did my homework! Ha, ha! I'm smarter than you!" I told him that I would need to verify it. Nelson had, in fact, completed all his homework, apparently without hiding his books or any delay. I then spoke to Nelson about his accomplishment, "This is amazing. I can't believe it. I've never been outsmarted by a 12-year-old. Congratulations. But we both know it won't happen again. I'm sure it was all luck." "No it wasn't. You'll see!" responded a riled-up Nelson. He was right. Nelson maintained his new homework practices and thrived on the praise staff gave him for completing his homework. He found that positive attention felt much better.

Change the Location of the Performance of the Complaint

Problems occur in some places but not others. Invite youth or others involved to continue the complaint but in a location in which the problem has not occurred.

Case Example 6.4

The mother of a family of four had the complaint that dinner was a "nightmare." She stated that there were "constant" arguments that made it "nearly impossible to enjoy each other's company." Family members were asked about the length of their arguments, the general sequence of events, and so on. It was learned that although there were other periodic conflicts, dinner was by far the most troublesome time of day. It was suggested that the family have dinner as usual, but as soon as an argument began, they were all to proceed directly to the garage (which was connected to the kitchen), which was deemed the "crisis room." Once there, they were to continue the argument until each person had a chance to fully express himself or herself or agree to refrain from arguing. They were to take as much time as possible and return as many times as necessary to restore peace to dinner time. If arguing broke out again they were to return to the crisis room.

Change the Complaint's Time (Hour/Time of Day, Week, Month, or Year) of the Pattern around it

Time is one of the more predictable elements of problem patterns. Like changing the location of complaints, small changes in time can be enough to disrupt repetitive sequences. Time includes small (i.e., seconds, minutes, hours) or large (i.e., days, weeks, months, years) increments depending on the problem.

Case Example 6.5

A grandparent who was raising two grandchildren was concerned about the behavior of her oldest grandson. She stated that the 9-year-old would wait until just before bedtime to talk about "serious" issues. She was concerned that the time just before "lights out" should be reserved for reading or telling relaxing stories. It was learned that when bedtime conversations turned serious her grandson would become upset, which would, in turn, affect his sleep. It was suggested that the grandmother reserve a set time each evening when they could talk about the events of the day and any worries her grandson might have.

Case Example 6.6

A woman was frustrated with her 12-year-old son because he would sneak out late at night. It was suggested that she schedule "sneak out" time each morning. She was to wake him up at 5:00 am every morning and sit on his bed until he got up and went outside for at least 15 minutes. Her son was annoyed with being woken so early each morning and quit sneaking out.

Change the Sequence (Order) of Events Involved in or around the Complaint

Because patterns involve events, an obvious point of entry is the sequencing of those events. Once patterns are mapped out, work with youth and others involved to determine what might be changed in the sequence.

Case Example 6.7

A youth was concerned that each time she tried to get in a word with her father he would start giving her advice. The sequence was that he would make a comment, he would begin to give advice, she would try to interrupt and tell him what she needed, and he would talk over her. She appreciated his advice but was not always asking for it. Sometimes she just wanted him to listen. The end result was her giving up on conversations. It was suggested that she determine what kind of conversation she wanted with her father prior to calling him. Then, she was to call him and before raising an issue, tell her father what she needed from him, thus changing the sequence of their conversations. If he continued to talk over her, she was to tell him she had to get off the phone. After getting off the phone one time, her father began listening to her requests and accommodating them in conversation.

Interrupt or Otherwise Prevent the Occurrence of the Complaint

Change problematic patterns by interrupting or stopping complaints altogether. This is generally done by "beating the other person to the punch." Once problem patterns have been identified, YCWs or others involved "step in" to alter patterns.

Case Example 6.8

A youth in a residential program would refuse to do his chores each afternoon. Chores were to begin at 3:15 pm and just a minute or two prior the youth would approach a YCW on shift and state his refusal. To avoid inevitable power struggles, as a group the YCWs decided they would "go with it" and even encourage the youth to refuse more often than usual. At the start of a new week, the youth was approached at 3:00 pm and told, "There is no reason to wait until 3:14 to refuse to do your chore. You should probably get it over with and refuse now." The youth stared back at the YCW and said nothing. A couple minutes later the YCW again approached the youth, "It's 3:02. Why not refuse to do your chore now and get it out of the way?" The youth replied, "What? You're crazy." At 3:05 a different YCW said to the youth, "There's still plenty of time to refuse to do your chore. How about it?" This time the youth said, "You guys are all messed up. Just tell me what my chore is so I can get it over with."

Add a New Element to the Complaint

Patterns can be helpful to youth, particularly when they are in the form of routines that keep them on track with important life tasks. If such routines are well established, youth are likely to be resilient to small changes. When patterns are problematic, however, the addition of new elements can be enough to disrupt those patterns. The idea is for YCWs to think of little things that can lead to big changes.

Case Example 6.9

A YCW in a residential program had a pattern of debating the rules of the program with staff. The youth's routine would begin with the question, "Why do we have that rule?" He would then draw staff into a debate, which, in many instances, led to a power struggle in staff and resulted in loss of privileges or consequences to the youth and/or frustration for staff. The YCWs created a "Debate Sheet." The youth was notified that whenever he was unhappy with the first response of the YCWs on shift to his questions he would be required to complete the form. The form would be reviewed within 24 hours and a hearing would be scheduled in which he would be required to appear to engage in a formal debate. The youth dropped the staff debates that had become routine.

Break up Any Previously Whole Element of the Complaint into Smaller Elements

Another way to change problem sequences is by breaking them up into smaller parts. This can be an effective approach because it takes youth and others involved out of the rhythm and spontaneity associated with their patterns. Youth can become unknowingly caught up in the blow-by-blow of problematic patterns. Building deliberate breaks into patterns makes it difficult for those involved to both maintain patterns and the intensity that can accompany them.

Case Example 6.10

A father and his teenage son were having disagreements over household chores. Each time they would try to discuss a topic, it turned into an argument. It was suggested that a timer be set for two minutes, allowing each that amount of time to state his point of view. Once the timer went off, it was the other person's turn. The father and son were to argue no more than one household chore at a time.

It can be helpful to think of depatterning as "running interference" in problem sequences. Because patterns represent what is familiar, trying something different or new can be difficult. As an experiment, try saying the word "yes" while shaking your head from left to right indicting "no." Or do the opposite by saying "no" and moving your head up as if to indicate "yes." What was that like? If it felt awkward at all, you can relate, on some level, what it is like to change a pattern.

In choosing methods, we keep in mind that patterns can be difficult to change. Youth and supportive others must decide whether or not they are willing to carry out suggestions. With this in mind, it can be helpful to say, "Change involves work." YCW recommendations or suggestions for changing patterns represent ideas that they believe may be helpful but are not directives.

Finally, the methods outlined in this section represent general categories to change problem sequences. Some methods overlap with others, and it is possible to combine two or more at the same time. It is also possible, although unnecessary, to target multiple aspects of problem patterns. Small alterations are usually sufficient to trigger changes in the performance of symptoms.

Changing Actions and Interactions, Pathway 3: Repatterning

A third sub-pathway of changing views is through *repatterning*, which involves eliciting and highlighting previous solution patterns, strengths, and resources. It casts YCWs as detectives who investigate areas that are likely to yield exceptions and contexts in which youth have demonstrated competence and mastery over problems. As discussed, YCWs do not try to convince youth of their strengths or imply that all they need to do is think positively. Such efforts (e.g., "I can see you're full of strengths" and "Just go out there and do it") may be interpreted as invalidating, condescending, disingenuous, or as a form of "false cheerleading" (Bertolino, 2010). Being strengths based means evoking what youth have already done that demonstrates competencies and solutions. When youth are able to connect with concrete examples of solutions, strengths, and resources through repatterning processes, they are more likely to convince themselves of the influence they have over problems. Next are multiple ways of repatterning.

Find any Helpful Changes that have Happened before Services Began

Depending on the circumstances, there may be occasions in which the road to positive change began prior to the start of formal services. Researchers refer to this phenomenon as *pretreatment change* (referred to here as preservice change), and studies indicate that up to two-thirds of clients coming for their first sessions report positive changes in reference to the complaints that brought them to services (Lawson, 1994; Ness & Murphy, 2001; Weiner-Davis, de Shazer, & Gingerich, 1987). As with exceptions, determining what youth or others involved did differently is important in addition to identifying preservice change and corresponding solution patterns. To find out about this kind of change, YCWs ask about any differences youth or others noticed prior to the start of formal services (i.e., typically, face-to-face contact). The following questions can assist with this process:

- What's been different between the time you decided (or informed that you were) to come here and now?
- What have you noticed that's been just a little better?
- What ideas do you have about how this change came about?
- What did you or others do differently?
- What difference has the change made for you?
- What will it take to keep things going in a better direction?
- What will you need to do to make that happen a little more beginning today?
- What else will you need to do?
- What, if anything, can others do to help you to continue to move forward?

Case Example 6.11

An uncle who was the primary caregiver of a 17-year-old male named Jerome called to set an appointment to see a case manager with a transitional living program. According to the uncle, Jerome had dropped out of school and was refusing to return to school, work, or follow the rules set in the home. He wanted to explore options for Jerome to live outside of the home since according to the uncle the situation had become "unmanageable." An appointment for an interview was set for eight days later. The day before the interview the uncle called and said that Jerome had "made a huge turn-around." Without prompting, Jerome had returned to school and started following the rules at home. The uncle considered cancelling the interview but after talking to the YCW (case manager) decided to keep it so options could be left open. During the interview the YCW worked with Jerome and his uncle to identify what had changed since the interview had been scheduled. With ideas about how to handle future stuck points and leaving the option of transitional living open in the future, Jerome remained with his uncle.

Preservice change can help to encourage solution patterns in two ways. The first is by highlighting what youth or others have done to "get the ball rolling" to make positive strides in relation to their concerns. With the expectation of starting services as a kind of "flossing" effect (flossing more vigorously or more often in preparation of visiting the dentist), youth begin to direct more attention and effort to their problems (Bertolino & O'Hanlon, 2002). A second way to encourage solution patterns is by giving youth and others credit for their actions. When positive change is already in motion, YCWs can talk about how that change came about and who did what. As we will learn in the next chapter, talking about how change occurred is essential because the more youth attribute change to themselves and their actions rather than external factors or chance events the more likely the change is to remain in the long term.

Search for Contexts that Indicate Competency and/or Good Problem-Solving or Creative Skills

Because problems can dominate attention, they often affect other aspects of youth's lives. Problems can appear as all encompassing, thereby clouding competencies that youth have used in other areas and contexts of their lives. These contexts can include employment, school, hobbies, sports, clubs, or other areas in which clients have special knowledge or abilities that they can tap into as resources for solving problems. These contexts of competence offer possibilities for transferring the ability from one area of a youth's life to another in which it is not currently being employed. YCWs use this form of "linking" to identify situations in which problems would not have occurred and connect them with areas with present concerns.

Case Example 6.12

Keon, a 12-year-old middle school student had been getting into trouble in class. He would make animal sounds, mock other students, speak out of turn, and touch others as they walked by. He was being sent to the principal's office on a daily basis. His behavior had affected his grades and he was at risk of being held back.

It was learned that Keon was an avid basketball player in his CYC (Catholic Youth Council) league. Keon was asked the difference between personal and technical fouls in his league. Personal fouls were as expected, interfering with another person when they had the ball, and so on. Technical fouls could involve purposely hitting another player, yelling at others, using profanity, and the like. When asked how many technical fouls he had accumulated in CYC play Keon looked surprised. He said, "None. I've never got a technical." It was proposed to Keon that he was getting technical fouls regularly in school, whenever he was being sent to the principal's office. How was it that he was able to keep things in check on the basketball court? No matter the situation—whether he became upset or frustrated or angry, Keon was able to temper his responses. Keon remarked that when he got "riled up," his coach would give him a hand signal to remain calm.

To connect the competence he displayed on the court, a meeting was held with Keon, his mother, stepfather, teachers, a school case manager, and CYC coach. A plan was created to signal Keon, as his coach would, in the classroom, when his behavior was approaching a "technical foul." Keon's behavior quickly improved in the classroom. His history of technical fouls ended.

The key to identifying contexts of competence is to be on the lookout for them. Abilities, strengths, and resources come out in different contexts. YCWs assume that youth have abilities. Asking questions can help to pan their lives to identify those abilities and then link them to problem contexts. The following questions assist with this process:

- How have you managed to hold the problem at bay when you're at (place)?
- What do you do differently when you're (action description) as opposed to (action description) that helps you to manage your life a little better?
- How can being able to (stand up to, better manage) when you're (action description) be helpful to you in dealing with (problem)?
- How can you use that ability in standing up to (person's name or position)?

In most instances, at least some part of the competencies utilized are transferable and provide solutions to problems experienced elsewhere. It can also be helpful to find out about times when youth or those involved have faced similar problems and resolved them in ways that they liked. This provides a pathway for transferring knowledge and associated actions from one person to another.

Find out what Happens as the Problem Ends or Starts to End

The problems that youth experience in services have endings or at least points at which they are much less evident and intrusive. One way to evoke solution patterns is to explore the sequences that lead to those endings. Once identified, RYCWs can work with youth to use those sequences in the present and future. The following questions elicit information about these solution sequences:

- How do you know when the problem is coming to an end?
- What do you do when this is happening?
- What is the first sign that the problem is going away or subsiding?
- How do you usually react to this?
- How can your friends/family/supportive others/coworkers tell when the problem has subsided or started to subside?
- Is there anything that you or supportive others have noticed that helps the problem subside more quickly?
- What have you noticed helps you to wind down?
- What is the smallest thing you could do when you notice the decline of the problem?
- What do you do when the problem has ended or subsided?
- What will you do in the future when the problem is no longer a problem or more consistently out of the picture?
- How might these problem-free activities differ from what you do when the problem is happening or present?

Case Example 6.13

A mother stated that she and her 16-year-old daughter would get into "screaming" matches that would result in terrible things being said to one another. They were asked what brought the screaming to an end in the worst situations. The mother stated that after an hour or so she would reach a point where she would refuse to talk about the issue at hand any further and go sit in her car. She would do this for no less than 15 minutes and no more than an hour. The mother agreed to import her action earlier in those interactions that she recognized were escalating.

Identify Previous or Partial Solutions or Successes to Problems (Exceptions) and Associated Actions

We have learned about a direct pathway to solutions by focusing on exceptions to problems. All patterns of action and interaction have exceptions—it is just that they are more difficult to notice in the midst of problems. To reorient youth toward previous exceptions and successes, YCWs invite youth and others to reexamine, not reprocess, events to flesh out details that run counter to problem descriptions and patterns. In searching for exceptions, a YCW might say, "Tell me about a time when you expected the problem to (surface, get worse, continue) but it didn't." This would be followed by questions that identify how and what youth did—the competencies associated with those exceptions. Specifically, the therapist asks, "How were you able to do that?" and "What did you do differently?"

This process seeks more than an attentional shift that comes from asking questions that elicit exceptions. The intent is to tap into youth's motivation to take action. This requires YCWs to maintain their investigative stance and identify those actions and interactions that represent the influence youth or supportive others have had in the past over their problems and that can be re-engaged in the future. The following questions can elicit exceptions:

- Tell me about a time during the past (day/week/month) when (the problem) happened to lesser degree or not at all? What happened? What specifically was different? Who did what?
- Tell me about a time when (the problem) happened and you were able to get somewhat of a handle on it. What was different about that time? What did you do?
- You said that you've felt a little better over the past (days, weeks, months). What has been different? How did that happen?
- You mentioned that you've had trouble with (the problem) three of the last four days. How did you manage to (hold the problem at bay, stand up to the problem) on that one day?
- You commented that you and (other person's name) have had a lot of conflict recently about (problem). Yet when (the problem) came up you said that you didn't (fall back into the old pattern, engage in the conflict as in the past). What happened so that the situation didn't (do that, get stuck in the conflict)? What did you do? What did (other person's name) do?
- You told me that you've done (action) (two, five, 10) times in the past week. Even though you had the chance and may have thought about it, how did you manage to keep from drifting back into the old pattern the rest of the time?
- You didn't (action) last night. How did you keep yourself from doing what you usually have done? What did you do this time instead of (action)?

Because problematic patterns have exceptions, YCWs assume that there have been times when things have gone better and problems have been less apparent and influential in youths' lives. YCWs do not ask whether but when things have gone differently. In effect, they presuppose exceptions and move to gain clear action descriptions of what youth did when things went a little differently in regard to their problematic patterns. This involves gaining details about what happened, when it happened, and what needs to happen in the future so the solution patterns occur more deliberately and with more frequency.

Case Example 6.14

Lakesha had been in conflict with another female youth, Donnell, who was in the same residential facility. Just a week earlier the two girls had been in a physical fight. Both girls were at risk of being discharged from the program because of the incident. But Lakesha's involvement was being further reviewed because Donnell was the aggressor and had started the fight.

In a one-on-one session with her case manager, Laskeha expressed her frustration with Donnell, "She's always in my face—saying shit and running her mouth. Donnell gonna get her mouth popped one of the times." The case manager responded, "You and Donnell have been in this program together for six months. Tell me about a situation when you weren't getting along with Donnell or another resident, and that situation could have got worse but you chose to do something else." Lakesha said, "Two weeks ago Donnell was all in my face—callin' me 'bitch' and I was ready to drop her. I wanted to, but I knew if I did I would probably get kicked out of here and back living on the streets." "What did you do?" Laskesha was asked. "I just said "forget it, you ain't worth it." Then I went in the other room and talked to staff. "So you told yourself it wasn't worth it, walked away, and sought out staff?" "Yeah, that's what I did. And I tried to walk away this last time but she came up behind me and jumped me." "Would you say you know what to do when there's conflict—do you have a plan?" "I do have a plan, but sometimes there are crazies around and you got to stay away from them." So maybe another part of your plan is being clear who you are around." "That's right," said Lakesha.

It is common for youth to focus primarily—and sometimes exclusively—on what is not going well in their lives and situations. YCWs do not want to force solutions on youth and others but want to help to reorient them to other aspects of the problem that have gone unnoticed and abilities that have been underutilized. Exception-oriented questions provide a doorway for youth to reorient themselves to moments when they had influence over the problems. It also can be helpful for YCWs to offer multiple-choice options to youth to see whether something that emerges from conversations resonates with youth and to offer other possibilities for future situations. The following points can serve as guides in focusing on previous solutions patterns and associated actions.

Ensure that Youth Feel Acknowledged and Validated

YCWs remain youth driven and use feedback processes to ensure that youth feel heard and understood. A push toward solutions can lead to invalidation, discouragement, and what can appear to be resistance. Refer to the processes described in Chapters 3 and 4 and continue to employ feedback processes on an ongoing basis.

Explore Shades of Difference by Working from Worst to Best

Before exploring any shades of difference regarding the intensity of problems, youth and supportive others involved need to feel heard, acknowledged, and validated. Creating this feeling can help to let such persons know that the severity of their concerns has been noted. To do this means learning from youth how "bad" problems are, including how they affect their well-being and everyday functioning. Reflecting, paraphrasing, and summarizing are used to convey this understanding. YCWs can then begin to move toward differences in problem intensity in ways that are less abrupt.

Case Example 6.15

YCW: You've said that Trevor's behavior has been very bad lately and you're most worried about his tantrums. When he's had these tantrums, he's scratched and kicked you. Is that right?

Parent: Yes. He scratches and kicks.

YCW: Tell me about a time recently when he seemed a little more manageable.

Parent: I don't think you understand. His tantrums are always bad. They're very bad. They just go on and on.

YCW: Okay. Help me to understand what you've been going through with Trevor because I don't think I'm getting how it's been affecting you.

Parent: Well, it's just flat out frustrating. He just seems to be getting worse.

YCW: I can see and hear your frustration.

Parent: It's been really hard because it doesn't seem to let up.

YCW: It seems like it's always there . . .

Parent: . . . exactly . . . it's like it's always there.

YCW: How have you managed to hang in there?

Parent: It hasn't been easy.

YCW: That's what it sounds like . . . and I'm wondering, because you've been through so much, how you think I might be able to help you with this?

Parent: If we could just see any change with him, then I think I would have some hope.

YCW: I see. If it's all right with you, I'd like to ask you a few more questions to help me better understand how it's been with Trevor.

Parent: Sure.

YCW: So which day this week was the worst regarding Trevor's scratching and kicking you?

Parent: Thursday. Definitely Thursday,

YCW: What happened on Thursday?

Parent: He kicked me so hard that he bruised my arm. It also took me a long time to calm him down once he got going.

YCW: Are you okay?

Parent: Oh yeah. It'll go away.

YCW: I'm sorry that Thursday was such a difficult day.

Parent: Thanks. I'm guess I'm used to it.

YCW: Well, I appreciate your persistence. And I'm curious as to how the other days stacked up against Thursday—because that was the worst day.

Parent: You know, Tuesday wasn't quite as bad.

YCW: What happened on Tuesday?

Parent: He slept more and the one time he started to get riled up, he calmed down pretty quickly.

YCW: How did that happen?

Parent: I think maybe I caught it as he was getting riled up and I distracted him with a puzzle.

Youth or their supportive others who do not feel listened to or heard are more likely to shut down verbally, give up, and dropout of services. They can also appear to YCWs to be resistant and unmotivated. The YCW in Case Example 6.15 moved forward toward exceptions before the parent was ready, recognized this, and backtracked to ensure that the parent felt heard and understood. This was done by attending more to the problem and then by searching for a small opening to create an inroad for exploring exceptions.

Focus on Small Changes Instead of All-or-Nothing or Sweeping Changes

A further consideration relates to youth and supportive others answering queries such as "Tell me about a time recently when you didn't have the problem?" or "When have things been better?" They often say, "I always have the problem!" or "It's never better!" This happens because these types of questions represent too big a leap for most youth. Because people generally orient toward problems and what is not working, it is too much for them to turn 180 degrees and consider when problems are completely absent and what is working. Instead, YCWs search for small movements and indicators of success as opposed to sweeping, all-or-nothing exceptions. To do this, YCWs ask questions such as, "Tell me about a time recently when things went a little better" or "What's been different about the times when the problem has been a little less dominating in your life?" Smaller increments of change when things were a little better or more manageable are typically more palatable for youth and easier to identify.

Rituals of Connection and Continuity: Balancing Security and Change

A final but often overlooked area is rituals. Of the various forms of rituals, here the focus is on those involved with connection and continuity, which offer stability and consistency. These rituals consist of activities that take place daily, weekly, monthly, yearly, seasonally, on holidays, or at other intervals with regularity. Examples include activities such as exercising, writing in a journal, having dinner with family, or going out for dinner with friends.

Rituals are, in effect, solution patterns. In addition to connecting youth with others and bringing stability, they serve as protective factors in the face of adverse conditions such as child abuse, neglect, substance abuse, divorce, or the loss of loved ones. In fact, research indicates that everyday routines and activities that remain constant in the lives of children can contribute to increased levels of resilience in adulthood (Wolin & Wolin, 1993). Most people's lives involve some form of rituals whether they involve their families, friends, or others who are close to them.

Rituals that provide connection help youth who have come from or are in chaotic, disruptive, and potentially detrimental environments to have greater consistency in their lives. Regardless of the context (e.g., home, residential placement, foster care), YCWs can help youth to create, implement, and engage in those activities that are meaningful, create stability, and increase connections. These rituals can make a significant difference in helping them to deal with the adversity they face in life. The problem is that when disruptions occur, they disrupt rituals as well.

Part of what YCWs can do is to help youth and those involved with youth to either restore rituals that have been interrupted by their life changes or help them create new ones.

Case Example 6.16

Zac and his father had been very close since he was about seven years old. Zac would follow his dad around the house, and they would spend lots of time together. One of their favorite things was to attend baseball games together. As time passed, Zac began to spend more and more time with his friends. This meant less time with his father. Around the age of 15, Zac began getting into trouble. Initially, he was charged with stealing and breaking and entering. As a result, he was ordered to placement at a juvenile facility.

Over the course of a year, Zac was able to earn the right to go on weekend passes with his father. One August weekend, Zac's father picked him up from the juvenile facility. As they were driving along not saying much, Zac noticed a pair of baseball tickets above his father's sun visor in the car. He asked his dad, "How come you don't want to go to games with me anymore?" His father, surprised, responded, "When your friends changed and you started to get into trouble, it seemed like I was the last person you wanted to be around. So I just stopped asking." A tearful Zac sat quietly for a moment, then spoke, "I miss going to the games with you." The father and son restored their ritual of going to baseball games together. This helped to bring stability to Zac's life and reconnect father and son.

Many situations can disconnect youth and families from their rituals. These events do not have to be traumatic, just unsettling in some manner. For example, events such as the birth of a child or the change of a job can disrupt them. As in the preceding example, rituals that help to reconnect youth can also provide continuity (stability) to relationships. Rituals of stability can also help youth to reconnect with themselves. People, like organisms, have a tendency to withdraw and protect themselves when they are traumatized. This means that some will withdraw from aspects of themselves or others and as a result struggle to reconnect. YCWs therefore want to encourage patterns that help youth to feel safe and secure and experience increased stability in their lives.

The methods outlined in this chapter offer ideas for helping youth and supportive others involved to change actions and interactions. These changes can be enough to bring about positive change. It is important to keep in mind that in nearly every situation views and actions go hand in hand. That is, action must follow to experience the benefits of changes in views. In accordance, a change in what one does involves, at least to some degree, a change in perspective.

seven
Exchanges: Progress and Transitions

There are two kinds of people, those who do the work and those who take the credit. Try to be in the first group; there is less competition there.

—Indira Gandhi

On January 15, 2009, Captain Chelsey B. "Sully" Sullenberger executed a "controlled ditch" to safely land US Airways flight 1549 in the Hudson River, off midtown Manhattan in New York. Captain Sullenberger's action saved the lives of 155 passengers and crew and was dubbed the "Miracle on the Hudson." The world celebrated his heroism. But Sully himself was clear from the outset: The successful landing was "a crew effort." It wasn't just the crew itself Sully was referring to—it was their *adherence to discipline and teamwork*. But most of us did not hear that part of the story. It was as if we couldn't process what he was saying. The myth of the hero was too compelling.

With the passage of time and Captain Sullenberger's persistent statements about the actions of the crew, a new narrative began to emerge for those who would hear it. Sullenberger made it clear that adherence to rigid discipline including following various series of checklists was what preserved the safety of all on board. Because there *were* checklists and because everyone used them, Sully could rise above any unnecessary distractions and focus on the one key decision for which human judgment was required. The heroic part of that flight was not the flight ability of Captain Sullenberger, it was the willingness of the entire team—including the flight attendants, who then acted through their protocols to get the passengers off that plane in three minutes—to acknowledge their fallibility, admit that they could fail by relying only on training and memory, and exercise the discipline to overcome that fallibility. Sullenberger summed it up by stating, "There was nothing hard about the physical navigation of this plane—what worked was teamwork and adherence to protocol." Indeed, the hero was the team.

What messages can YCWs take away from the heroic efforts of the crew of flight 1549 and how do they apply to YFS and YCWs in particular? The purpose of this chapter is to answer this and other questions as they relate to the success of YFS. To do this we will first study the role of teams in YFS. Whether speaking of flight, surgical, or construction crews, effective execution of services is reliant on teamwork. Next, this chapter builds on previous ones by exploring how to monitor the progress of youth in services and determine next steps.

Team Positive Deviance

In the first chapter, we learned about the Pillars of Positive Deviance. Here we explore the second pillar—how teams in YFS affect services. To do this, we will investigate several ways in which teams can better work together to benefit youth, services, programs, and agencies.

There are few instances in which a single YCW is the only professional in contact with a youth or family. More often there are multiple persons involved. In the case of residential programs, there may be several YCWs, for example, responsible for the same tasks. In other instances, multiple front line and specialized staff (e.g., psychotherapists, psychologists, teachers, nurses, etc.) work together as a team. The structure of teams may vary in size, function, and responsibility, but at core are common characteristics that contribute to efficient and effective teams. For the purposes of review, refer to Table 2.1. What stands out in terms of the characteristics of effective YCWs and effective teams? As you probably surmised, the skills that YCWs rely on in working with youth are also necessary when it comes to teams. Now let's explore three points that can guide YCWs and other YFS staff in terms of teamwork.

Have Confidence in Yourself and Your Team Members

Despite every reason to be fearful—and the crew of flight 1549 were fully aware of their potential fate—Captain Sullenberger remained calm and his "team" followed suit. Every day YCWs experience stress on the job. As a coworker and/ or leader and team member, how can you convey calmness to others? You may feel as if you are becoming unraveled inside *and* you still have the capacity to remain confident and calm. Your coworkers will look to you and reassurance can emanate from confidence. When it comes to teams, confidence can be contagious. Be a staff person who soothes situations rather than throwing gasoline on the fire. Being confident does not mean being a "know it all." Instead, it is a belief that you can maintain a safe climate and get the job done. An overconfident team makes mistakes because they tend to lack balance between intuition and training. Trust yourself but always balance your personal insights with evidence.

Expect the Best but be Prepared for the Worst

In the interviews following his Hudson River landing, more than one reporter asked Captain Sullenberger what he had been thinking. His response was straightforward, "I must, and I can, land this plane safely." This kind of thinking comes from training. Pilots train rigorously under stressful conditions. You don't land an Airbus A320 smoothly in a river by working only on ordinary approaches on calm, sunny days. Research makes it clear that practice is much more effective when it done in situations that replicate the real-life conditions (Ericsson, 2009). As discussed in Chapter 6, practicing in stress-free conditions will not do the job. Preparing for the worst is strengths based. In effect, we are using our abilities to deal with whatever comes our way by using staff abilities and wherewithal. No matter the protocols they have to be executed.

Teams in YFS have to learn how to respond in uniform ways. This requires preparing for both routine occurrences and crises and going through protocols then comparing responses to the philosophical underpinnings of the organization. In other words, does the response match what the agency purports to do in its services? For example, agencies that have no physical restraint policies have to determine responses that all staff are trained in that do not involve "take downs" and the like.

It should be noted that adhering to protocols does not mean that creativity goes away. On the contrary, creativity is a necessity. For example, a YCW who knows a particular youth well may use humor or distraction within a protocol that has been established for maintaining safety. Ultimately, YCWs must execute designated procedures. To this end, one of the ways that teams become divided is when there are differences in how to respond among staff. These differences have to be worked out within teams or those differences will lead to larger, perhaps more serious threats to safety. Quite simply, teams that are on the same page provide more consistent and reliably effective services.

Work Together

"It's my airplane." Those were the first words of Sully Sullenberger when the effect of the birds being pulled through the engines became evident. His actions were not an attempt to exude control. Rather, they were part of the emergency protocol. His first officer knew that and complied. From there each person had a role to fulfill to maintain the safety of airplane and a state of calmness. When roles are carried out the chances of success greatly improve. YCWs must rely on each other and know when to defer to another. To effectively work together, team members have to both know their roles and responsibilities and be flexible enough to step out of those roles when the situation arises. There can be no competitions for heroism—our success lies in the ability to work collectively without losing focus of the tasks at hand.

There are aspects of being a YCW that are out of our ability to control. For example, we cannot always predict what a youth will do in a given situation. What we can do is follow Captain Sullenberger's lead by controlling our responses to every circumstance, which begins with remaining calm. High levels of stress can fuel a furnace of emotions. We can be conduits of confidence, being prepared for the worst but expecting the best. Doing so will increase discipline and flexibility. Confident teams are positive deviants in their own right because they concern themselves not with norms but with clear goals in mind. In the case of YFS, this translates to safety and services that benefit. When YCWs work together in a unified direction there are few situations that will evolve to a degree of unmanageability, and like Captain Sullenberger, they are able to safely pilot their own Hudson River landings.

The Wisdom of Teams

In his book, *The Wisdom of Crowds,* author James Surowiecki (2004) tells a story about British scientist, Francis Galton. In 1906, at the age of 85, Galton attended a country fair in the town of Plymouth. The same curiosity that won him notoriety for his work on statistics and the science of heredity remained, and on this day he was interested in livestock. The fair was the annual West of England Fat Stock and Poultry Exhibition, a gathering of people interested in appraising the quality of one another's livestock. Galton's interest was undeniable and was focused on two things: The measurement of physical and mental qualities and breeding. He believed that only a few people had the characteristics to keep societies vibrant and healthy. In fact, he was utterly convinced of this idea.

As he moved through the exhibition he came across a weight-judging competition for an ox. The ox had been placed on display for the gathering crowd to place wagers on the weight of the ox. For sixpence, a wager could be made and the best guesses would receive prizes. The nearly 800 who tried their luck varied from butchers and farmers—those with some knowledge of the weight of livestock—to those with very little or no expertise in such judgments. Galton was interested in the judging capabilities of the "average voter," those with limited expertise, which he assumed to be poor. What, in effect, began as a walk through the fair became an on-the-spot experiment for Galton.

When the contest had ended and the prizes had been distributed, Galton was able to borrow the tickets and run a statistical analysis of the guesses. In all, 767 tried their luck (of which 13 had to be discarded because they were illegible). Among the statistical analyses run by Galton was calculation of the mean, the average of the entire group. Galton sought to determine what the crowd as a whole would guess as the weight of the ox were they to make a single wager. Given his beliefs, Galton would have posited that a few smart people in the mix of many mediocre to unintelligent ones would lead to an abysmal guess that was way off the actual weight of the ox. But Galton was wrong. The crowd guessed the ox would weigh 1,197 pounds. The ox's true weight turned out to be 1,198 pounds. The crowd's judgment was right on. Galton later wrote about his finding: "The result seems more credible to the trustworthiness of a democratic judgment than might have been expected."

What Galton stumbled on represents a simple but important and powerful consideration when it comes to groups. Groups are often more intelligent than the smartest people in them. Even when groups are comprised of members with varying degrees of knowledge or are not especially well informed or rational they can still reach collectively wise decisions. Surowiecki (2004) refers to this ability as "the wisdom of crowds."

It can be argued that guessing the weight of an ox is hardly complex and certainly not as serious a matter as making decisions about youth and families. Yet, the evidence suggests that when structured properly, groups such as those comprised of YCWs and other support staff, on average, make better collective decisions than those made by even the smartest individuals in those groups. Teams in YFS can apply Surowiecki's ideas by following a few simple structural guidelines:

1   Encourage diversity of opinion: Each member of a team should have her own point of view, even if it's just an interpretation of the known facts. Teams that are able to explore differing points of view generate more, and a wider range of, possibilities for action than those that tend to be homogenous.
2   Value independence: Team members' opinions are free of manipulation and corrupting influences and are not determined by the opinions of those around them. The process of arriving at a collective decision should not be through coercion, force, or subversion. Instead, collective decisions result from each team member having the freedom to convey his or her thoughts and ideas in a supportive context.
3   Decentralize to strengthen: Some team members will specialize and/or have specific roles and responsibilities based on their local knowledge, which continues to evolve over time through experience, practice, and relationships. Team members' differing roles in YFS can benefit collective decision-making and in what happens when putting those decisions into action.
4   Aggregate: Some mechanism exists for turning private judgments into collective decision. In YFS, the process of moving from multiple sometimes disparate viewpoints is part of the structure implemented from the start. In other words, there is a rationale and method in place to move conversations toward collective decisions.

Teams in YFS create conditions for success by balancing the information that each member holds and common information shared by its members collectively. Decisions are arrived at not by team members modifying their positions or through compromise but when teams embrace and encourage diversity and independence and figure out how to use mechanisms that support the group as a whole. As discussed throughout this book, an example of one such mechanism in YFS is outcome measurement. Although there are different forms of outcome measurement, the concept of using outcome as a factor in decision-making with youth is independent of any one staff member.

In the next section, will explore the role of collective decision-making with staffings, case consultations, and meetings.

Positive Deviance in Action: Staffings, Case Conferences, and Meetings

At the core of YFS is collaboration. One specific form of interdisciplinary collaboration is meetings in which youth and families are discussed. Generally referred to as "staffings" or "case conferences," these meetings usually involve discussion of concerns and goals, issues related to safety, treatment planning, updates on what is and is not working, and clarification of "who is doing what." Staffings are not competitions for the best idea; rather they are forums for generating many ideas for the purpose of improving the care of youth. They also present opportunities to get everyone on the "same page." Lack of unity with a team or clarity with roles can spell a myriad of problems with consistency and follow-through.

Considerations for Staffings

Staffings are an integral aspect of decision-making and service coordination. To ensure representation of the views of youth and others who may be involved, the following ideas can be used as a general guide:

- Involve youth and supportive others in meetings whenever possible.
- If youth cannot be present, invite them to contribute any thoughts or questions they might have.
- Share with youth any points that you would like to make in upcoming meetings, providing rationale and allowing them the opportunity to edit your comments.
- Update youth on the outcome of staffings, case conferences, or meetings including any ideas or questions that may have been generated.
- Act "as if" youth are present at meetings to keep conversations respectful and focused.
- Use person-first language and youth's real names, avoiding depersonalizing labels such as "the bipolar kid," "the overreactive grandma," or "the crisis-oriented family."

The focus of staffings is on youth, however, most staff gatherings do not actually involve the most important determinant in outcome—youth themselves. Being strengths based means going beyond the ideas listed earlier by scanning for opportunities to both include and highlight the perspectives of youth.

Structuring Staffing Conversations

A core idea throughout this book has been the 80/20 rule. Because too much information can hinder the collective intelligence of teams and hamper decision-making we ask: What information is most essential to conversations about youth? To address this question, we again refer to the strengths-based principles to underscore conversations:

- Identify and utilize the strengths of youth.
- Engage youth through supportive alliances.
- Consider cultural influences and how they shape youth's lives.
- Promote growth, development, and well-being.
- Create or rehabilitate hope.

Next, is to structure conversations by determining what will be of focus. Here we will use a three-point strategy to provide structure and direction. The three points are:

1 outcome rating
2 provider rating
3 action plan.

Outcome Rating

In Chapter 3, we learned that the severity of the youth's distress at the start of services is the most consistent and reliable predictor of eventual outcome. This point is underscored by research that indicates that mental health professionals are poor at identifying both client progress and deterioration (Bertolino et al., 2012). These findings accentuate the importance of employing some form of reliable and valid outcome measurement at the start of services. In staffings, outcome scores serve as a starting point.

For the purposes of illustration we again refer to the Outcome Rating Scale (ORS) and Child Outcome Rating Scale (CORS) which were discussed in detail in Chapter 4. The ORS and CORS are self-report measures that provide information about a youth's level of distress and are administered at the start of services and each session or meeting thereafter (or one time per week for programs in which there are multiple sessions or meetings). Scores are transferred to a graph (see Appendix A) or input into an electronic system. Caregivers or collaterals can also complete the measures which can be used as comparisons.

As discussed in Chapter 4, the ORS and CORS measures have age-contingent clinical cutoffs. To summarize, the clinical cutoff for adults ages 19 and over is 25, 28 for ages 13 to 18, and 32 for children 6 to 12. The clinical cutoff is an important statistic because it helps YFS personnel to determine a youth or supportive other's level of distress at the outset. Lower scores on the ORS and CORS measures indicate greater degrees of distress and impaired functioning. According to studies, clients who rate their levels of distress lower (as indicated through high scores) and above the clinical cutoff are far more likely to dropout and/or have a negative outcome.

In initial staffings—the first time a youth is discussed with a team or group—the YCW or other staff member shows intake or first session scores and if available provides a graph (see Appendix A). Again, particular attention should be given to lower scores. For example, at Youth In Need, scores of 15 or below are considered cause for more detailed risk assessment.

In subsequent staffings or when there multiple scores (data points), the progress of youth is discussed. The graphs provided in Appendix A once again offer a visual way of monitoring progress. We also want to balance ORS and CORS scores with any other forms of self-report we have from youth. As mentioned earlier in this chapter, the "Who I Am: What I Want Staff to Know About Me" form provides a possible option. With this information teams want to know: Is the youth reporting progress? No progress or change? Deterioration? Later in this chapter, we will learn about various ways to respond to each of these variations.

The significance of measuring outcome on a routine and ongoing manner cannot be overstated. Knowing a youth's level of distress helps to determine the type and intensity of services, with matching services (see Chapter 5) to youth, and most importantly, whether services are benefitting youth. We ask not whether youth need services but rather, are youth benefitting from our services? Monitoring outcome provides a scientific basis to services.

Provider Rating

Next to youth the second largest contributor to the variance in outcome is who provides the service, which in YFS is most often teams. Since YCWs are at the heart of YFS and spend more time with youth than other staff they have to rely heavily on their experience, education, and intuition. YCWs are responsible for the safety of youth and will need to use their observational and interviewing skills to identify concerns that may indicate risk (i.e., suicidal ideation, substance abuse, etc.). To assist YCWs with determining degree of risk there are numerous forms of assessment. An example of a tool that can be used to rate the functioning of youth is the Children's Global Assessment Scale (C-GAS). The C-GAS is a measure of the overall severity of disturbance in children (Shaffer et al., 1983). The measure has a range of 0 to 100, with lower scores suggesting greater degrees of impairment with functioning. The C-GAS is completed by YCWs or other YFS staff and can be used in conjunction with other measures of distress and improvement. As an alternative to the C-GAS, another possibility might be to use a scale of 1 to 10, similar to what health professionals might use to track things such as level of pain.

Staff reports will vary given that staff are trained differently and see things differently. The aim is to identify areas that may indicate risk of harm to self or others and act as hurdles to youth achieving their preferred futures. Including staff ratings as part of staffings provides further points of reference and a more encompassing perspective of the youth.

Action

The third point of structuring conversations about youth in staff meetings is *action*, which serves as a conduit for the first two points. Action involves determining "what to do" to address concerns or problems, building on positive change and exceptions, and supporting youth and others to achieve positive outcomes. Crucial to discussions about actions is "action talk." As discussed in Chapter 4, action talk helps with clarifying vague descriptions. For example, if a youth has a CORS score of 22, which is just below the clinical cutoff, we want to know what is happening in the youth's life that led him or her to provide that rating. In other words, what did a youth say when asked what a score of 22 represented or "looked like?" Or, if a YCW assigns a rating of 65 on the C-GAS, we want to know what the YCW observed that led to assignment of that score. Further, through action talk we inquire as to what the YCW would indicate as improvement.

There is no room for ambiguous language in staffings. Minimally, ambiguity can lead to confusion in terms of what team members are going to both individually and collectively do to help youth. In worst cases, ambiguity can increase threats to safety and well-being, particularly when staff are unclear about their roles and the actions they are expected to carry out.

Beyond collective decision-making made about services is how information from staffings will be shared with youth. As mentioned earlier, youth are frequently left out of discussions about their welfare. One possibility for encouraging youth participation with staffings is to write down various ideas that were generated and sharing them with youth. What follows is an example of how this idea might be employed with a youth.

Case Example 7.1

YCW: Erica, as you know we had a staff meeting this morning. Do you remember the form you filled out the other day?

Erica: The one about things I want staff to know about me?

YCW: Right. That's the one. Staff were impressed about what you wrote and we had a chance to talk about it. We also talked about how we might help you to accomplish the things you wrote about. Staff had some ideas that I wanted to share with you. Are you interested in hearing them?

Erica: Yeah.

We strive to include youth in decisions—not to make promises we are not in a position to follow through on. Simply, engagement strengthens YCW–youth relationships and increases the probability of success. Productive staffings—ones that are efficient and lead to specific plans of action—not only focus on youth, they maintain their structure. Other practices that assist with structure include *time limits* and *simplicity.* By time limits we mean establishing a set amount of time to discuss youth. A common range would be 5–10 minutes, using the three conversational points as a guide. Although there will be exceptions such as with safety planning, as a rule, longer discussions about youth do not typically translate to better ideas and better outcomes. Time limits also help to keep staffings moving, discussions focused, ensure that all youth are discussed, and keep staff engaged.

A second additional structural consideration is to keep things simple. Einstein once said, "If you can't explain your theory to a six-year-old you probably don't understand it yourself." A risk with staffings is they can quickly turn into philosophical or theoretical discussions, which may be interesting but more often will complicate matters and be unproductive. A further side effect is that YCWs and other staff leave staffings without a clear idea of what to do. Youth are far more interesting to talk about than theories. To be sure that what has been discussed is clear, we ask each staff person to describe, in one minute or less, what he or she will do differently in working with a youth as a result of the conversation. If staff cannot do this the team as a whole should regroup and revisit their collective decisions.

Subsequent Interactions: Monitoring Progress

Second and subsequent formal interactions with youth are not necessarily "continuations" of previous ones. Sometimes conversations pick up where they left off, at other times entirely new ones emerge. Being on the front lines, it is understood that YCWs interact with youth on a frequent basis, however, for the remainder of this chapter, we will concentrate on those interactions that are considered formal, most commonly in the form of sessions or meetings. These interactions are characterized by a focus on specific problems or concerns and may require YCWs to use more thought-out strengths-based interventions.

We begin subsequent interactions the same way as initial ones by extending permission to youth to begin where they are most comfortable. Doing so helps to convey respect, enhance collaboration, and strengthen the alliance. YCWs continue to acknowledge, validate, and create a climate that promotes hope and possibilities for future change. To get things started YCWs can use opening questions such as those posed in Chapter 3 by asking, "How have you been?" or "Where would you like to start today?" There are, of course, many ways that youth might respond to such questions. The task of the YCW is to gain a sense of direction to use action talk to determine how subsequent conversations might benefit a youth. Of the different ways in which youth might respond, there are two general categories that will be the focus of the remainder of this chapter: *No improvement or deterioration* and *improvement*. Both categories of response are contingent on the use of outcome measurement and feedback described in previous chapters.

Better or Not? That is the Question

As youth convey that which has transpired between formal sessions or meetings YCWs attend to two forms of information. The first relates to what youth communicate verbally and nonverbally through language and interaction. For example, does a youth talk about things going better? Unchanged? Worse? What can be drawn from their body language? As described throughout this book, youth will often give vague, non-descriptive answers, which calls for YCWs to use action talk to gain clarity.

The second level of information YCWs attend to is the ongoing distress of youth as captured through outcome measurement. We want to learn through instrumentation whether or not things are improving and whether or not services provided are of benefit. Consistent with initial sessions and meetings, youth are asked to complete an outcome measure. The measure is then scored and the results are plotted on a graph (see Appendix A). What follows is discussion about the actual scores and more importantly, the meaning of those scores.

Review of two (or more) data points on a graph will only reveal so much about a youth and his or her progress. And even though youth are asked to complete the ORS/CORS based on what has transpired over the past week or since the last meeting, sometimes scores go up or down based on events. A youth may have a good or bad day or something could have happened just prior to the meeting which in turns affects how the youth rates his or her degree of distress. In addition, YCWs should monitor for sharp increases or decreases. Although we strive for early change, with few exceptions (i.e., so-called "epiphanies" or life-changing experiences) change that "sticks" tends to be gradual. When large increases or decreases occur YCWs will want to consider further risk assessment. Big changes have to be followed up quickly, which can be done by YCWs checking out the meaning of individual scores to learn their significance in the eyes of the youth.

Before exploring the two categories of response, it is necessary to learn about key terms that assist YCWs and other YFS staff to determine whether or not a self-report change by a youth is considered statistically robust. First, when services are successful, scores on the ORS/CORS should increase over time. To be able to attribute such changes to nonrandom, substantial changes in well-being, the difference between two scores must meet or exceed a statistical index known as the *reliable change index* (RCI). The RCI is a measure used to assess the magnitude of change necessary to be considered statistically reliable rather than due to chance or maturation (the passage of time), or measurement error. It is an average based on the reliability or consistency of an instrument. The RCI for the ORS and CORS (see Chapter 4) is 5. That is, a 5 point increase on the ORS *at the end of services* is a considered reliable change. The RCI can prove useful in separating successful and unsuccessful cases; however, it can also result in over- or underestimates of the amount of change depending on level of severity (Duncan et al., 2004).

A second key term, *clinical significance,* refers to reliable improvement that also corresponds to a change in clinical status, which involves movement from a clinical (often referred to as dysfunctional) range to a nonclinical (functional) range. YCWs work with youth to achieve an overall change on the ORS or CORS that is above the clinical cutoff (see Chapter 4) at the end of services. YCWs are also mindful that the absence of subjective improvement in the first few sessions suggests that the youth is at much greater risk for negative outcome (Brown, Dreis, & Nace, 1999).

Category 1: No Improvement or Deterioration

When a youth's current ORS/CORS increases or decreases but remains within four points of his or her initial ORS/CORS score, it can be said that there is "no improvement." "Deterioration" is when a youth's most recent ORS/CORS score decreases by five or more points as compared to the initial ORS/CORS. YCWs are mindful of overall change as an indicator of successful outcome. However, it is also important to compare the most recent ORS/CORS scores to the previous session ORS/CORS scores to determine immediate progress and next steps. In this section, we explore both forms of response.

No Improvement

YCWs listen closely to the descriptions youth provide of their situations and their reports of distress through the use of outcome measurement such as the ORS or CORS. In this and upcoming sections, we use examples of graphs to track the responses of youth. Graphs also serve as visual aids for both YCWs and youth. For some youth, the use of graphs will generate conversation and better connect them with YCWs, therefore strengthening the alliance.

For the purposes of discussion, refer to Figure 7.1, which provides an example of an 18 year-old youth who has an initial ORS score of 26.2, a second session score of 22.1, and a third session score of 25.8. In this example, the variance in scores remains small—with no sharp increases or decreases. When the first session ORS score is compared with the most recent session score the change is −0.4, which is a decrease, but not a significant one. If the same youth were to instead have a third session score of 28.2, which would represent a two point numerical increase from session one (and an overall improvement), it still would not be statistically *reliable* or *clinically significant* based on the properties of the ORS/CORS measures. The point is that there are occasions in which small degrees of change may not be considered change at all.

A second example of "no improvement" can be found with Figure 7.2, in which the opening ORS for a 15-year-old youth is 32.6 and at the fifth session the ORS is 28.8. (Note that the opening ORS score in Figure 7.2 is above the clinical cutoff, which

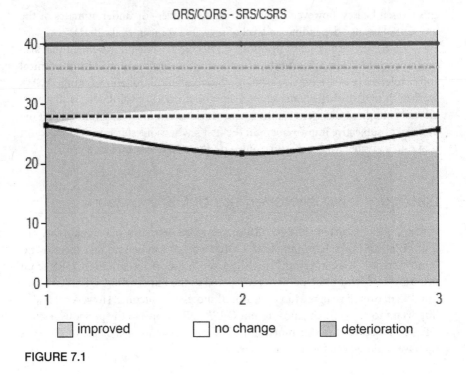

FIGURE 7.1

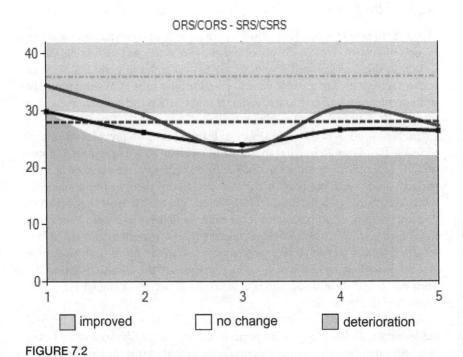

FIGURE 7.2

as detailed in Chapter 4, indicates a lower level at the start of services which without prompt attention by the YCW may put the youth at greater risk of dropout and negative outcome.) Small changes as indicated in Figures 7.1 and 7.2 are usually supported by statements such as, "Things are the same as last time" or "There's nothing new."

If a youth's verbalizations conflict with ORS/CORS scores (i.e., verbalizations are higher or lower than what was reported on the measures) the YCW checks it out. For example, a YCW might say, "From what you said it sounds like things have gotten worse over the past week but your ORS is very similar to last time. Can you tell me about that?" or "From what you've described things have been pretty much the same as last but your ORS has gone up. What can you tell me about that?" Oftentimes differences between what a youth says and actual ORS/CORS scores are small and may be statistically insignificant. At the same, small variations can be building blocks for exploring exceptions and can be meaningful.

Another possibility is when improvement has occurred at some point in services prior to a regression. Figure 7.3 provides an example of ORS scores for a 17-year-old that improved between sessions one and five (from 28.3 to 33.4), but dropped at session six (26.8). Later in this chapter, we learn about ways to build on the "in-between" progress, at this juncture we refer to the current status of

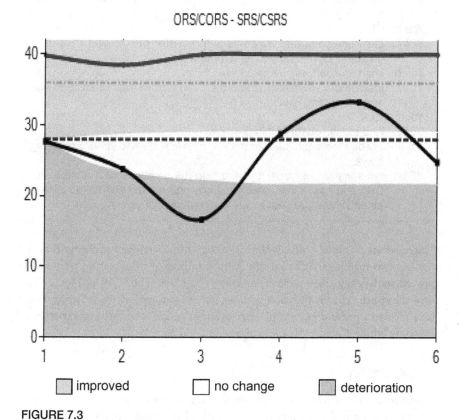

ORS/CORS - SRS/CSRS

☐ improved   ☐ no change   ☐ deterioration

FIGURE 7.3

the youth, which indicates a drop from session five to session six and no overall improvement between session one and session five (from 28.3 to 26.8). The drop at session six is not considered deterioration because it was less than 5 points as compared to session one. Although the youth's beginning and most recent scores fall into the "no improvement" category, YCWs express interest in both short-term and overall change. Here's how a YCW might explore both types of change, using Figure 7.3 as a reference.

Case Example 7.2

YCW: If we look at how you rated things now compared to when you first came here your scores are pretty much the same. Does that seem right to you?

Youth: Yeah. It's not any better. I'm still fighting with my dad. I thought things were getting better but I was wrong. It's a bummer.

YCW: That's got to be hard on you. You're wanting things to be better—and there were signs of that—but then things went backwards a little.

Youth: Right. That's what happened.

YCW: If it's okay I'd like to hear more about that. But before we do that I wondered if I could ask you about the difference between the last time we met and now.

Youth: Okay.

YCW: Last time you rated things as a little better. In fact, you were up a good five points. Do you remember that?

Youth: Yeah, my dad was being cool.

YCW: I remember you talking about that. You said he was listening to you and not cutting you off.

Youth: Exactly.

YCW: And today you rated things lower.

Youth: My dad went right back to the way he was—back to yelling and being a jerk.

YCW: I'm sorry to hear that. It would help me greatly to hear more about that, and how things have gone downhill a little. And I'm also interested in how you kept things from getting worse.

The previous example involved inquiries about overall change and change between the last two meetings. Although the youth's ratings of his situation were unimproved statistically, there were exceptions to build on. The YCW also focused on how the youth kept his situation with his father from getting worse, which could be a factor in preventing overall deterioration, which is the second variation of response within Category 1, and will be discussed next.

Deterioration

When scores from both initial and most recent sessions decrease by 5 or more points it can be said that there is "deterioration." As discussed in earlier chapters, research makes it clear that mental health practitioners often struggle to identify deterioration. This finding underscores the importance of YCWs paying close attention and responding to variations in outcome scores. Attention of this sort reduces the chances that deterioration will go unnoticed.

Youth whose outcome scores trend downward will typically say things such as, "My life is going downhill," "My life sucks," or "It's worse than before." Again, reports of this kind are not unusual because youth will have ups and downs. And yet, what accompanies deterioration is frustration and loss of hope, which are precursors for dropout (Garcia & Weisz, 2002) and negative outcome (Warren et al., 2010), two of the most significant threats to YFS.

Figure 7.4 provides an example of a 16-year-old youth in services whose ORS scores indicate deterioration. The youth had an initial ORS of 21.6, then a series of three sessions in between in which the scores remained consistent with the opening session (i.e., no increases or decreases of 4 or more points). In the fifth session the youth's ORS score dropped to 14.8, a decrease of 6.8 points. It can be said that the youth has deteriorated in services. In contrast, Figure 7.5 shows a 12-year-old youth with an initial ORS score of 26.1, who demonstrated improved scores through session five and a sharp decrease at session six as evidenced by an ORS score of 18.9, an overall decrease of 7.2 points. Without prompt attention the youth described in Figures 7.1 through 7.5 are four times more likely to have a negative outcome, with the last two at the greatest risk.

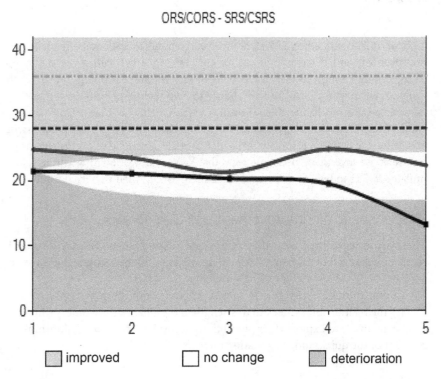

ORS/CORS - SRS/CSRS

☐ improved   ☐ no change   ☐ deterioration

FIGURE 7.4

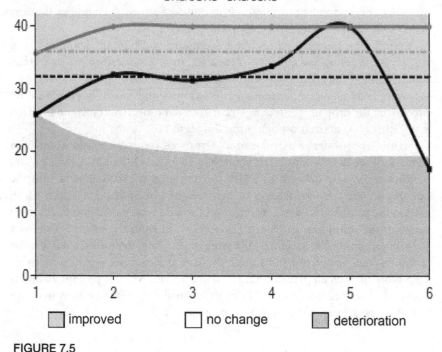

FIGURE 7.5

How YCWs and other YFS staff involved respond to situations involving no improvement and deterioration can be the difference between a youth staying engaged long enough to reap the benefit of services and dropping out. If youth dropout, we may not have another chance to help them and perhaps worse, they may shy away from future mental health services, believing that it won't do any good. When faced with deterioration, YCWs must be prepared to respond in a swift and deliberate manner. Failing to do so increases the likelihood of premature dropout. Next, we investigate two main ways that YCWs can work with youth to reformulate services to benefit youth and move them toward their preferred futures.

Responses to No Improvement and Deterioration

There are at least three ways that YCWs can respond when ORS/CORS scores remain unchanged or decrease. Each will be explored in the sections that follow:

1   Coping through exceptions: What's kept things from getting worse?
2   It's the relationship! Check in to strengthen the alliance (and others who may be involved) to explore their perceptions of service-oriented relationships.
3   Out of the quicksand: Negotiating impasses.

Coping through Exceptions: What's Kept Things from Getting Worse?

When progress with youth stagnates or things deteriorate it is essential that YCWs not lose sight of their personal philosophies. The best resource we have is our perspective. Perspective is expressed through character, which, in turn, reveals itself in adversity. And youth need the support of YFS staff most in the midst of adversity. YCWs who maintain clear perspectives are less vulnerable to negativity. They are better able to stand up to views that hold that youth are oppositional, defiant, or unwilling to change, or in some cases, worse. For example, it is not uncommon when things are not going well for YFS staff to fall prey to ideas such as "youth have to get worse" and perhaps even "bottom out" before they get better. This type of generalization is not only empirically unsubstantiated, at minimum it closes down possibilities for change (Timko et al., 1999). In worst cases there, are negative consequences when youth are left to deteriorate without concerted efforts to intervene. Letting youth fall into a downward spiral without intervention poses threats to their health and well-being and raises serious ethical and legal concerns.

Having a clear perspective, YCWs can "lean into" the search for exceptions as a means of countering situations in which there is no progress or deterioration. As always, we take care to acknowledge youth, letting them know we understand their concerns and are not glossing over problems. In addition to using the methods detailed in previous chapters, we specifically scan for evidence of how youth and/or others have been able to keep situations from getting *even worse*. Things can always get worse. Doing so involves tapping into resilience, including the ways youth cope with and keep problems from completely overtaking them. The strengths and resources that youth use, often unknowingly, serve as coping mechanisms. The following case example illustrates how strengths are present even in situations that appear to be heading the wrong direction.

Case Example 7.3

I was working in a program set up to serve youth who had been in trouble with the family court. Not long after I started the job, 14-year-old Jacques was referred after being charged with stealing. According to his mother, Jacques also had a history of taking drugs and stealing from her. During our third meeting, his mother said, "It can't get any worse. I've just had it." I acknowledged her feelings of frustration and then asked Jacques, "How come you're not already locked up?" He seemed confused by my question. I continued, "I see quite a few teenagers, and by the time they've done what you've done, they're either headed for out-of-home placement or have already been there. What's kept you from being sent away?" Jacques's demeanor changed and he looked down. "Apparently someone believes that you should have another chance and has given you a pass. And I wonder how you have kept things from getting any worse, knowing that one more charge would most certainly get you placed?" Jacques replied, "I don't want to be sent away." I replied, "I hear you. Tell me what have you done since your last offense to prevent that from happening?" "I've listened to my mom more," he answered. "What else?" I countered. "I haven't stolen since I got in trouble," a teary Jacques replied. I learned that it had been nearly six weeks since Jacques had last stolen, which began a shift to focusing on the specific things Jacques had been doing and could do to get his life back on track.

Focusing on factors that prevent things from getting worse is a way to acknowledge pessimism while maintaining an eye on possibilities. In subsequent sessions or meetings when youth or others involved say "Every week it's the same old same old," "Nothing is going to work," or "Things will never change," YCWs combine acknowledgment with exception-oriented questions. These questions can foster resilience and draw out underutilized strengths and resources. For example, a YCW might say to a youth, "From what you've described, things have been worse. I'm sorry to hear that things have been sliding downward. I'm also curious about what has kept things from completely bottoming out. How have you done that?" The questions that follow can help with identifying exceptions in cases in which there appears to be no improvement or deterioration:

- How come things aren't worse with your situation?
- What have you done to keep things from getting worse?
- What steps have you taken to prevent things from heading downhill any further?
- What else has helped things from getting worse/deteriorating further?
- How has that made a difference for you/with this situation?
- What is the smallest thing that you could do that might make even more of a difference with your situation?
- How could we get that to happen a little now?
- What could others do?
- What might help you to hold steady once you leave here today?
- What will you think to do the next time you feel yourself slipping?
- What specifically will you do?
- What could you do on a more regular basis to keep things from slipping?

Asking about what has kept things from getting worse may surprise youth who are used to talking almost exclusively about problems. The questions offered help orient youth to whatever aspects of themselves, others, or their situations, however small, have worked to any degree. The preventative mechanisms can help build hope for youth when they feel or think that nothing is going right. The following example illustrates how a YCW might work with a youth to build on small change to help move things in a better direction. Such small changes can lead to more substantial, statistically measurable ones.

Case Example 7.4

Youth: Nothing's better. I still feel like crap.

YCW: Nothing seems better—you've been feeling like crap.

Youth: Yep, nothing's working for me. I'm sinking further and further.

YCW: Nothing's worked so far . . . I can see why it would seem like you are sinking further and further.

Youth: I just want to feel better.

YCW: I want you to feel better too. Tell me about a time recently when you felt like you had your head slightly above water.

Youth: I can't think of one. There hasn't been a time.

YCW: I want to be sure I understand. Please tell me a little more. Let's start with last week. Even though every day was crappy, which one was the worst?

Youth: Wednesday.

YCW: Tell me about that. What was it like?

Youth: I didn't make it to school . . . my mom kept trying to get me to wake up, I don't know how many times . . . but I didn't listen. And I didn't eat until that night . . . it was a bad day.

YCW: I see. Not the kind of day that you want to repeat too often.

Youth: No way.

YCW: Okay, then tell me about Thursday because even though that wasn't a great day either, it wasn't as bad as Wednesday. What was different about Thursday?

Youth: I slept too long.

YCW: Alright. How was Thursday different than Wednesday?

Youth: Well, I did finally get up about nine-thirty. Wednesday I didn't get up until three in the afternoon.

YCW: Wait, hang on a second. Instead of sleeping late on Thursday like you did on Wednesday you put on the brakes and got up earlier?

Youth: Yeah, a little earlier.

YCW: How did you manage to get yourself up earlier on Thursday?

Youth: I just knew that I had to get to school. I can't miss any more or I'll flunk my classes.

YCW: That's what you said to yourself, "I can't miss anymore." What did you do then?

Youth: I just got dressed and my mom took me and signed me in. I only missed one class. I just told myself, "You can get through it."

YCW: And that worked . . .

Youth: It did.

YCW: And Friday?

Youth: Ha. I went the whole day. It sucked but I went.

YCW: It sounds like you surprised yourself. Even though you have been depressed you mustered up the wherewithal to go.

Youth: I didn't think about it until now. But I totally did. When I went to bed Thursday night I had no plan to go on Friday. But I woke up about six and started to feel guilty. I hate feeling guilty more than I hate going to school. So I went.

YCW: Ok, you don't like feeling guilty. But there's more to it, isn't there? At some point you decided enough is enough. You decided to not let the situation get any worse and you took action. Maybe I'm wrong but was there something else other than guilt going on with you that you decided to go on Friday?

Youth: Maybe. I won't know have to do this forever. I can deal with that if it means I can do what I want in the future.

YCW: Ah yes, the future.

Youth: Yeah, that's all I'm interested in.

YCW: Maybe thinking about the future you want for yourself can help you stay focused and give you traction when you need it.

Youth: If I can just keep focused. Sometimes I get frustrated and start to give up.

YCW: Is that something we could work on? How to stay focused on your future so that when you have tough times you don't get sidetracked?

Youth: That would be cool.

To identify and build on exceptions YCWs exercise patience and take care to acknowledge the experiences of youth and supportive others who may be involved. Otherwise closed-down situations can produce opportunities for positive change when YCWs start small. YCWs do not try to convince youth that things are better than they perceive them. This can prove invalidating. Instead, they assume there are exceptions by virtue of the fact that things can get even worse. Questions are aimed at helping youth to do their own surveys to convince YCWs of their abilities by identifying what they have done to keep things from getting worse. In the previous case example, the YCW exercised patience by first acknowledging how bad things had been going for the youth and asking for more information. From there, the YCW sought a way of comparing the worst day to another bad day. In doing so, small differences were identified, including how the youth managed to cope when things were heading downhill. In this sense, the youth provided exceptions and the YCW built on them.

It is imperative that we respond to the absence of change or deterioration in a timely manner. The risk of negative outcome with youth who do not show improvement in the first few sessions or meetings is high and that risk increases without adequate response. Also important is to note fluctuations that may occur over time. Some youth will demonstrate greater highs and lows than others or have patterns that will repeat. Later in this chapter, we will focus on ways to build on positive changes—the "ups" in services—at the same time it remains imperative that deterioration on outcome measures be considered along with professional expertise with an eye on reducing risk. Deterioration is cause for further risk assessment and if necessary, action, including intensifying or modifying services. In other cases, YCWs will need to talk with youth and their caregivers about whether the services provided are good fit at this point in time, which may lead to a referral.

It's the Relationship! Check in to Strengthen the Alliance

No idea in this book is more crucial in working with youth than Principle 2: *The therapeutic alliance makes substantial and consistent contributions to outcome* (see Chapter 2). In Chapter 4, we learned about SRS, CSRS, and GSRS (for groups) measures as a way to monitor the alliance. In review, the SRS/CSRS/GSRS is administered near the end of sessions or meetings to capture youth, and supportive others', perceptions of the therapeutic relationship. We are reminded to use some form of alliance measure as a way of gathering feedback. The clinical cutoff for the SRS/CSRS/GSRS measures is 36, meaning that any overall score of 36 or below or any single subscale score of 8 calls for YCWs to respond. Figures 7.1 to 7.5 provide example SRS scores in the top lines of the charts.

The quality of feedback YCWs receive from youth and others involved will largely depend on how measures were introduced to begin with. YCWs who discuss the value of feedback and frame as a means of quality improvement or even professional development are much more likely to receive helpful feedback. It takes little effort to get high alliance scores from youth so YCWs have to take it on themselves to communicate the importance feedback and its role in providing the best "fit" possible regarding services.

When a score falls at or below 36, the YCW follows up to gain more information. For example, a YCW might say, "Compared to our last meeting it seems the scores went down a bit. Could you tell me a little about what the meeting was like for you today?" Sometimes youth will shy from giving direct feedback out of fear of hurting the YCW or other's feelings. To take the pressure off the youth the YCW strives to frame the feedback as an "opportunity" to make changes or adjustments that will help the youth. This may involve reorienting the youth to the purpose of the measure, "It's okay. By giving me feedback you're helping me to help you. You won't hurt my feelings or make me feel bad. You'll actually be helping me to be a better helper."

There will be times that that youth will not assign high scores. For example, a youth may give an SRS score of 31. When asked about the meaning of the score the youth may provide feedback that is similar to that of someone who gave a score of 38. In other words, all scores are relative. The task of the YCW is to elicit feedback about what can be done to strengthen the relationship. Oftentimes attention to subscales reveals more information than total scores. We'll continue to use the SRS as an example. The SRS has four subscales: Relationship, goals and topics, approach and method, and overall (see Appendix A). Let's say a youth gives scores of 9.4, 9.1, 7.4, and 8.5 for a total score of 34.4. Because the total score is below 36 the YCW would request feedback about the session or meeting in general. There is a single domain "approach and method," however, that is lower than the others. Therefore, the YCW might summarize the results by saying, "It seems that you felt listened to and that we worked on what you wanted to work on but perhaps the way we approached your concern was a bit off. Does that seem right or am I missing something?" The YCW's aim is to generate conversation to learn what he or she can do differently should services continue. Failure to respond to feedback is a missed opportunity and can contribute to dropout.

In Chapter 4, a series of questions for checking in with youth was provided. In addition to using formal instrumentation, these questions can be used at any time to help YCWs to monitor the pulse of the relationship. Because problems can occur at any time, YCWs aim to respond quickly to avoid the frustration and demoralization that can occur if problems are left unresolved (Safran, Muran, Samstang, & Stevens, 2002). When ruptures or problems occur, YCWs consider doing the following:

- Discuss the here-and-now relationship with the youth or others involved.
- Ask for further feedback about the therapeutic relationship.
- Create space and allow the youth or others to assert any negative feelings about the therapeutic relationship.
- Engage in conversations about the youth or supportive other's expectations and preferences.
- Spend more time learning about the youth or supportive other's experience in services.
- Readdress the agreement established about goals and tasks to accomplish those goals.
- Accept responsibility as a service provider for your part in alliance ruptures.
- Normalize the youth or supportive others' responses by letting them know that talking about concerns, facing challenges, taking action, and/or services in general can be difficult.
- Provide rationale for techniques and methods.
- Attend closely to subtle clues (e.g., nonverbal behaviors, patterns such as one-word answers) that may indicate a problem with the alliance.
- Offer more positive feedback and encouragement (except when the youth communicates either verbally or nonverbally that this is not a good match).

There will be times that an adjustment made in one meeting will not apply to another, underscoring the importance of routine and ongoing monitoring of the alliance. Relationships will change, sometimes requiring frequent adjustments. Although there are no one-size-fits-all methods, because YCWs most often work as part of teams, discussion of factors that both strengthen and threaten relationships with youth should be shared.

Joining the Pessimism

No matter how insightful or creative a YCW is, some youth will remain steadfast in their perspectives. They will counter attempts by YCWs to join them in conversation by expressing annoyance or pessimism or even frustration. YCWs will find themselves challenged to avoid the pull of impossibility—seeing youth as resistant or unmotivated or that their situations, circumstances, or problems are unchangeable. When youth or others involved respond to YCWs' attempts to elicit exceptions or differences with negative or closed-down statements, it is up to the

YCW to make a change. This is because many youth are communicating that what YCWs are doing to relate is not working.

When all paths seem to have been exhausted, joining in the pessimism can prove beneficial. An example might be for a YCW to say, "You've convinced me just how bad things really are. I don't think I understood at first. Even though I think things can get better, I really don't have a clue as to what to do to help you. I'm sitting here wondering what I must be missing about your situation and where to go with this." Another option is to say, "It really does sound like a dreadful situation. I think maybe I didn't see that at first. Maybe we should spend more time on this so it really sinks in with me." Statements should match the youth or other's degree of pessimism and not trivialize their concerns. The following example offers a way of using pessimism to join with a mother.

Case Example 7.5

A mother was frustrated with her 15-year-old son, Miguel. She described how the two would yell at each other, leading to them both feeling hurt and angry. Their arguments had become increasingly intense according to both. I searched about for exceptions by asking, "When have things been just a little better between the two of you?" and "What is different about times when your arguments are less intense?" These questions were met with terse, short answers that things are "never better" and "will always be that way." It seemed that whatever I tried was met with trepidation. I shifted my approach to join their sense of pessimism. I said, "You've convinced me." The mom raised her head and inquired, "Of what?" "Well, you've convinced me that your relationship isn't really worth talking about anymore. It's beyond help." The mom and Miguel looked at each other. Miguel, on the edge of tears, replied, "It's not that bad." I responded, "What's not that bad? I haven't seen one indication that you are able to handle your disagreements in any other way but to argue until one or both of you suffers." The room fell silent and then the mom spoke, "Actually, there have been a couple of times recently when we've been able to stop things from getting too bad." Miguel nodded in agreement. At that point an exception emerged which we were able to use as a starting point to rebuild their relationship.

Joining the pessimism is not a first choice, but an option in circumstances in which other possibilities have been exhausted. As a result, some youth will reverse gears and reveal exceptions that can then be amplified and built on. Joining with youth and others involved means YCWs are putting relationships first, knowing that "better" relationships yield better outcomes.

Responding to "No-Talk" Youth

It is not unusual to encounter youth who speak very little or not at all. Most youth will usually break their silence sooner or later. For those youth who do not it is important that YCWs remain patient. Although youth may not be talking they are still communicating nonverbally. It is a task of the YCW to pay attention to these communications and extend permission not to speak. A YCW might say, "It's okay if you don't want to talk. Sometimes I feel that way." Another possibility is, "You're the only one who will know when it's right for you to talk. I'll leave it up to you" or "If you want to talk later that's fine. If you don't, that's okay too." The following example offers a way for YCWs to take the pressure off youth to talk.

Case Example 7.6

An 11-year-old boy came to see me because he had been isolating himself from other children and appeared despondent. When he did not speak or respond verbally to questions, I said, "I just wanted to let you know that it's okay if you don't want or feel like talking. I've felt that way at times. And, if you want or feel like talking later, that's okay too—but there's no pressure to have to say anything. And you know, today might be a good day to not talk. You know why? Because I have a lot to say! You see, I wanted to tell you about this TV show I saw last night. It was about UFOs. It was really cool but weird too." As I continued to talk, the young man smiled and seemed ready to say something so I said, "Ah, you know what I mean. But wait, I'm not quite finished yet." By the time I did finish, just a minute or so later, he was bursting with excitement and couldn't wait to tell me about his favorite movie, which was about an alien invasion. The rest of our meetings were filled with conversation.

Conversation is more likely to blossom when YCWs are themselves. There is no substitute for genuineness. YCWs might also consider self-disclosure and stories as encouragers. When attempts to spur conversation fall short, we bear in mind that youth may not say much at times but are still listening.

Out of the Quicksand: Negotiating Impasses

When situations with youth are not improving or getting worse desperation can easily set in. YCWs and teams can become frustrated, which, in turn, threatens judgment and effectiveness. What follows are strategies for YFS staff to consider when services appear at a standstill:

- Assess the youth's current stage of change. (Ask: What is the youth's state of readiness for change?) (See Chapter 5.)
- Focus more on the youth's view of the problem or situation.
- Ask open-ended questions that will allow the youth to notice one or more aspects that have been downplayed or have gone unnoticed (take care not to imply that the youth's perspective is "wrong"; instead, try only to introduce other ways of viewing that may offer new possibilities or will encourage the youth to talk about the problem or situation differently).

- Help the youth to weigh the possible positive and negative effects of his or her behavior.
- Help the youth to weigh the possible benefits and drawbacks of change.
- Offer straightforward feedback without imposing it. (For example, "From where I am standing, I'm concerned about what might happen if this continues. Of course, that is for you to decide, but I believe it's my responsibility to speak about it.") (Note: Always provide more directive feedback and make necessary safeguards if there is risk of harm to self or other.)
- Demonstrate genuine confidence that the youth has the strength to face his or her challenges.
- Avoid a "solution-forced" situation when the youth's preference is to talk more about problems and his or her ambivalence.
- Acknowledge further—ensure that the youth feels heard and understood and verifies this either verbally or nonverbally (ask questions or use an alliance measure as needed).
- Reorient to the youth's concerns to ensure that you and the youth are focusing on the same issue.
- Discuss with persons who have the authority to begin or end services whether the level of services is a good fit.

Lack of progress and deterioration are signals to YCWs to respond as opposed to react. Accordingly, the strategies discussed throughout this book place youth and those involved with youth at the center of decision-making processes. We work *with* youth, not *on* youth. Success in YFS is contingent on strong working alliances at all levels of services and relationships are no more critical than when things are not going well.

In both cases of no improvement and deterioration, our aim is to partner with youth to improve the fit of services and the effect—the benefit to youth. From our conversations with youth, several possible options will emerge. First, for a youth who has remained in services for a reasonable amount of time (depending on the program) but demonstrated no measurable improvement, referral to another service is an option. A youth who has made has made a reliable change that exceeds 5 points, however, remains in the clinical range; we consider changing the type of services, making a referral, or ending services.

Category 2: Improvement

Arguably, it matters little whether or not youth *need* services if they do not *benefit* from those services. As detailed in the previous section, because we are monitoring progress from the outset of services, we are able to distinguish those who are reporting no improvement or deterioration. And we are also able to identify those who are rating their lives as improved, which will be the focus of this section.

As discussed, when a youth's current ORS/CORS increases but remains within four points of his or her initial ORS/CORS score, it can be said that there is "no improvement." This is because the improvement is not considered reliable (i.e., greater than chance, measurement error, or maturation). At the same time, YCWs want to explore any form of positive change as it may serve as a building block to more significant, sweeping changes. In contrast, change that is considered reliable is five points or greater on the ORS/CORS as compared to the initial score. To further recap, *clinical significance* results when there is both reliable improvement and the youth's score ends at or above the clinical cutoff, indicating a change in clinical status.

Figures 7.6 and 7.7 provide two variations of improvement. Figure 7.6 is of an 11-year-old whose primary caregiver, his grandmother, has reported gradual improvement over the course of five meetings, which then appears to stabilize at session six. Figure 7.7 shows a 16-year-old female who reports improvement early in services and then maintains that progress over an extended period of time. In both cases, the YCW's task is to help youth and others involved to build on change to a point at which that change rises above the clinical cutoff and the concerns that led to services have been resolved.

To identify change, YCWs scan for exceptions, indicators of improvement in relation to the problems that led to services. The questions that follow can assist in identifying change:

- What have you noticed that has changed with your concern/problem/self/ situation?
- What specifically seems to be going better?

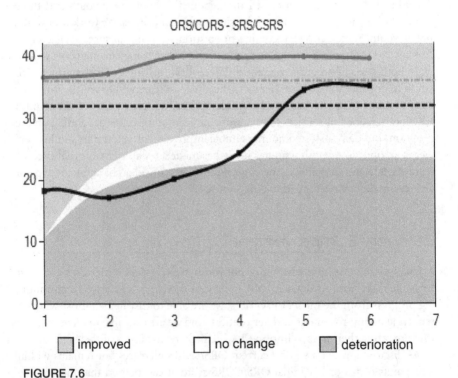

FIGURE 7.6

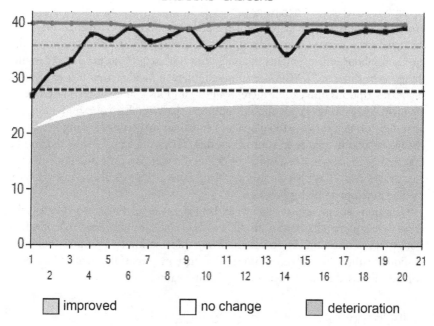

FIGURE 7.7

- Who first noticed that things had changed?
- Who else noticed the change?
- When did you first notice that things had changed?
- What did you notice happening?

Next, YCWs focus on *how* the change occurred and *what* factors appeared to contribute to it. This process involves asking questions that draw on specific actions of youth and others who may be involved. In addition, YCWs emphasize any differences that the change has made in relation to goals. The following questions are used to amplify change:

- How did the change happen?
- What do you think might have influenced that positive change (e.g., family, other support, culture)?
- What worked for you?
- What specifically did you do?
- How did you get yourself to do that?
- How was what you did different than before?
- Where did you get the idea to do things that way?
- What role, if any, did others play in helping to move things forward?
- How specifically did others support and/or help you?

Answers to these questions can help to better understand how youth use their strengths and resources to manage problems. Doing so is an integral part of change processes because it often helps youth and others around them to recognize abilities that have gone unnoticed or underutilized. Because youth or others can respond to questions about improvements in ambiguous ways (e.g., "I just did it"; "I wanted things to be different"), YCWs continue to follow up with action talk to translate vague descriptions into clear, concrete ones. Questions that focus on how and what are pivotal to gaining clarity. Should youth struggle with these questions, it may be an indication that they are too global or general. In such cases, looking for smaller changes may prove more fruitful. To do this, YCWs might say, "How did you get that change to happen just a little?" or "What did you do a little differently than in past situations?" YCWs need only identify granules or ripples of change, which can then be developed into bigger ones.

Questions about improvement can be separated into two broad categories: Ones that explore what the youth did and ones that emphasize the role of others. Both types of question can reveal important information and yet how that information is situated in relation to overall change matters significantly. This point will be addressed in detail in the two sections that follow.

Self-Change: Attribution and Speculation

Throughout this book, we have focused on the most influential factor in the change process—youth. Youth are the engineers of change. Herein is a challenge for YCWs. Youth do not make lasting change without the help and support of others. In contrast, if youth see YCWs or outside helpers, medication, or other external entities as primarily responsible for their improvements, the likelihood that the change they have experienced will "stick" decreases. This is, in part, because personal accountability dissipates once external factors have been removed or diminish as causal agents of change.

A task of the YCW, then, is to help to attribute the significant portion of positive change to those who receive services. Whether change happens before or during services, whether it results from youth or others' actions, or by happenstance, YCWs want to enhance the effects of change by helping youth to see change and its maintenance as a consequence of their own efforts. In a sense, YCWs "blame" youth for changing for the better. To do this, YCWs ask questions to assist in assigning change:

- How is that you have been able face so many challenges and not lose sight of _____?
- Who are you such that you've been able to _____?
- What does the fact that you've been able to face up to _____ say about you?
- What kind of person are you that you've been able to overcome _____?
- Where did you get the wherewithal to _____?

YCWs take care to acknowledge and not dismiss the contributions of external influences. Instead, YCWs work with youth to acknowledge the contributions of external factors while simultaneously attributing change to their own actions:

- You said that _____ (i.e., parent, caregiver, other form of support, etc.) has always been there for you. How has _____'s involvement helped you with what you've been going through? How did you use _____'s support as a stepping stone to take steps toward your future?
- You mentioned that you feel/think that (e.g., medication, services) is helping. How are you working with the (e.g., medication, services) to better your life?

Even the most experienced YCWs encounter youth who struggle to identify what has brought about or contributed to positive change. Youth often respond to YCWs' questions with "I don't know" or by shrugging their shoulders. These kinds of "empty" reply do not mean that youth are withholding information or are resistant; they may not have given much thought to it, really do not know, or perhaps are not interested. Rather than pushing youth to come up with an answer or labeling them "resistant" or "oppositional," YCWs consider the aforementioned responses of youth only as communication; and such communication calls for YCWs to *do something different.*

An effective way of attending to "empty" replies of youth is through *speculation.* Speculation involves YCWs combining conjecture or curiosity with guesswork about how change might have come about (Bertolino, 2003). For example, a YCW might have a youth speculate or guess by asking, "If you had to guess, and there were no wrong answers, what would you say made a difference for you?" or "If (e.g., a close friend, mother, teacher) were here, what would he/she say has contributed to things changing?" If these sorts of question do not reveal anything, YCWs can do their own speculating, "What do you think about the idea that you might have had a role in your situation improving?" This inquiry can then be followed up with questions to assist with developing speculation:

- I'm wondering if perhaps part of the reason things are going better for you is that you are becoming (e.g., more in tune with what you want, more responsible, more mature, wiser, growing up). Perhaps you are becoming the type of person you want to be and learning new ways of managing your life. What do you think about this idea?
- Is it possible that the change you've experienced might be related to your (action)?
- What do you think about the idea that the change you've experienced might be related to your (e.g., wanting to lead a different life, being ready for the next stage of your life)?
- What do you think about the idea that the change you've experienced might be an indication that you're taking back control of your life?
- How might the change you've experienced be a sign of a new, preferred direction for you?

YCWs leave it up to youth to either accept or reject the speculations. It is noteworthy that when YCWs' speculations involve the attribution of positive qualities and actions, they are less likely to be rejected. It is unlikely that a youth will say, "No, I'm becoming less responsible." Even if speculations are off target, because they highlight competencies, youth will at least ponder them. This may trigger new youth-initiated speculations. It is hoped that YCWs' speculations will lead youth and those involved to come up with their own.

Case Example 7.7

Trey, a 14-year-old, was mandated to therapy by the family court. He and a friend had stolen his friend's mother's ATM card and withdrawn more than $2,000. Trey had also been failing his classes at school. Over the course of seven months, Trey made amends and paid restitution for the theft and raised his grades in school. He did this by turning in his homework and doing extra credit. To his mother's surprise, he also began helping out at home by mowing the lawn and cleaning. When asked what he thought led him to make so many changes, Trey appeared somewhat confused and answered, "I'm not sure. I guess I just did it." I followed this by speculating about some possibilities by saying, "I wonder if it's because you are becoming more mature and responsible. Maybe you're also thinking more about others, like your mom." His eyes glistening, Trent leaned forward and said, "Yeah I think that's part of it. I also think I'm just seeing that things need to be done and no one can do them but me. I've done it and I'm proud."

Attribution and speculation not only draw attention to the roles youth have in creating positive change, they also support evolving new stories of growth, resiliency, and hope that run counter to the problem-saturated ones. New stories serve as an "anchor" for change, meaning that youth are better able to connect with their internal experiences, including feelings and sensory perceptions (Bertolino, 1999). By moving to an experiential level, the change may be more profound. To further assist youth in connecting with internal experiences, YCWs ask questions such as these:

- When you were able to (action), what did that feel like?
- How did you experience that change inside?
- How was that feeling similar or different than before?
- What does it feel like to know that others may also benefit from the changes you've made?

The Contributions of Others: Sharing Credit for Change

Although change involves the individual actions of youth, it can be particularly helpful to share the credit for it, especially with caregivers and families. Unlike attribution, sharing the credit involves focusing on relationships and acknowledging each person's contribution to improving overall situations. Sharing the credit serves several purposes. First, as you have learned, the quality of the client's (in this case, youth and families') participation in services is an important factor in outcome. When involved persons are left out of therapeutic processes, they can appear as noncompliant, resistant, and unmotivated. By recognizing the contributions of supportive others, YCWs are extending change to those who may be more peripherally involved but are nonetheless important to the stability of the youth's relationships and/or social networks.

A second purpose of sharing the credit is to use it as a countermeasure in situations where positive change has occurred but is being negated in some way. This is most often evidenced by caregiver statements such as, "It will never last"; "He's done that before"; or "You haven't seen the real (name) yet." These comments sometimes originate from caregivers or supportive others who do not feel as if they have made a valued or positive contribution to the improvement of the youth.

To better understand this idea, consider what a caregiver, such as a parent, might experience when change happens quickly in services. A parent gives her all to raise her son. Because her son gets into trouble she begins to feel her efforts were to no avail. So the mother seeks services for her son and he begins to turn things around. Although problem resolution is the goal, positive change can also raise feelings of self-blame ("I'm a bad parent"; "I clearly did a bad job") or inadequacy ("I obviously don't know what I'm doing"; "Anyone could do a better job than me"). Some caregivers or supportive others experience both feelings of being a failure for not being to fix problems and also invalidation when a stranger—a YCW, for example—is able to "fix" the situation.

Caregiver experiences of invalidation and feelings of failure can undermine services. The irony is that although family members are sometimes considered the cause of problems they do not always get credit for their contributions when things go better. By identifying the contributions of everyone who may be involved, YCWs counter negative statements that can minimize change and prove invalidating. There are several possibilities for sharing the credit for change. One way is to give others involved with services credit by saying:

- I wonder how you were able to instill the value of (specific value) in (name).
- Like you, (name) seems to hold the value of (specific value). I can't help thinking that he/she learned it from you.
- It seems to me that (name) has learned the value of (specific value) from you.

A second possibility is to evoke from those involved something that they feel contributed to the change process:

- How do you think your (relationship, parenting, etc.) has contributed to (name)'s ability to (action)?
- In what ways do you think you have been able to help (name) to stand up to adversity?
- In what ways do you think you were of assistance in helping (name) to stand up to (concern/problem) and get back on track?

A third way is to ask the youth what contributions others have made to his or her life and then to share the answers with others who are involved:

- What did you learn from (name) about how to overcome (concern/problem)?
- Who taught you the value of (specific value)?
- From whom did you learn about (action, thing)?

These questions do not create conflict in attributing change to the qualities and actions of individuals but offer "both/and" as opposed to "either/or." YCWs both attribute the major portion of significant change to youth and share the credit with those who have provided care and support. Doing so can neutralize each person's feelings that their efforts have been acknowledged but are valued negatively. As a result of sharing the credit for change, it is not uncommon for youth and supportive others to experience a new sense of togetherness or spirit of family.

Following the Ripples of Change

When identifying and amplifying improvement, it is important to keep in mind that a change in one area can lead to one or more changes in another. YCWs continue to scan for ways in which positive change may be creating a "ripple effect." Like a snowball traveling downhill, expanding as it gains speed and momentum or a domino starting a chain reaction of knocking over others, YCWs search for other changes in the lives of youth. Questions to assist with the ripples of change include:

- What else have you noticed that has changed?
- What else is different?
- How has(have) that(those) difference(s) been helpful to you?
- What difference has the change made with school/home life/friends/work, etc.?
- Who else has noticed these other changes?
- Who else has benefited from these changes?

Consistent with exploring changes that have occurred in relation to goals, YCWs clarify ambiguous responses to understand "what" is different and "how" those changes came about. In addition to recognizing the changes themselves, YCWs orient youth to other changes in their lives.

Although specific goals are identified from the outset of services, it is not uncommon to learn that secondary concerns or areas are affected and change in some way. Secondary changes suggest that although identified goals are the main focus, YCWs must remain on the lookout for ways to promote change in general. Doing so can indirectly lead to gains in meeting established goals. It is therefore crucial to ask youth about positive changes or benefits that may have occurred elsewhere in their lives and how those might relate to the concerns that led to services.

What Does it Mean? Revisiting Goals and Outcomes

When determining improvement, YCWs keep in mind that there are different ways to both gauge progress and its meaning. Throughout this book, we have focused on two different forms of corroborating improvement: Goals and outcomes. To restate, goals are clearly delineated, observable changes described through action talk. Outcomes refer to youth or supportive others' ratings of progress in the areas of individual, interpersonal, and social functioning. The meaning of goals and outcomes can vary depending on the youth and situation.

YCWs remain cognizant that those responsible for the start and end of service determine relative significance of positive change. The task of the YCW is to engage youth and supportive others in conversations to understand the meaning of change. With both goals and outcomes a central question is: How does the change that has occurred relate to the goals and outcome defined at the start of services? Further questions include: Have the concerns or problems been resolved? What else needs to happen for services to be considered successful/for goals to be met? To understand how change is situated in relationship to goals, the following questions can be helpful:

- What difference has the change made in your life?
- How are you benefiting from the change you've experienced?
- What will be different in the future as these changes continue to occur?
- In the future, what other changes do you think might occur that might not have otherwise come about?
- Who else might benefit from these changes? How?
- In the future, what will indicate to you that these changes are continuing to happen?
- How does the change that's happened relate to the goals that we set?

An outcomes focus differs from a goals focus by emphasizing the use of real-time data. The use of reliable and valid methods of measurement raises the bar of accountability for YFS organizations that claim to do "good work for good causes." When outcome improvement occurs, YCWs explore the meaning of that improvement through the questions listed and by reviewing the stability of progress over time. For example, Figure 7.7 reveals a youth who experienced improvement that has remained relatively stable between session 4 and 21—with no decreases of 4 or more points. When improvement seems to have maintained YCWs discuss possible options with youth and others involved. We will return to these options shortly.

Throughout this book, we have reviewed the benefits of monitoring both goals and outcomes. And yet, because not all YFS-based organizations will track both, let's review some concerns with evaluating progress exclusively on the basis of one or the other, beginning with goals.

A primary concern is that youth can meet goals without necessarily having an improved outcome. For example, a youth may report that she is meeting goals such as getting to school on time, completing her homework, and getting better grades. However, if the same youth does not report improvement on an outcome measure, further exploration is necessary. This is because the youth may reach concrete goals yet remains depressed or anxious or continue to have trouble in relationships with peers, and so on. If goals have been met but are inconsistent with outcome scores, a YCW might approach the youth by stating, "You've accomplished the goals you set out to achieve and yet you've expressed some _____ (summarize what has been indicated in the outcome measure) in the instrument you completed today. Please tell me about that."

The same can also occur when outcomes improve without goals being met. Because real-time data can provide snapshots of recent times, YCWs are reminded that single scores can indicate one-time fluctuations. Large changes in scores are likely to reflect situational changes (e.g., positive events, crises) that may not give an accurate depiction of youth's lives as a whole. YCWs serve youth best by comparing and contrasting scores over several sessions. Improvement, deterioration, or flattening of scores (i.e., very small changes over a span of multiple sessions) is likely to provide a more reliable picture.

Since both goals and outcomes can produce anomalies, using multiple sources of data while sticking to the 80/20 rule (i.e., focus on information that is most meaningful and essential to decision-making) is a best practice. In YFS, the duo of goals and outcomes provides a consistent way of evaluating improvement. At the same time, research makes it clear that if a choice has to be made in terms of what kind of data best indicate improvement an outcomes focus is considered far more reliable.

Preparing for Transitions: Youth Development in Context

A focus of YFS (see Chapter 2, Principle 4) is to help youth to grow, develop, and experience positive well-being. As aspect of growth is age-appropriate independence. For some youth, the path to independence will differ due to circumstances such as being in the custody of the state or moving from program to program throughout childhood and adolescence. For other youth (and their families) chronic situations and perpetuating cycles will translate to services over a lifespan. No matter the situation, YCWs maintain an unwavering commitment to preparing youth for greater self-sufficiency.

An emphasis on independence is reflected in the principles of positive youth development (PYD) described in Chapter 5. In sum, a focus on PYD involves promoting and fostering characteristics of youth such as rewarding bonds with supportive others, self-determination, positive identity, a future focus, and prosocial norms that reflect clear, healthy, responsible beliefs and behavior. The addition of PYD to goals and outcomes forms an excellent trio of markers for evaluating overall improvement in YFS. And yet, improvement is not an end point in YFS but rather an indicator of current functioning as compared to the start of services. Therefore transition is a focus from the outset of services. We plan for the end at the beginning.

Transition will vary based on factors such as the current type of service, program, and improvement achieved. Options can include: decreasing service dosage or type of service, establishing new goals—particularly if residential or long-term (foster care) services, and/or transition from services, also known as termination. An example of adjusting the service dosage would be by lengthening the time between meetings, which can help with managing "bumps in the road." Another way to transition youth is through "check-ups"—having youth return periodically for meetings (i.e., a few weeks to months) (Bertolino, 2010). Check-ups can keep youth with more severe or chronic concerns to stay on track and maintain their improvement.

New goals can be developed if needed, particularly in long-term programs. There are, however, several points for YCWs to be mindful of when it comes to forming new goals. First, in any service there is a maximum benefit that can be achieved. Keeping youth in services too long can lead to regression. The issue is time. As long as youth are benefitting services ought to continue. When the benefit of services appears to have leveled out and mutually agreeable new goals are not developed relatively quickly the risk the youth will deteriorate increases substantially. As a parallel, consider that physicians do not continue to treat patients for problems that have been resolved. They conclude services and suggest that patients return if there is a reoccurrence of the same problem or if they should experience a new concern.

A further indicator that youth may have reached the maximum benefit of services is when discussion about new concerns is characterized by vague problem descriptions. For example, a youth may have achieved a goal of improving her social relationships by making more friends. This may be supported by improved outcome scores that move her into the nonclinical range and are both clinically significant and reliable. A caregiver, however, reports that there is "something else" that needs to be worked on. The YCW, youth, and caregiver talk about the caregiver's concerns, yet despite concerted efforts and the use of action talk no specific concern is identified. As discussed, if a new goal is not negotiated in a reasonable amount of time youth may regress; however, there is also a risk of becoming dependent on YCWs or other program staff. One way to identify dependence is by referring back to outcome measurement. A combination of high alliance scores (i.e., the youth's rating of the relationship with the YCW on the SRS/CSRS is consistently 36 or above) without any discernible change in outcome (i.e., scores that have become flat on the ORS) often indicates dependence.

An additional area to re-evaluate in the context of improvement is the purpose of YFS. As we have learned, YFS is characterized by services that help youth and families with a wide range of concerns. And an integral aspect of successful services is support. It is clear that youth who have stable support systems have better outcomes. Herein is the conundrum. Support is not a service—it is an adjunct to services. As social beings, we all need support in life. Because youth are a vulnerable population they often need more support. As discussed earlier in the section on wraparound, a task of the YCW is to work with youth and others who may be involved to both utilize existing and develop new external resources and systems of support.

Apprehension to Transition

Some youth and/or families may express apprehension about transitions, particularly when it involves ending services altogether. These concerns can be perpetuated by the difficulties associated with accessing services to begin with. Long waitlists, limited access to services, and issues related to funding are but a few of the challenges families face. Other families will have more concerns with the prospect of setbacks. They will describe worries about ending services and experiencing a subsequent reoccurrence of the problem. Later in this chapter, the topic of setbacks will be explored. In terms of access to services, it can be helpful for agencies to practice an "open door" philosophy (Bertolino, 2010). An open door approach parallels the general practitioner (GP) model employed by physicians. The idea is that families are encouraged to make contact when they first have concerns, instead of allowing those problems to exacerbate. The response of YFS agencies is to reduce barriers to re-entry by having personnel and time allotted to see those requesting services. Doing so can prevent pain and suffering from problems worsening, reduce the intensity and length of services, and the cost of those services.

A theme throughout this book has been the importance of accountability in YFS. It is essential that we demonstrate the benefit of services and exercise stewardship with program and community resources. Nowhere is the issue of accountability more significant than with transitions. Discussions regarding accountability underscore the point that for most youth services are a pit-stop in the road of life. With exception, services are a vehicle for traveling through the rocky terrain faced by many youth and families. To this end, our aim is to provide services that target a concern or series of concerns without losing sight of the importance of youth growing up in environments that are least restrictive and as "real world" as possible.

Seeding Future Change

Part of helping youth to transition from one service to another or out of services altogether is to engage in conversations about potential setbacks and hurdles. These kinds of conversation are preventative because they involve the use of strengths and resources as a buffer to challenges that may arise as youth continue to grow. Next we explore a few ways to seed future change.

Setbacks as Opportunities

Adolescence is characterized by developmental challenges and unexpected hurdles. Progress is rarely, if ever, linear. Youth will make progress then face a new challenge. And although they may raise frustration, setbacks or lapses are to be expected and seldom indicate a loss of gains and full-blown return to old patterns. YCWs help to prepare youth and supportive others involved for *potential* future obstacles by openly discussing them. We are not suggesting that there will be setbacks, only that setbacks are a part of life and do not need to knock youth off track. By taking stock of progress made to date and having a realistic view of the future, youth will have a solid foundation for handling whatever comes their way.

One way to prepare youth for the future is by noting their "muscles of resilience"—strategies that they have used in the past to minimize the impact of setbacks and get back on track (Bertolino, 2003). This can be done by using questions offered previously (see Chapters 5 and 6) to learn how youth and others kept problems from getting worse. For example, a YCW might ask, "When you had trouble with _____ what did you do to keep things from getting worse?" Central to exploring this kind of resilience is to help youth to identify *what* they did and *how* they did it as opposed to *why*. The following questions can assist with the identification of small differences that demonstrate how youth managed those setbacks to any degree:

- Given what you've been through, how did you manage to (continue to go to school or work, make it to this appointment, etc.)?
- When you hit that rough spot, what kept things from going downhill any further?
- How did you manage to bring things to a halt?
- What did you do?
- What helped you to bring it to an end?
- Who else helped you?
- How were those persons helpful to you?
- How might they be helpful to you in the future?
- What signs were present that things were beginning to slip?
- What can you do differently in the future if things begin to slip?
- What have you learned about this setback?
- What will you do differently in the future as a result of this knowledge?
- What do you suppose _____ (name) would say that you will do differently as a result of this knowledge?
- What do you suppose will be different as a result of your doing things differently?
- What might be some signs that you were getting back on track?
- How will you know when you're out of the woods with this setback?

Setbacks are also opportunities to learn more about youth's lives in the real world. Specifically, we want to know how youth coped differently in the past as well as what has and has not worked. As discussed, although setbacks can be serious, in nearly every situation at least some gains have been retained. And, in most cases, setbacks are more similar to a brief rain shower than a hurricane. The following example illustrates this point.

Case Example 7.8

Fourteen-year-old Zoe and her mother had been working with a case manager after Zoe had been suspended from school for fighting. Zoe had returned to school after three weeks and after two months of working together it appeared she was ready to transition out of services. Once argumentative with the case manager and her mother and refusing to talk about her troubles at school and conflicts with her peers, Zoe had opened up. She described her hopes for the remainder of the school year and how she would use her new "calming" skills when called names by others or taunted to fight. Her calming skills involved humming her favorite song to herself and smiling as she walked away. Zoe's new skills had even caught the attention of teachers who described the youth's change as both "inspiring" and a "lesson to other students."

As the case manager, Zoe, and her mother talked about the transition from services, which involved her checking in with her school counselor twice a week, Zoe declined to talk. She sat silently, with a sense of sadness about her. Then she began to cry. After a short while, Zoe began to talk. She said there had been a "problem" at school and that "things are back to the way they were." The following conversation ensued:

Case manager: It's okay to cry.

Zoe (Sobbing): I did something bad.

Case manager: Tell me about that.

Zoe: Things are now backwards.

Case manager: It seems to you like things have gone backwards . . . .

Zoe: I was doing good and now I'm back to where I was.

Case manager: Can you tell me what has given you the idea that you're back where you were?

Zoe: Yesterday I was walking down the hall and this girl, Sharita, starting talking stuff. I didn't listen to her. I walked away and hummed. But she kept following me.

Case manager: You did what we talked about and she kept following you . . .

Zoe: Yeah. I told her to knock it off but she didn't listen. And there weren't any teachers around. I didn't know what to do so I walked as fast as I could. She jumped in front of me and blocked my way out of the hallway.

Case manager: I'm sorry that happened to you. What happened next?

Zoe (Intense sobbing): I just pushed right through her and she fell against the locker. Then I ran to my class. I'm sorry. I didn't mean to push her that hard.

Case manager: Zoe, it sounds to me like you did what you could to get away from her. Is there anything you could have done differently?

Zoe (Wiping her tears): I needed a teacher but there was no one to help me. I was scared and I didn't know what else to do.

Case manager (To Zoe's mom): Is this the first time you've heard of this or did you already know?

Mother (Appearing surprised): I had no idea.

Case manager: What do you think about calling the school?

Mother: Absolutely. I want to call right now.

Case manager: You did the right thing, Zoe. And from what I understand the situation could have been much worse. While your mom calls the school, please tell me a little about how you kept things from getting worse.

Zoe: But I pushed her to get out of the hallway.

Case manager: Yes, you did. She was blocking your way out, right?

Zoe: She was.

Case manager: It is not okay for someone to block an exit. You had a right to exit that hallway. But it could have turned into a very bad situation. It could have turned into a fight with Sharita. What did you do to keep things from getting worse?

Zoe: I just did what I had to do to get away. I didn't want to fight. So I guess I ran to my class so it didn't get worse.

Case manager: That was wise. What made you think to do that?

Zoe: I remembered we talked about walking fast if I needed to. I tried that but she jumped in front of me so when I got past her I ran. We're not supposed to run in the halls but I had to get away from her.

Case manager: It's okay that you ran. This was a special circumstance.

Mother (Interrupting): I just talked to the assistant principal. He knew about the incident in the school hallway. They have it on video because it was a main hallway and they all have security cameras.

Case manager: What did he say?

Mother: He said Zoe was walking down the hallway when Sharita cut her off and wouldn't let her get by. Sharita blocked Zoe from getting out of the hallway. Then Zoe pushed through Sharita and ran. The assistant principal is on the phone now and wants to talk to Zoe.

Case manager: Can we put him on the speaker phone? Would you both be okay with that?

(Zoe and her mother nod in the affirmative.)

Mother (To assistant principal on phone): I would like to put you on speaker so we can all hear you. Is that okay?

(The assistant principal agrees.)

Mother (To assistant principal): Okay, we are all ready.

Assistant principal: Zoe, I have seen the video. I want you to know that you did the right thing. You had the right to leave that hallway and no one should ever prevent that. I am very sorry we did not have any school personnel there to assist you. We will from now on. And the student who blocked you will not cause you any more trouble.

Zoe: I didn't mean to push her. I didn't know what else to do, cause I was scared.

Assistant principal: In this case, you had limited options. You could have yelled for help. But pushing your way through was okay in this situation. You and I have talked before and I know you know the difference between this situation and just being violent for the sake of being violent. Right?

Zoe: Yes, I do.

Assistant principal: And from what I understand you have put violence behind you. Is that right too?

Zoe: That is totally right.

Assistant principal: Okay then. You come see me if you need anything, okay? I'm looking forward to hearing more great things about you. Goodbye.

Zoe (Smiling): Thank you. Goodbye.

Case manager: That was amazing, Zoe. What do you think about what your assistant principal had to say?

Zoe: He was nice. I'm glad I'm not in trouble. I thought he would be mad at me and I might get suspended again.

Case manager: It was a difficult situation that you handled to the best of your ability. And you did not turn a difficult situation into a terrible one. A few months ago you might have acted differently. But not anymore. You have taken your life back from fighting.

Zoe: Yeah, I don't fight anymore.

Case manager: Right. And let's say you have to deal with another student or kid who gives you a hard time and maybe doesn't block your way out of a hall, but angers you, what will you do?

Zoe: I will hum my song and walk away. Just like I tried to do with Sharita.

Case manager: What else?

Zoe: I will do like Mr. Stallings (assistant principal) said—yell for help.

Case manager: Those are excellent ideas. And maybe your mom can help you to prepare for other situations in the future if you are going to do something new.

Mother: Right. We have already been talking about Zoe going to the movies with friends this coming weekend and what she can do to protect herself.

Zoe: Uh huh.

Case manager: That's good planning. And mom, what do you think of how Zoe handled the situation at school?

Mother: I am proud of her. She did the best she could in that situation. What I'm most proud of is that she now knows the difference between protecting herself and purposely getting in fights. I really believe fighting is now a thing of the past.

Zoe: It is.

Case manager: Okay. So we will meet once more next week but it seems like things are right where they should be.

Zoe: Me too.

A task of the YCW is to remain calm and patient when exploring setbacks with youth. Acknowledgment that setbacks are part of life often adds perspective which can neutralize disappointment that youth or others may express. In contrast, when single setbacks become patterns of (i.e., two or more instances) YCWs become more explicit in the search for triggers or precursors to those setbacks. Detailed information can help to determine what methods are most applicable in preventing future setbacks.

YCWs also inquire about supportive others who may have also played a key role in helping youth to manage setbacks. Particularly important is *how* others provided support to youth. And while we share credit, as discussed earlier in this chapter, we want youth to attribute the majority of the preventative efforts to their actions.

A final consideration with setbacks relates to outcome measurement. By monitoring outcome scores patterns sometimes become evident, bringing forth some predictive value. The example that follows illustrates this point.

Case Example 7.9

I supervised a case manager who worked with an 18-year-old who had see-saw scores on her ORS. One meeting the scores would be high, the next they would drop significantly. They would then rise again and this pattern revealed itself over the course of about 10 weeks. It seemed she would make progress only to have a setback shortly thereafter. After one particularly rough stretch, the case manager asked the youth if she noticed anything about her ORS scores over the time they had met together. The youth said, "Wow. I never noticed how up and down they were. All those low scores are times my boyfriend has been off work and we hung out more. I love him, but, I mean, it's stressful. He says mean stuff to me and makes me nervous." The case manager followed up, "Does that mean the higher scores were around times when he was working more and you spent more time apart?" The young woman confirmed this and said, "It's so tense around him. The rest of my life is going much better now but I don't know what to do when it comes to him." The case manager asked her if she wanted to work on a plan to address her relationship." The young woman answered, "No. I really just want to get away from him. He only brings me down and I'm sick of it." The pair then proceeded to develop a plan for how the young woman would separate from the boyfriend, which included a safety plan given her fear of him.

Outcome scores can also be helpful with youth who are involved with services sporadically (i.e., their periodical attendance is mixed with cancellations and "no shows") and then call in crisis. Exploration of their scores often reveals distinct patterns that may be helpful in predicting more challenging or stressful times and an increased risk of setbacks. Services become more preventative when possible "trouble zones" are identified and plans are created by which youth use their strengths and resources to stay on track.

Potential Hurdles and Future Change

As youth transition from services, hurdles or perceived barriers may pose a threat to maintaining the changes they have made. At other times, YCWs may initiate conversations about possible areas of future concern. We are careful to not state that that youth will hit roadblocks but rather on the road of life they will likely face some hardships. By discussing possible future hurdles, YCWs maintain a focus on prevention and normalize apprehension and fear about what may come down the road. They also increase the likelihood that current changes will continue in the future.

To talk with youth about conversations regarding possible future hurdles or perceived barriers, we ask, "Is there anything that might come up between now and the next time we meet that might threaten the changes you've made?" or "Can you think of anything that might come up over the next (few weeks/months) that could present a challenge for you in staying on track?" If a youth responds "yes," we then explore, in detail, what those challenges might be and how the youth and supportive others will meet them. The following questions help to identify and address perceived hurdles or barriers:

- What have you learned about your ability to stand up to _____?
- What might indicate to you that the problem was attempting to resurface?
- What might be the first sign?
- What will you do differently in the future if you face the same or a similar problem?
- How can what you've learned help you in solving future problems?
- If you feel yourself slipping, what's one thing that can stop that slipping and get you back heading in the direction you prefer?
- What's one thing that can bring a slippage under control or to an end?

YCWs can also create scenarios that would require a youth to use new understandings and skills in the future. For example, a YCW might say, "If you were to encounter a new concern such as _____ and it caught you off guard, how might you use what you've learned to keep it from overwhelming you?"

Case Example 7.10

A 16-year-old boy was in services for fighting at school. During his last session, he was asked if he could think of anything that might throw him off track. When he said he couldn't, he was asked specifically how he might handle things in the future if someone were to start something with him. He immediately said, "That already happened. A kid threatened to pop my bike tire. I stood back and told him to go ahead. I wasn't going to fight him. The kid walked away."

It is not possible neither is it necessary to cover every situation that could derail a youth. Our aim is to remind youth to use what they have learned more deliberately in the future. In the same vein is a focus on future change in general. Effective services prepare youth for coping with life beyond the concerns that led to services. By asking questions that orient youth toward future change and progress, they often become more resilient to everyday problems. It is as if their psychological and relational immune systems are less likely to be compromised because they are focusing on health, well-being, and the future. To invite clients into conversations to explore how change can be extended into the future, YCWs ask:

- How can you put your new understandings to work in the future?
- What have you been doing that you will continue to do once services has ended and in the future?
- How will you continue to solidify and build on the changes that you've made?
- What will you be doing differently that you might not have otherwise been able to do?
- After you leave here, what will you do to keep things going in the direction you prefer?
- What else will you do?

A vision of the future can have an effect on how youth act in the present and view the past. Instead of focusing on how they are held captive by past events, youth and persons involved in the lives of youth focus on where they are going and the kind of futures they want for themselves. Further, when youth remain connected with their strengths and resources they are less vulnerable and more resilient to life changes, developmental challenges, and spontaneous threats.

The End is the Beginning

For some youth it will be important to mark transitions from services with some form of transition or celebratory ritual. These rituals are rites of passage that signify new beginnings, helping youth to move from one role or developmental phase to another. They can be particularly helpful in signifying the achievement of goals and in accentuating changes youth have made. Context is the determinant in how and to what degree such rituals are used. For example, in residential facilities, transition/celebratory rituals are commonly used to symbolize the mastery of skills or movement from one program level to another. It is especially important to engage youth in conversations to determine whether and what kinds of ritual would be meaningful for them. To do this we might say to youth, "Sometimes it's fun to celebrate changes. Is there anything that we might do here to put an exclamation point on the changes you've made or punctuate the work you've completed and your transition from here?" There will be youth who will want to move forward without any symbolic event, preferring that their transitions be subtle. Others will request things such as exchanging cards or sharing stories. The point is to ask.

As services draw to a close YCWs use discharge plans or summaries to capture the changes made to that point in time. As with service plans or assessments, discharges can include information required for funding purposes and/or that which is consistent with the program philosophy (i.e., strengths of a youth or gains he or she has made, goals accomplished, etc.). Another point of inclusion is progress made as indicated through outcome measurement. That is, a discharge form might list initial and ending ORS/CORS scores. Appendix B includes an example of a discharge summary.

A final consideration is to continue to view change on a developmental continuum. As youth move from one form of services to another or out of services altogether we are reminded that problems may reoccur and/or that they may return for "check-ups" at a later time. As discussed previously, services should accommodate the needs of youth and families, allowing for re-entry with minimal hurdles. Doing so can contribute to more sustained well-being while simultaneously reducing stress on youth and families along with future health, mental health, and social services expenditures. Because youth experience different problems at different times in childhood and adolescence, it is necessary that systems of care be responsive and flexible.

eight
Better: Achieving Excellence in Youth and Family Services

Whoever destroys a single life destroys the entire world.
Whoever saves a single life saves the world entire.

—Talmud

Throughout this book, stories from both in and outside of YFS have served as illustrations for unique ideas and new perspectives. The purpose of these illustrations is to provide examples of excellence that serve as a guide to the development of best practices in YFS. Because success in YFS is reliant on openness to that which is new and willingness to embrace that which will strengthen, one of the ways YCWs can promote current and future generations of excellence is through ongoing, purposeful study of fields and disciplines not typically considered reference points for YFS. In this final chapter, we continue the pursuit of excellence as we delve into training and supervision. In each of the aforementioned areas, we address the question: How do we create and sustain excellence?

Born That Way? The Myth of Talent

Consider that Wolfgang Amadeus Mozart wrote his first composition at the age of five and symphony by the age of eight. In all, he wrote over 600 pieces of music, including 41 symphonies during his short life of 35 years. Pablo Picasso made over 20,000 paintings in his lifetime and created a new type of art called "cubism," comprised of different overlapping shapes. Hockey player Wayne Gretzky holds 61 National Hockey League records including most all-time goals, assists, and points.

Many of his records are considered unbreakable. The Beatles, disbanding in 1970 after just seven years together, remain the top selling musical group of all time with estimates of having sold over 1,000,000,000 discs and tapes worldwide. And Bill Gates, well, his accomplishments are, of course, part of everyday life. These are just a few of the remarkable achievements of people considered by many as gifted and perhaps even geniuses.

Unbelievable abilities, right? It's hard to look at the lives of such people and not think, "They're naturals." But to view such persons—and countless others not listed here—in a way that suggests they were born with exceptional abilities and skills, would be to overlook the very heart of what led to their success. This point also rings true with YCWs and behavioral health professionals who seem to be better at their jobs and more importantly, have better outcomes than the rest. We find ourselves saying, "She is so gifted. I'll never be that good." According to research the idea of talent has been greatly exaggerated when it comes to success. Although there may be at some point, there exists no evidence to support the theory that genetics account for people's abilities. Widely regarded as the world's leading "expert on expertise," researcher K. Anders Ericsson and colleagues have studied the likes of musicians, chess players, and athletes, to name a few, only to find a distinct lack of "naturals" (Ericsson et al., 2006). Instead, they identified variables that serve as a roadmap for how excellence develops over time. And this roadmap provides direction for YCWs and those who work in YFS to improve their practice.

Getting Better all the Time: Pursuing Excellence in Youth Care Work

If performance is not based on natural ability and talent, then how do people become the best at what they do? More importantly, how can YCWs use these ideas to improve their practice? Let's first consider that very word, "practice." Research makes it clear that practice based on specific principles helps to improve skill and develop excellence. It is both *what* and *how* we practice that makes a difference in performance. Before we learn about principles for improving practice let's consider an important variable shared among all the very successful people listed earlier. At some point, each made a deep commitment, most but not all at a relatively early age, to put in the time and effort necessary to get better.

Top performers accept that commitment and passion are accompanied by failure. Mozart may have played and wrote music at a very young age but the consensus is that he did not produce his first masterwork (N. 9, K. 271) until the age of 21—which of course, is still remarkable, but nonetheless relative to his years of practice (Howe, 1999). Bill Gates spent hours and hours building computers and developing software that did not see the light of day. Even Einstein and Edison had far more failures than successes. They accepted the probability of failure as part and parcel to success. We can follow suit through what is known as "error-centric" learning, in which development occurs when small errors in the application of knowledge and skills are identified thereby allowing remedial action to be taken. Rather than focusing energy on the skills already mastered, energy is on areas less developed. Only by decreasing these "deficits" can performance rise above average (Ericsson et al., 2006). Maintaining an error-centric focus, and developing and implementing "deliberate practice" strategies, which will be discussed later in this chapter, to improve areas of weak performance can improve effectiveness. The idea of focusing on deficits may appear counter to a strengths-based philosophy but is not. Rather attention is placed on the perseverance and commitment of learners to build further skills and capacities to better themselves and in the case of YCWs, the lives of others.

There are no shortcuts to excellence. Putting in the work is part of a process of learning and developing. By the time the world had heard the Beatles they had played hundreds of gigs (which translated to thousands of hours) in clubs throughout Europe. They played the same songs (a mixture of original tunes and covers of other artists) over and over, sometimes multiple times a night in venues with poor acoustics, often unable to hear themselves or their band mates. Central to the group's development was repetition in "real-world" situations. It's one thing to practice in settings where you can stop and start again and there is no added pressure. It's another to practice in the type of climate that more closely resembles that in which the skill will likely be used.

The amount of practice time also matters. Ericsson and colleagues have estimated that it takes about 10,000 hours (about 10 years) to achieve the kind of expertise shown by people such as *international chess champions and Olympic athletes* (Ericsson, Krampe, & Tesch-Romer, 1993). Pop culture writers have taken the "10,000 hour rule" as a generality in an effort to challenge the notion of talent and unpack the mystery of success (see Colvin, 2008; Gladwell, 2008; Syed, 2010). This has sparked a debate with dissenters arguing that 10,000 hours in and of itself does not make one an expert—once again, missing the point.

There are two issues here. First, Ericsson and colleagues do not say that all domains of expertise require the same amount of deliberate practice. Many domains will require fewer hours (5,000–6,000 in many cases) to achieve what is considered expertise for that specific skill set. Second, not just any kind of practice counts when it comes developing ability. Ericsson is fond of saying: "Just because you've been walking for 50 years doesn't mean you're good at it." Development of expertise requires focused, deliberate practice. Said differently, the amount of time invested on improving ability is dependent on both what is practiced and more importantly, how practice occurs. Bruce Lee once said, "I fear not the man who has practiced 10,000 kicks once, but I fear the man who had practiced one kick 10,000 times." Practice dedicated to intensive honing of skills is what seems to matter. Let's now explore how practice can improve performance specific to YFS.

Five Steps to Improve Skills in YFS

In this section, we explore a process for helping YCWs and other YFS professionals to improve both skills and effectiveness. These steps are meant to serve as a guide for *how* to practice and learn rather than instructions. Before exploring these steps we consider *what* skills are most important for YCWs to develop. A starting point is the five principles of strengths-based youth care work outlined in Chapter 2. Each principle has a key competency and a series of key tasks. These tasks are discussed further throughout the chapters in this book. It is recommended that the process outlined next is used to develop skill with these key tasks.

Cultivate a Mindset

In Chapter 1, we learned about factors such as personal philosophy and positive deviance, both of which reflect the personal stance of those who have elected to work in YFS. Passion is an incredible motivator. It fuels focus, resilience, and perseverance. If your mindset does not evolve around doing what you really love it will be difficult to fully apply yourself. A starting point is to discuss in pairs or as a group, the passion and drive each person has to do their very best as a YCW or other working in YFS. It can be helpful to make a list of the things that feed that passion and discuss how those things can remain a driving force when difficulty is encountered.

Equally essential is to carry that attitude into practice. "It's not that I'm so smart," Einstein once said, "It's just that I stay with problems longer." Practice without commitment to learning and getting better will certainly reduce its benefits. Beginning practice with a positive outlook also cultivates a "growth" mindset in which one is both not threatened by failure and sees failure as opportunity. At this juncture, it can be helpful to talk about expectations for improving and the benefits of entering into new learning experiences with both an open mind and commitment to doing what it takes to improve beyond one's current level of ability.

Establish a Baseline Performance Level

Whether in sports, music, medicine, or behavioral health, top performers are able to accurately assess their knowledge, skills, and effectiveness. What's more, the best are consistently comparing their current performance to: (1) their own personal best; (2) the performance of others; and (3) a known national standard or benchmark (Ericsson et al., 2006).

In YFS, there are numerous ways to establish benchmarks. One way would be to focus on individual skills YCWs should be adept at. For example, research has demonstrated that the most effective behavioral health practitioners are able to accommodate the different relational styles of clients. That is, they vary their approach depending on how the client presents and his or her relational preferences. To create a baseline, YCWs could be asked to role play brief interactions in which the persons(s) playing the youth or others varies the relational style (i.e., being passive, or aggressive, or dependent, etc.). Supervisors or colleagues would rate the performance of the YCW thereby creating a baseline to improve from. Alliance measures such as the SRS (as detailed in Chapter 4) can also be used as a way of establishing baselines. A caveat here is that the raters must agree on what is valued in terms of YCW skills and be able to identify those skills. To reiterate a point from Chapter 2, the alliance is an excellent place to start in terms of developing ability because there are over 1,100 studies on it. Further, the client's rating of the alliance is the best process-related predictor of outcome. Chapter 2 details the four empirically established components of the alliance that can be used for areas of skill development.

Because YFS often involve teams some benchmarks will apply to group performance as opposed to individual performance. Therefore, another way to establish benchmarks relates to tracking the overall progress of youth in programs. For example, using an outcome measure such as the ORS (see Chapter 4), a baseline rate of improvement can be created by collecting data on youth that receive services through the program. Programs could then compare data over specific periods of time, other similar programs, or national norms. As a further example, my agency (Youth In Need, Inc. www.youthinneed.org) compares data from outclient counseling, school-based counseling, emergency shelter, transitional living, and independent living programs every six months.

Engage in Deliberate, Reflective Practice

The next step is to teach a particular skill and have the YCW or other use deliberate, reflective practice to both learn and improve on that skill. Deliberate practice is different than typical practice. It entails considerable, specific, and sustained efforts to do something you can't do well—or even at all. Research shows that it is only by working at what you can't do that you turn into the expert you want to become. Deliberate practice involves two kinds of learning: Improving the skills you already have and extending the reach and range of your skills. The enormous concentration required to undertake these twin tasks limits the amount of time one can spend doing them. It is interesting to note that across a wide range of experts, including athletes, novelists, and musicians, very few appear to be able to engage in more than a few hours of high concentration and deliberate practice at a time. In fact, most expert teachers and scientists set aside only a couple of hours a day, typically in the morning, for their most demanding mental activities, such as writing about new ideas. While this may seem like a relatively small investment, it is two hours a day more than most executives and managers devote to building their skills, since the majority of their time is consumed by meetings and day-to-day concerns.

Because YCWs spend much of their time with youth, focusing on day-to-day tasks, deliberate practice has to be planned for and factored into daily activities such as meetings, trainings, and "down time," when full attention can be given to practicing. Mornings are often a good time because we have more energy and fewer distractions. To determine a plan we ask: When is the best time to reflect? When am I best focused and for how long? Define the time and place specifically. Be consistent and persistent about the habit; consistency is key (Ericsson et al., 2006).

What constitutes deliberate practice differs across domains of expertise (i.e., musicians practice differently than athletes). All forms, however, include the highly focused, repetitious practice of skills focused on improving the parts of performance that are not yet mastered. Over time, deliberate practice results in the development of what researchers refer to as, "deep domain-specific knowledge." The best not only know more, but when, where, how, and with whom to use what they know.

To better understand deliberate practice, using the first example in Step 2, YCWs would be introduced to and practice skills—one at a time—as to how to accommodate the expectations and preferences of youth and others involved such as those outlined as collaboration keys in Chapter 3. As with Step 2, YCWs would then role play brief interactions in which the persons(s) playing the youth or others vary the ways of relating (i.e., passive, aggressive, dependent, etc.). Each skill needs to be broken down into sharply defined elements. The focus is then entirely on that one minor element—over and over. The focus must be narrow—be it asking great questions; establishing rigorous peer feedback, and so on—otherwise we will not be able to make exacting improvements. Following practice there should be pause, with sufficient time to stop and reflect.

Most deliberate practice occurs outside of formal training. So much so that it is sometimes difficult to notice subtle differences in how YCWs do their jobs. In fact, two YCWs could appear to be doing similar things and simultaneously be doing very different things in the eyes of youth. This is why alliance ratings are crucial. They tease out those differences. A more reliable gauge of identifying skill development is by examining what YCWs do *before* their interactions with youth and how they reflect *afterward*. A specific example would be to explore the differences in how YCWs think about situations that did not go well and what could be done differently in the future. A final consideration here is that deliberate practice can include reading journal articles, reading books, studying video, and observing colleagues (other YCWs).

Obtain Ongoing Feedback/Coaching

Without feedback our attempts to improve are suspect to "conformation bias," we believe what we want to believe. And, in some cases, subpar performance is reinforced because there is not enough feedback for a person to accurately reflect on the performance itself. The Beatles ultimately stopped playing live when they could no longer evolve as a band outside the studio. Onstage sound-monitoring systems were woefully inadequate and the band continued to struggle to hear what they were playing. Although the young band's performances in live settings had benefits in terms of gaining experience through repetition in a "natural" environment, the Fab Four reached a point in which they could not improve further without hearing the nuances of their playing. The studio, by way of contrast, provided an opportunity to listen very discretely break down each track into smaller segments, reflect on their individual and collective performances, and then work to improve on them. In short, the Beatles had feedback on their performances in the studio and could work to improve.

Because the bulk of learning occurs during reflection, we want to concentrate on methods of documenting experience and engaging in processes that are reflective in nature. One way to do this is for YCWs to keep journals or notebooks that include reflections. Documenting reflections should occur within close proximity of the interaction, role play, or event. This allows for more details to be recalled. YCWs will want to record their own.

A second way for obtaining feedback in YFS is via real-time measurement, which provides both outcome and alliance feedback directly from clients. As discussed throughout this book, this type of feedback creates an opportunity to respond. It is also part of "error-centric" learning.

A third way to gain feedback is through supervision or coaching. Coach John Wooden used to refer to "checking for understanding." He wanted players to continuously seek feedback as they went through basketball drills. Similarly, continuing with the first example in Step 2, observers of role plays can provide ongoing feedback to YCWs about their performance. The purpose of this form of feedback is to push YCWs just beyond their current realm of reliable performance.

As a supervisor or coach, we want to concentrate on providing simple and precise feedback; when it comes to early learners, the simpler the better. Too much feedback, too continuously can create cognitive overload, increase anxiety, and interfere with learning. As expertise develops the feedback should also evolve, meaning that persons providing feedback need to have evolved with their own expertise. For advanced learners, feedback that is too fundamental can actually inhibit development.

A fourth and final way to obtain feedback is through communities of practice. Researcher Etienne Wegner refers to "communities of practice" as "Groups of people who share a concern or a passion for something they do, and who interact regularly to learn how to do it better" (Bertolino, 2011, p. 35). Communities of practice have a common interest, work together, and share information and resources. More than a group of friends or network of personal connections, a community of practice is formed, often spontaneously and informally, by practitioners of a "domain of interest"—a profession, a hobby, a field of expertise, an art or craft, even a common concern. Such communities, Wenger writes, "Engage in a process of collective learning in a shared domain of human endeavor: a tribe learning to survive, a band of artists seeking new forms of expression, a group of engineers working on similar problems, a clique of pupils defining their identity in the school," or, he might have added, the members of a community agency working with youth and families (pp. 35–36). The central insight to this intuitively simple idea is that learning is primarily a social phenomenon, rather than—as we so often think—a purely individualistic activity. In fact, as we were discovering at YIN, people learn, acquire competency and expertise, gain genuine knowledge and understanding through practice in community (Bertolino, 2011).

By creating a community of practice around the common theme of a strengths-based philosophy, we were trying to capture the elusive passion and deep commitment of each individual at YIN and funnel this energy into a collective effort to achieve excellence as an agency. We believed we could do this by shifting the prevailing culture from one reflecting division, mistrust, and resentment to one reflecting a collective vision, a shared body of knowledge, a general pattern of open, undefensive communication, and a common purpose: To make this the best agency possible.

The predominant process here is to share, reflect and repeat . . . and repeat . . . To get better at anything takes a grinding determination for betterment. Some people simply don't care enough to face the difficulty—this is true in all professions and walks of life. Repetition is dull. It is why so few people become true experts. The good news is that our end goal is not expertise. As we learned in Chapter 4 from surgeon Atul Gawande, we simply need to be better than average.

Rest and Ritualize

Learning can be a strenuous process. It is imperative to take regular renewal breaks. Relaxing after intense effort not only provides an opportunity to rejuvenate, but also to metabolize and embed learning. It's also during rest that the right hemisphere becomes more dominant, which can lead to creative breakthroughs.

Finally, try to ritualize practice. The best way to insure you will take on difficult tasks is to build rituals—specific, inviolable times at which you do them, so that over time you do them without having to squander energy thinking about them.

To make significant improvements YCWs, like any professional, must be willing to devote more time than could be realistically allocated within work hours. This is where passion and dedication become even more important. To keep on task we must maintain our sense of purpose and passion.

"Better" than Average: Staff Development Planning

In YFS, an ideal plan for training, learning, and staff development will involve a simple, straightforward process that includes (1) measuring outcomes and determine overall rates of effectiveness; (2) identifying areas of practice just beyond a YCW or other professional's current level of proficiency; (3) developing and executing a plan of deliberate practice; (4) obtaining coaching, instruction, training; (5) measuring the impact of the plan and training on performance; and (6) adjust the plan and steps.

To move beyond the realm of reliable performance, the best engage in forethought—setting specific goals for improvement and developing a plan to reach those goals (Bertolino et al., 2013). Therefore, the TAR framework—think, act, and reflect—can be also useful here. In the act phase, YCWs track their performance by monitoring on an ongoing basis whether they used each of the steps or strategies outlined in the thinking phase and the quality with which each step was executed. The sheer volume of detail gathered in assessing performance distinguishes exceptional from average performers. During the reflection phase, YCWs review the details of their performance, identifying specific actions and alternative strategies for reaching their objectives or goals. Where unsuccessful learners paint in broad strokes, attributing failure to external factors and uncontrollable events, the best know exactly what they do, most often citing controllable factors.

Pursuing Growth as YCWs

Achieving excellence in YFS is hard work. It is also doable. Again, our end goal is not to reach expert status but to continue to get better. In Chapter 2, we learned about essential characteristics of YCWs. These characteristics serve as a foundation on which to build. To improve beyond these characteristics YCWs maintain a growth mindset (Dweck, 2006). Study of the most effective psychotherapists, or "supershrinks," as they are sometimes called, reveals a series of additional characteristics that provide direction for YCWs. These characteristics include:

- Maintaining a posture of awareness, being alert, observant, and attentive in service-related encounters.
- Comparing new information and what is learned with what is already known.
- Remaining acutely attuned to the vicissitudes of client engagement—actively employing processes of gaining ongoing formal feedback and incorporating that feedback into services on a consistent basis.
- Spending more time on strategies that might be more effective and improve outcomes as opposed to hypothesizing about failed strategies and why methods did not work.
- Expanding awareness when events are stressful and remaining open to options.
- Evaluating and refining strategies and seeking outside consultation, supervision, coaching, and training specific to particular skill sets (Miller, Hubble, & Duncan, 2007; Ricks, 1974).

As in other fields, working hard and demonstrating interest in outcome are clearly characteristics of effective YCWs. They go several steps beyond what other YCWs do. This requires ongoing self-examination and exposure to feedback that although sometimes painful, contributes to growth. There is no known shortcut to this kind of commitment to excellence in helping relationships.

Staying the Course: Getting the Most out of Your Experience

We now come full circle regarding professional development. Due to factors discussed early in this book such as job responsibilities and pressures, hours, and pay, YCWs are vulnerable. A strengths-based philosophy not only provides a way of neutralizing many these threats but of actually improving effectiveness and job satisfaction. But again, mindset and hard work are necessary. Next are a few reminders for each of us as we strive to get the most out of our experiences in YFS:

- Believe in what you do.
- "Walk the talk" by practicing what you preach both personally and professionally.
- Be action oriented.
- Stand by your word.
- Be an energy-giver, not an energy-drainer.
- Be a source of optimism, inspiration, and support to others.
- Give your unconditional energies (body, mind, heart, and soul).
- Be strengths based, not just "positive."
- Recognize what others have to offer—their contributions to change.
- Be a resource to others (clients and colleagues).
- Check in with yourself regularly. (What kind of day have you had? What else is going on with you?)
- Build in restorative "recovery time" every day.
- Find what inspires and gives you hope—this can create more personal energy.
- Remember that hope is contagious!

Further recommendations come from Shawn Achor (2010), who in his book, *The Happiness Advantage: The Seven Principles of Positive Psychology that Fuel Success and Performance at Work,* suggested the following:

- The more you believe in your own ability to succeed, the more likely it is that you will.
- Beliefs are so powerful because they dictate our efforts and actions.
- Constantly scanning the world for the negative comes with a great cost. It undercuts out creativity, raises our stress levels, and lowers our motivation and ability to accomplish goals.
- Optimism, it turns out, is a tremendously powerful predictor of work performance.
- The key is not to completely shut out all of the bad, all of the time, but to have a reasonable, realistic, healthy sense of optimism.
- The best leaders are the ones who show their true colors not during the banner years, but during times of struggle.
- One of the biggest drivers of success is the belief that our behavior matters; that we have control over our future.
- Knowledge is only part of the battle. Without action, knowledge is often meaningless.
- Habits are like financial capital—forming one today is an investment that will automatically give out returns for years to come.
- When we encounter an unexpected challenge of threat, the only way to save ourselves is to hold on tight to the people around us and not let go.

- We are more equipped to handle challenges and obstacles when we pool the resources of those around us and capitalize on even the smallest moments we spend interacting with each other.
- Studies show that the more team members are encouraged to socialize and interact face-to-face, the more engaged they feel, the more energy they have, and the longer they can stay focused on a task.
- The people who actively invest in their relationships are the heart and soul of a thriving organization, the force that drives their teams forward.
- Studies have found that the strength of the bond between manager/supervisor and employee is the prime predictor of both daily productivity and the length of time people stay at their jobs.
- Smiling tricks your brain into thinking you're happy, so it starts producing the neurochemicals that actually do make you happy.
- Each one of us is like that butterfly (the Butterfly Effect). And each tiny move toward a more positive mindset can send ripples of positivity through our organizations, our families, and our communities.

Perhaps former North Carolina basketball coach Jim Valvano provided us with the best possible advice: "To me, there are three things we all should do every day. We should do this every day of our lives. Number one is laugh. You should laugh every day. Number two is think. You should spend some time in thought. And number three is, you should have your emotions moved to tears, could be happiness or joy. But think about it. If you laugh, you think, and you cry, that's a full day. That's a heck of a day. You do that seven days a week, you're going to have something special." If we allow ourselves to become fully immersed in YFS, we will experience such a range of emotions. We again heed the challenge of David Whyte (see Chapter 1) to turn toward rather than away from the great experiences of life.

There are, of course, many "moving parts" when it comes to effectiveness, career longevity, and job satisfaction. Be reminded of what led to you to work in YFS to begin with. Now, consider what keeps you in the field? If you haven't already made the commitment what will it take to make YFS a career? Our field needs people like you—who dedicate themselves to bettering the lives of others. When we have enough good people we can create organizations of excellence.

Unwavering Integrity

It is my hope that, as you finish this book, you feel appreciated and valued. I also hope that you have a renewed or improved sense of what you can do to be an even more effective in your role, YCW or otherwise. It has been said that "integrity is revealed behind closed doors." There may not be a truer statement when it comes to YFS. We do what we do not for accolades but because it is the right thing to do. We lead by example, ambassadors for the promise of the future.

And so we end with a baseball reference, this one of the great ambassadors of all time, Stan "The Man" Musial.

When Musial passed away on January 19, 2013, broadcaster Bob Costas remarked that the lifetime member of the St. Louis Cardinals lacked the demarcation of some of his counterparts. There was no Hollywood-worthy sensationalism—just 22 years of brilliance in baseball and 92 years as a wonderful human being. Beyond his Hall of Fame career and honors such as the Presidential Medal of Freedom . . . was as Costas put it, a man who held the "all-time record for autographs signed, spirits lifted, and acts of kindness large and small." Just as Stan led by example, so can we. It is, after all, what we do that defines us.

Appendix A

Outcome Rating Scale (ORS)

Name: _____ Age (Yrs):____ Sex: M / F
Session #: ____ Date: _____
Who is filling out this form? Please check one: Self_____ Other_____
If other, what is your relationship to this person? _____

Looking back over the last week, including today, help us understand how you have
been feeling by rating how well you have been doing in the following areas of your
life, where marks to the left represent low levels and marks to the right indicate high
levels. *If you are filling out this form for another person, please fill out according to
how you think he or she is doing.*

Individually
(Personal well-being)

|---|

Interpersonally
(Family, close relationships)

|---|

Socially
(Work, school, friendships)

|---|

Overall
(General sense of well-being)

|---|

International Center for Clinical Excellence

www.centerforclinicalexcellence.com

Child Outcome Rating Scale (CORS)

Name: _____ Age (Yrs):____ Sex: M / F
Session #: ____ Date: _____
Who is filling out this form? Please check one: Child_____ Caretaker_____
  If caretaker, what is your relationship to this child?
_____

How are you doing? How are things going in your life? Please make a mark on the
scale to let us know. The closer to the smiley face, the better things are. The closer
to the frowny face, things are not so good. *If you are a caretaker filling out this form,
please fill out according to how you think the child is doing.*

Me
(How am I doing?)

I--I

Family
(How are things in my family?)

I--I

School
(How am I doing at school?)

I--I

Everything
(How is everything going?)

I--I

International Center for Clinical Excellence

www.centerforclinicalexcellence.com

Young Child Outcome Rating Scale (YCORS)

Name:_____ Age (Yrs):____
Sex: M / F_____
Session #:____ Date: _____

Choose one of the faces that shows how things are going for you. Or, you can draw
one below that is just right for you.

International Center for Clinical Excellence

www.centerforclinicalexcellence.com

Session Rating Scale (SRS V.3.0)

Name: _____ Age (Yrs):_____ Sex: M / F
Session #: _____ Date: _____

Please rate today's session by placing a mark on the line nearest to the
description that best fits your experience.

Relationship

I did not feel heard,
understood, and   I--I
respected.

I felt heard,
understood, and
respected.

Goals and Topics

We did *not* work on or
talk about what I   I--I
wanted to work on and
talk about.

We worked on and
talked about what I
wanted to work on
and talk about.

Approach or Method

The therapist's
approach is not a good   I--I
fit for me.

The therapist's
approach is a good
fit for me.

Overall

There was something
missing in the session   I--I
today.

Overall, today's
session was right
for me.

International Center for Clinical Excellence

www.centerforclinicalexcellence.com

Child Session Rating Scale (CSRS)

Name: _____ Age (Yrs):_____ Sex: M / F
Session #: _____ Date: _____

How was our time together today? Please put a mark on the lines below to let us know how you feel.

Listening

did not always
listen to me.

😦   🙂

listened to
me.

How Important

What we did and
talked about was not
really that important
to me.

😦   🙂

What we did
and talked
about were
important to
me.

What We Did

I did not like
what we did
today.

😦   🙂

I liked what
we did
today.

Overall

I wish we could do
something different.

😦   🙂

I hope we do
the same kind
of things next
time.

International Center for Clinical Excellence

www.centerforclinicalexcellence.com

Young Child Session Rating Scale (YCSRS)

Name: _____ Age (Yrs):____
Sex: M / F____
Session #:____ Date: _____

Choose one of the faces that shows how it was for you to be here today. Or, you can draw one below that is just right for you.

Group Session Rating Scale (GSRS)

Name: _____ Age (Yrs):____
ID#: _____ Sex: M / F
Session #:____ Date: _____

Please rate today's group by placing a hash mark on the line nearest to the description that best fits your experience.

Relationship

I did not feel heard,
understood, respected,
and/or accepted by the
leader and/or the group.

I---I

I felt heard,
understood, respected,
and accepted by the
leader and the group.

Goals and Topics

We did *not* work on or
talk about what I
wanted to work on and
talk about.

I---I

We worked on and
talked about what I
wanted to work on and
talk about.

Approach or Method

The leader and/or the
group's approach is
not a good fit for me.

I---I

The leader and
group's approach is a
good fit for me.

Overall

There was something
missing in group
today—I was not
engaged.

I---I

Overall, today's group
was right for me—I felt
engaged.

International Center for Clinical Excellence

www.centerforclinicalexcellence.com

© 2007 Barry L. Duncan, & Scott D. Miller

Client Outcomes Graph v25

(Ages > 19 – Clinical Cutoff = 25)

Client Name: _____   Age: _____

ID: _____

40												
35												
30												
25												
20												
15												
10												
5												
0												
Session Number	1	2	3	4	5	6	7	8	9	10	11	12

------------- SRS Cutoff

━━━━━━━━━━━ ORS Clinical Cutoff

Session #	ORS/CORS	SRS/CSRS
_____	_____	_____
_____	_____	_____
_____	_____	_____
_____	_____	_____
_____	_____	_____
_____	_____	_____
_____	_____	_____
_____	_____	_____
_____	_____	_____
_____	_____	_____
_____	_____	_____
_____	_____	_____
_____	_____	_____
_____	_____	_____
_____	_____	_____

Client Outcomes Graph v28

(Ages 13 to 19 – Clinical Cutoff = 28)

Client Name: _____   Age: _____

ID: _____

	1	2	3	4	5	6	7	8	9	10	11	12
40												
35												
30												
25												
20												
15												
10												
5												
0												
Session Number	1	2	3	4	5	6	7	8	9	10	11	12

------------- SRS Cutoff

▬▬▬▬▬▬▬ ORS Clinical Cutoff

Session #	ORS/CORS	SRS/CSRS
_____	_____	_____
_____	_____	_____
_____	_____	_____
_____	_____	_____
_____	_____	_____
_____	_____	_____
_____	_____	_____
_____	_____	_____
_____	_____	_____
_____	_____	_____
_____	_____	_____
_____	_____	_____
_____	_____	_____
_____	_____	_____
_____	_____	_____
_____	_____	_____

Client Outcomes Graph v32

(Ages ≤ 12 – Clinical Cutoff = 32)

Client Name: _____ Age: _____

ID: _____

Session Number	1	2	3	4	5	6	7	8	9	10	11	12
40												
35												
30												
25												
20												
15												
10												
5												
0												

-------------- SRS Cutoff

━━━━━━━━━ ORS Clinical Cutoff

Session #	ORS/CORS	SRS/CSRS
_____	_____	_____
_____	_____	_____
_____	_____	_____
_____	_____	_____
_____	_____	_____
_____	_____	_____
_____	_____	_____
_____	_____	_____
_____	_____	_____
_____	_____	_____
_____	_____	_____
_____	_____	_____
_____	_____	_____
_____	_____	_____
_____	_____	_____
_____	_____	_____

Appendix B

Initial Service Plan (ISP)
(To be completed at intake/admission)

Date of Admission _____ **YIN #** _____
Name of Client _____ **Date of Birth** _____
Guardian Name and Address _____
_____
_____

Reason for Admission: □ Family Timeout □ Homeless □ Children's Services □ Other _____

Brief Statement of Presenting Concern _____
_____

Initial ORS/CORS Score: _____

Immediate Goals (Should include any Immediate Risks and/or Needs identified in Sections 1 & 5)
1. _____
2. _____
3. _____

Summary of Services to be Provided and Estimated Frequency (Check all that apply)
□ Individual Sessions (#)_____   □ Family Sessions (#)_____   □ Group Sessions (#) _____
□ Case Management (please describe) _____
_____

□ Visitation Plan (see attached)

Preliminary Plan for Discharge_____
_____

_____   _____
Signature of Staff Completing Intake   Signature of Parent/Legal Guardian

_____   _____
Date   Date

_____   _____
Signature of Youth   Date

Reviewed by

_____   _____
Signature of CCM or Shelter Director   Date

□ Copy of ISP given to parent/legal guardian

Revised Service Plan (RSP)
(To be completed for youth with stays of 72 hours or more)
(Attach to ISP)

Date _____ Date of ISP _____ YIN # _____

Name of Client _____ Date of Birth _____

Rationale Regarding Extension of Stay _____

_____

_____

_____

Initial ORS/CORS Score (from intake assessment): _____

Intermediate Goals (In addition to those stated in ISP)

1. _____

2. _____

3. _____

Revised Summary of Services to be Provided and Estimated Frequency (Check all that apply)

☐ Individual Sessions (#)_____

☐ Family Sessions (#)_____

☐ Group Sessions (#) _____

☐ Case Management (please describe) _____

_____

☐ Visitation Plan (see attached)

Revised Plan for Discharge (if applicable) _____

_____

_____

_____   _____
Signature of CCM   Signature of Youth

_____   _____
Date   Date

_____   _____
Signature of Parent/Legal Guardian   Signature of Supervisor

_____   _____
Date   Date

☐ Copy of RSP given to parent/legal guardian

ASSESSMENT

Date of Assessment _____

Name of Client _____ **Date of Birth** _____

Names of Persons (excluding YIN staff) Present During Assessment _____

Name of YIN Staff Completing Assessment _____

1. Brief History and Immediate Risks

Answer to Question #1 on ORS/CORS Assessment: _____ * If any response other than "NO," assess for further risk and note date of last usage, type(s) of drug(s) used, and any current symptoms in section, "Substance Use/Abuse History"

Answer to Question #2 on ORS/CORS Assessment: _____ *If any response other than "NO," complete Suicide Assessment form

ORS/CORS Overall Score: _____

0	10	20	30	40

extremely high risk	high risk	moderate risk	low risk

ATTENTION:
If any single subscale score is <u>5</u> or below
or if the overall score is <u>20</u> or below assess further for risks of harm to self or other

Prior Placement(s)
(Inpatient psychiatric or substance-abuse related hospitalizations, foster care, residential, court-based, transitional living, independent living, job corps)

Where	*Placement Date*	*Length of Stay*
_____	_____	_____
_____	_____	_____
_____	_____	_____
_____	_____	_____

Prior Treatment
(Excluding placements—Including outpatient psychiatric services, counseling/therapy, psychological testing, etc.)

Where	*When*	*Length of Service*
_____	_____	_____
Where _____	*When* _____	*Length of Service* _____
Where _____	*When* _____	*Length of Service* _____

Currently Receiving Services □ Yes □ No **(if "Yes," please ensure contact information is provided in Intake Profile under "Community Resources" section)**

Incidences of Harm to Self or Other(s)

Incident	When	Outcome
_____	_____	_____
_____	_____	_____
_____	_____	_____

Current Risk of Harm   □ Yes □ No

□ To self (if score greater than *"No"* on ORS/CORS question #2 complete *Suicide Assessment* and consult with supervisor)_____

□ To other (if "yes" please explain and consult with supervisor) _____

□ Emotional well-being (i.e., depression, severe anxiety, panic, eating disorders, etc.) _____

□ Other (e.g., behavioral concerns) _____

Substance Use/Abuse

When	Substance(s) Used	Amount	Frequency of Use
_____	_____	_____	_____
_____	_____	_____	_____
_____	_____	_____	_____

Current Substance Use/Abuse (within past 30 days)   □ Yes □ No

(If "yes" to questions of abuse/use, or if concerns raised through observations, or if any score other than *"No"* on ORS/CORS question #1, explain and consult with supervisor) _____

□ Yes □ No   *Does youth smoke?*   □ *Offered information resources for smoking cessation*

Status Offenses

(i.e., runaway, curfew, truancy)

Date	Offense	Outcome
_____	_____	_____
_____	_____	_____
_____	_____	_____
_____	_____	_____

Current Risks   □ Yes □ No

(If "yes" please describe) _____

Legal

Type	*When*	*Disposition/Outcome*
_____	_____	_____
_____	_____	_____
_____	_____	_____
_____	_____	_____

Immediate Concerns   □ Yes □ No

_____

Abuse and/or Neglect

1. □ Physical   2. □ Sexual   3. □ Emotional   4. □ Neglect   5. □ Domestic Violence

_____

_____

_____

_____

Hotline Call Placed   □ Yes □ No

Name of Staff member placing call _____

   Date _____ Time _____ Hotline worker ID _____

   Was hotline call accepted?) □ Yes   □ No

   Other pertinent information _____

Immediate Concerns   □ Yes □ No

_____

Other Trauma/Loss

1. □ Death or Loss of a Loved One   2. □ Sexual Assault   3. □ Rape   4. □ Assault
   5. □ Harassment/Stalking   6. □ Dating Violence

_____

_____

_____

Immediate Concerns   □ Yes □ No

_____

2. **Strengths and Resources**

   Completed "My Strengths" (strengths-based inventory) □ Yes   □ No

   Completed Spokes of Life □ Yes   □ No

3. Reason for Assessment [immediate events and factors contributing to the problem(s)](attach additional sheets as needed). What are the concerns/problems that lead to the assessment? How are the concerns/problems affecting the youth? Family members?

_____
_____
_____
_____
_____
_____
_____
_____
_____
_____
_____
_____

What expectations do the youth and family members have about the type of services needed? What would the youth and family members like to have different/change as a result of services?

_____
_____
_____
_____
_____
_____
_____

Describe the youth and family members' physical and emotional states at the time of assessment.

_____
_____
_____
_____
_____
_____

4. Results of Assessment
- ☐ Admitted to Shelter
- ☐ Admitted to Shelter and Referred to Other Youth In Need Program(s) (Please explain)

  _____

- ☐ Referred to Other Youth In Need Program(s) (Please explain) _____

  _____

- ☐ Referred to Other Community Resource(s) (Please explain) _____

  _____

Complete Section 5 only if Youth is Admitted to Shelter:

5. Immediate Needs and Plan of Action (*If a need is identified, please explain)

Medical

Need(s): _____

_____

- 1) Is the youth currently taking any prescription medications? □ Yes   □ No (If "yes" please list under Section 2A: "Health"); 2) Does youth have enough of medication(s)? □ Yes   □ No (If "no" state plan to obtain meds)

Educational

Need(s): _____

Clothing/Supplies

Need(s): _____

Other

Need(s): _____

□ Releases of Information (excluding St. Charles School District and Medicaid) (please list)

    A _____

    B _____

    C _____

    D _____

□ Shelter program rules explained/discussed

6. Checklist (to be completed by CCM or other master's level staff within 48 hours of Shelter intake)

    □ Philosophy of Services provided to client
    □ Rights and Responsibilities provided to client
    □ Reviewed Intake Profile
    □ Reviewed Initial Assessment (including history, immediate risks, ORS or CORS, SRS or CSRS, Strengths and Resources Inventory, and Spokes of Life)
    □ ORS/CORS and SRS/CSRS data entered into outcome system
    □ Completed Initial Service Plan

_____   _____
Signature of Staff Completing Intake   Date

_____   _____
Signature of Clinical Case Manager   Date

VCRHYP Plan of Care Template

Youth Name: _____ DOB: _____

Youth Care Worker helping Youth Create Plan: _____

Date: _____

VCRHYP Program: ▢ BCP ▢ TLP

Reason for Accessing Services: *What are you most concerned about at this moment?*

_____

_____

_____

Housing Goal:	
What is it about me that will help me accomplish this goal:	
Things I can do to accomplish this goal:	
How will I know I am making progress:	
What strengths or assets am I building:	

Additional Goals: *Refer to Appendix 1 for help*

Goal:	
What is it about me that will help me accomplish this goal:	
Things I can do to accomplish this goal:	
How will I know I am making progress:	
What strengths or assets am I building:	

Goal:	
What is it about me that will help me accomplish this goal:	
Things I can do to accomplish this goal:	
How will I know I am making progress:	
What strengths or assets am I building:	

Goal:	
What is it about me that will help me accomplish this goal:	
Things I can do to accomplish this goal:	
How will I know I am making progress:	
What strengths or assets am I building:	

Potential Barriers To Your Progress – *What do you think are potential barriers to your progress? What are your plans to manage these barriers? (Examples of barriers may include transportation problems, cognitive and/or communication impairments, substance use, etc).*

_____

_____

_____

Strengths:

_____

_____

_____

Support Systems: *Who do you consider to be supportive people in your life?*

List specific individuals here and describe in what ways these people have been resources to you? How can they be helpful to your current situation or in the future?

_____

_____

_____

_____

_____

_____

_____

Coordination of Care – *Create a coordination of care plan if you are receiving services from multiple care providers. Include names and locations of other providers & services they are providing.*

_____

_____

_____

_____

Signatures of Plan Participants:

Signature of Youth: _____

Date: _____

Signature of Parent (*if appropriate*):
_____

Date: _____

Signature of Agency Youth Worker:
_____

Date: _____

Diagnosis Code: _____

Signature of Licensed Practitioner:
_____

Date: _____

My Strengths

My Name: _____   Date: _____

1. Things I like most about myself:

    _____   _____

    _____   _____

2. Things that are most important to me:

    _____   _____

    _____   _____

    _____   _____

    _____   _____

3. Things I like about myself:

    _____   _____

    _____   _____

    _____   _____

    _____   _____

4. Things I do well:

    _____   _____

    _____   _____

    _____   _____

    _____   _____

5. How I can use the things I do well to help me with hard times: _____

    _____

6. Other ways I could handle hard times is by: _____

    _____

7. Things I like to do for fun:

_____   _____

_____   _____

_____   _____

_____   _____

One new thing I would like to do but have not done is: _____

_____

8. I try to take care of myself by: _____

_____

9. What I like most about school is: _____

_____

10. People around me can me help me most by: _____

_____

11. One thing I do not have but would like to have is: _____

_____

12. I like to daydream about: _____

_____

13. If I could change one thing in my life it would be: _____

_____

14. When I think about my future I: _____

_____

15. I smile when: _____

_____

Spokes of Life

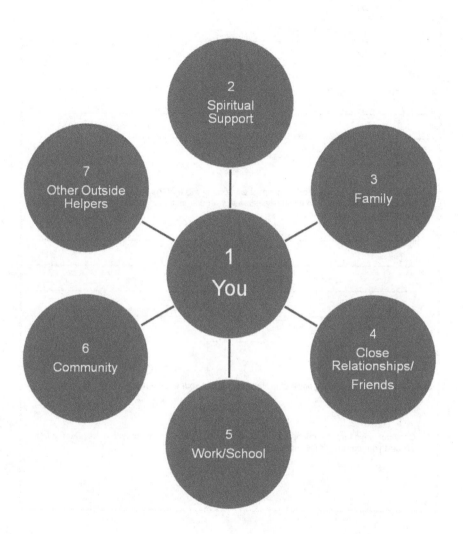

1. Make a list of those persons who fit into your current "Spokes of Life" and write their names in the spaces below. You may have more than person for each spoke or leave a spoke blank if it is not currently applicable to you. It is not the number of people in your life but the quality of your connection to those persons. Having one person you can count on and who supports you is a great place to begin.

_____   _____

_____   _____

_____   _____

_____   _____

_____   _____

2. Next, think about how you might connect with one or more of the persons you listed under Section #2. Make a plan to minimally increase your connection to that person or persons. Write your plan in the spaces below.

_____

_____

_____

_____

_____

3. Write or talk with a YCW or other professional about your experience with increasing your connection to others.

4. Consider ways that you might meet new persons or reconnect with others in the near future to expand your current social support system.

Note: No editing of this pdf as it is an extant, pre-published document.

VCRHYP Resiliency Assessment

Vermont Coalition of Runaway
& Homeless Youth Programs

Youth respond to each question with one of the following responses, followed by a comment line with prompts for voluntary qualitative responses:

No	A Little	Mostly	Definitely

Comment lines provide prompts for engaging in dialogue and better understanding why the youth has selected the response

Safety:

1. I feel safe where I live and/or stay.
Comment line: What are some of the things that help you feel safe where you live/stay?

2. I feel safe in my community.
Comment line: What are some of the things that help you feel safe in the community?

3. I feel safe from verbal and physical abuse.
Comment line: What helps you feel safe from verbal and physical abuse?

4. I am able to work through conflict without using verbal or physical violence.
Comment line: What helps you work through conflict?

5. I can identify healthy relationships.
Comment line: What are some of the characteristics of a healthy relationship?

6. I know how to keep myself out of trouble.
Comment line: What do you do to keep yourself out of trouble?

Well-Being:

7. At this time in my life, I like who I am.
Comment line: what would you change if you could?

8. I do at least one thing to be healthy.
Comment line: What do you do to take care of your health (ie: exercise, meditation, nutrition, primary care physician, dentist, etc).

9. I spend time doing at least one activity that I enjoy.
Comment line: What activity do you enjoy doing? What is your favorite activity?

10. I have healthy ways to manage stress or stressful situations.
Comment line: What do you do to manage stress?

Permanent Connections:

11. I have supportive relationships with one or more family members.
Comment line: What makes them supportive?

12. I have supportive relationships with one or more non-family adults, (i.e. mentor, teacher, counselor, employer, case manager).
Comment line: What makes them supportive?

13. I have one or more supportive friendships.
Comment line: What makes them supportive?

14. I feel that adults in my community respect young adults/youth.
What are some of the ways that adults demonstrate that they value youth?

15. In the past few months, I've done something to help someone else.
Comment: What was it that you did?

Self-Sufficiency:

16. I have done something I am proud of.
Comment line: What is something you are proud of?

17. I have a plan for the future.
Comment line: Tell me about your plan, and what you need to do to get there.

18. I can listen effectively.
Comment line: How do you know?

19. I can usually find the right words to share my thoughts, feelings, and ideas.
Comment line: Give an example...

20. I know what community resources are available to me.
Comment line: What are some of the community resources you have used?

21. I am comfortable accessing community resources.
Comment line: What makes you feel comfortable about accessing those resources?

22. When I have money, I think about saving some of it.
Comment line: Give me an example

Discharge Summary Report (DSR)
(To be completed within 30 days of discharge)

Date of Report _____   YIN # _____
Name of Client _____   Date of Birth _____
Admission Date _____   Disposition Date _____

Reason for Admission: □ Family Timeout □ Homeless □ Children's Services □ Other _____

Brief Statement of Presenting Concern _____

_____
_____
_____
_____

Goals Addressed During Stay
1. _____
2. _____
3. _____

High-Risk Concerns During Stay (i.e., threats of harm to self or other, substance abuse, issues pertaining to family or guardian, etc.) (Brief description, if applicable) _____

_____

* See attached documentation regarding high-risk concern(s) noted above

Services Provided
  □ Temporary Emergency Shelter (# of days) _____
  □ Individual Sessions (#)____ □ Family Sessions (#)_____ □ Group Sessions (#) _____
  □ Case Management (check all the apply)   Placement _____   Basic Needs _____
        Case Coordination _____   Medical Care _____ □ Educational

C/ORS Clinical Cutoffs: 25 (> Age 19)   28 (Ages 13-19)   32 (≤ Age 12)
Initial: C/ORS Score _____   Score above Clinical Cutoff?   Yes   No
Last: C/ORS Score _____   Score above Clinical Cutoff?   Yes   No

Disposition (Circle one)
1. Planned Disposition Above – Joint decision by client or guardian and provider to end services. Final ORS/CORS at or above Clinical Cutoff.
2. Planned Disposition Below – Joint decision by client or guardian and provider to end services. Final ORS/CORS below Clinical Cutoff.
3. Planned Disposition None– Joint decision by client or guardian and provider to end services. No ORS/CORS data.
4. Unplanned Program Disposition Above – Decision by program to discharge client. Final ORS/CORS at or above Clinical Cutoff.
5. Unplanned Program Disposition Below – Decision by program to discharge client. Final ORS/CORS below Clinical Cutoff.

6. Unplanned Client Disposition Above – Unilateral decision by client or guardian to end services. Final ORS/CORS at or above Clinical Cutoff.
7. Unplanned Program Disposition Below – Decision by program to discharge client. Final ORS/CORS below Clinical Cutoff.
8. Not Accepted – Client not admitted into program.
9. Drop out – Unilateral decision by client or guardian to end services. Final ORS/CORS below Clinical Cutoff.
10. No Show - Did not attend scheduled intake or initial session.

Explanation of Disposition: _____
_____
_____

To whom was the youth discharged? _____
Where is youth going?   _____

Aftercare Plan (Check all that apply)
☐ Referred to Other Youth In Need Program(s) (Please explain) _____
_____

☐ Referred to Other Community Resource(s) (Please explain) _____
_____

☐ Additional Recommendations (if any) _____
_____

Report Completed By: **Report Approved By:**

_____   _____
Clinical Case Manager   **Supervisor**

_____   _____
Date   **Date**

References

Achor, S. (2010). *The happiness advantage: The seven principles of positive psychology that fuel success and performance at work*. New York: Crown Business.

Anderson, T., Ogles, B. M., Patterson, C. L., Lambert, M. J., & Vermeersch, D. A. (2009). Therapist effects: Facilitative interpersonal skills as a predictor of therapist effects. *Journal of Clinical Psychology, 65*(7), 755–768.

Anker, M. G., Duncan, B. L., & Sparks, J. A. (2009). Using client feedback to improve couple therapy outcomes: A randomized clinical trial in a naturalistic setting. *Journal of Consulting and Clinical Psychology, 77*(4), 693–704.

APA Presidential Task Force on Evidence-Based Practice. (2006). Evidence-based practice in psychology. *American Psychologist, 61*(4), 271–285.

Appelstein, C. D. (1998). *No such thing as a bad kid: Understanding and responding to the challenging behavior of troubled children and youth*. Weston, MA: The Gifford School.

Bachelor, A., & Horvath, A. (1999). The therapeutic relationship. In S. D. Miller (Ed.), *The heart and soul of change: What works in therapy* (pp. 133–178). Washington, DC: American Psychological Association.

Baldwin, S. A., Wampold, B. E., & Imel, Z. E. (2007). Untangling the alliance–outcome correlation: Exploring the relative importance of therapist and patient variability in the alliance. *Journal of Consulting and Clinical Psychology, 75*(6), 842–852.

Bandler, R., & Grinder, J. (1975). *The structure of magic: A book about language and therapy*. Palo Alto, CA: Science and Behavior Books.

Barford, S. W., & Whelton, W. J. (2010). Understanding burnout in child and youth care workers. *Child Youth Care Forum, 39*, 271–287.

Barkham, M., Mellor-Clark, J., Connell, J., & Cahill, J. (2006). A CORE approach to practice-based evidence: A brief history of the origins and applications CORE-OM and CORE System. *Counselling and Psychotherapy Research, 6*, 3–15.

Bertolino, B. (2014). *The residential youth care worker in action: A collaborative, strengths-based approach* (2nd ed.). New York: Routledge.

Bertolino, B. (2011). Building a culture of excellence: Anatomy of a community agency that works. *Psychotherapy Networker, 35*(3), 32–39.

Bertolino, B. (2010). *Strengths-based engagement and practice: Creating effective helping relationships.* Boston, MA: Allyn & Bacon.

Bertolino, B. (2003). *Change-oriented psychotherapy with adolescents and young adults: The next generation of respectful and effective therapeutic processes and practices.* New York: Norton.

Bertolino, B. (2001). Lights, camera, action!!! Making new meanings through movies. In H. G. Rosenthal (Ed.), *Favorite counseling and therapy homework assignments: 56 therapists share their most creative strategies: Vol. II* (pp. 43–46). Philadelphia, PA: Brunner-Routledge.

Bertolino, B. (1999). *Therapy with troubled teenagers: Rewriting young lives in progress.* New York: Wiley.

Bertolino, B., Bargmann, S., & Miller, S. D. (2013). *Manual 1: What works in therapy: A primer. The ICCE manuals of feedback informed treatment.* Chicago, IL: International Center for Clinical Excellence.

Bertolino, B., Kiener, M. S., & Patterson, R. (2009). *The therapist's notebook for strengths and solution-based therapies: Homework, handouts, and activities.* New York: Routledge/Taylor & Francis.

Bertolino, B., & Miller, S. D. (Eds.). (2013). *The ICCE manuals of feedback informed treatment.* Chicago, IL: International Center for Clinical Excellence.

Bertolino, B., & O'Hanlon, B. (2002). *Collaborative, competency-based counseling and therapy.* Boston, MA: Allyn & Bacon.

Bertolino, B., & Schultheis, G. (2002). *The therapist's handbook for families: Solution-oriented exercises for working with children, youth, and families.* New York: Haworth Press.

Blackwell, L. S., Trzesbieswki, K. H., & Dweck, C. S. (2007).Implicit theories of intelligence predict achievement across an adolescent transition: A longitudinal study and an intervention. *Child Development, 78*(10), 246–263.

Bolin, I. (2006). *Growing up in a culture of respect: Child rearing in Highland Peru.* Austin, TX: University of Texas Press.

Bordin, E. S. (1979). The generalizability of the psychoanalytic concept of the working alliance. *Psychotherapy: Theory, Research, and Practice, 16,* 252–260.

Brendtro, L., du Toit, L., Bath, H., & Van Bockern, S. (2006). Developmental audits with challenging youth. *Reclaiming Children and Youth, 15*(3), 138–146.

Bringhurst, D. L., Watson, C. S., Miller, S. D., & Duncan, B. L. (2006). The reliability and validity of the outcome rating scale: A replication study of a brief clinical measure. *Journal of Brief Therapy, 5*(1), 23–29.

Brown, G. S., Lambert, M. J., Jones, E. R., & Minami, T. (2005). Identifying highly effective psychotherapists in a managed care environment. *American Journal of Managed Care, 11*(8), 513–520.

Brown, J., Dreis, S., & Nace, D. K. (1999). What really makes a difference in psychotherapy outcome? Why does managed care want to know? In M. A. Hubble, B. L. Duncan, & S. D. Miller (Eds.), *The heart and soul of change: What works in therapy* (pp. 389–406). Washington, DC: APA Press.

Brown, L. S. (2008). *Cultural competence in trauma therapy: Beyond the flashback.* Washington, DC: American Psychological Association.

Burlingame, G. B., Lambert, M. J., Reisinger, C. W., Neff, W. L., & Mosier, J. (1995). Pragmatics of tracking mental health outcomes in a managed care setting. *Journal of Mental Health Administration, 22,* 226–236.

Burlingame, G. B., Mosier, J. L., Wells, M. G., Atkin, Q. G., Lambert, M. J., & Whoolery, M. (2001). Tracking the influence of mental health outcome. *Clinical Psychology and Psychotherapy, 8*, 361–379.

Burlingame, G. B., Wells, M. G., & Lambert, M. J. (1996). *Youth Outcome Questionnaire.* Stevenson, MD: American Professional Credentialing Services.

Burlingame, G. B., Wells, M. G., Lambert, M. J., & Cox, J. (2004). Youth Outcome Questionnaire: Updated psychometric properties. In M. E. Maruish (Ed.), *The use of psychological testing for treatment planning and outcome assessment* (3rd ed.). Mahwah, NJ: Lawrence Erlbaum.

Cade, B., & O'Hanlon, W. H. (1993). *A brief guide to brief therapy.* New York: Norton.

Calhoun, L. G., & Tedeschi, R. G. (2012). *Posttraumatic growth in clinical practice.* New York: Routledge.

Campbell, A., & Hemsley, S. (2009). Outcome rating scale and session rating scale in psychological practice: Clinical utility of ultra-brief measures. *Clinical Psychologist, 13*(1), 1–9.

Catalono, R. F., Berglund, M. L., Ryan, J. A.M., Lonczak, H. S., & Hawkins, J. D. (2004). Positive youth development in the United States. *Annals of the American Academy of Political and Social Science, 591*, 98–124.

Chiles, J., Lambert, M. J., & Hatch, A. L. (1999). The impact of psychological interventions on medical cost offset: A meta-analytic review. *Clinical Psychology, 6*(2), 204–220.

Colvin, G. (2008). *Talent is overrated: What really separates world-class performers from everybody else.* New York: Portfolio.

DeChillo, S. (2009). Children on Medicaid found more likely to get antipsychotics. *New York Times,* December 11, 2009.

de Shazer, S. (1985). *Keys to solution in brief therapy.* New York: Norton.

de Shazer, S. (1991). *Putting difference to work.* New York: Norton.

Duncan, B. L., Hubble, M. A., & Miller, S. D. (1997). Stepping off the throne. *Family Therapy Networker, 21*(4), 22–31, 33.

Duncan, B. L., Miller, S. D., & Sparks, J. A. (2004). *The heroic client: A revolutionary way to improve effectiveness through client directed, outcome-informed therapy* (rev. paperback ed.). San Francisco: Jossey-Bass.

Duncan, B. L., Miller, S. D., Sparks, J. A., Claud, D. A., Reynolds, L. R., Brown, J., & Johnson, L. D. (2003). The session rating scale: Preliminary psychometric properties of a "working" alliance measure. *Journal of Brief Therapy, 3*(1), 3–12.

Duncan, B. L., Miller, S. D., Wampold, B. E., & Hubble, M.A. (Eds.). (2010). *The heart and soul of change: Delivering what works in therapy* (2nd ed.). Washington, DC: American Psychological Association.

Duncan, B., Sparks, J., Miller, S., Bohanske, R., & Claud, D. (2006). Giving youth a voice: A preliminary study of the reliability and validity of a brief outcome measure for children, adolescents, and caretakers. *Journal of Brief Therapy, 5*(2), 71–87.

Dunn, T. W., Burlingame, G. M., Walbridge, M., Smith, J., & Crum, M. J. (2005). Outcome assessment for children and adolescents: Psychometric validation of the Youth Outcome Questionnaire 30.1 (Y-OQ®-30.1). *Clinical Psychology and Psychotherapy, 12*, 388–401.

Dweck, C. S. (2006). *Mindset: The new psychology of success.* New York: Ballantine.

Erickson, M. H. (1954). Pseudo-orientation in time as a hypnotherapeutic procedure. *Journal of Clinical and Experiential Hypnosis, 2*, 261–283.

Ericsson, K. A. (2009). Enhancing the development of professional performance: Implications from the study of deliberate practice. In K. A. Ericsson (Ed.), *The development of professional expertise: Toward measurement of expert performance and design of optimal learning environments* (pp. 405–431). New York: Cambridge University Press.

Ericsson, K. A., Charness, N., Feltovich, P. J., & Hoffman, R. R. (Eds.). (2006). *The Cambridge handbook of expertise and expert performance*. New York: Cambridge University Press.

Ericsson, K. A., Krampe, R. T., & Tesch-Romer, C. (1993). The role of deliberate practice in the acquisition of expert performance. *Psychological Review, 100*(3), 363–406.

Ericsson, K. A., Prietula, M. J., & Cokely, E. T. (2007). The making of an expert. *Harvard Business Review, 85*(7–8), 114–121, 193.

Evans, C., Connell, J., Barkham, M., Margison, E., Mellor-Clark, J., McGrath, G., et al. (2002). Towards a standardised brief outcome measure: Psycho metric properties and utility of the CORE-OM. *British Journal of Psychiatry, 180,* 51–60.

Frank, J. D., & Frank, J. B. (1991). *Persuasion and healing: A comparative study of psychotherapy* (3rd ed.). Baltimore, MD: Johns Hopkins University Press.

Frankl, V. (1969). *Will to meaning: Foundations and applications of logotherapy.* New York: World Publishing.

Frankl, V. (1963). *Man's search for meaning: An introduction to logotherapy.* New York: Pocket Books.

Fredrickson, B. (2009). *Positivity: Top-notch research reveals the 3 to 1 ratio that will change your life.* New York: Three Rivers Press.

Frensch, K. M., & Cameron, G. (2002). Treatment of choice or the last resort: A review of residential mental health placements for children and youth. *Child & Youth Care Forum, 31*(5), 307–339.

Garcia, J. A., & Weisz, J. R. (2002). When youth mental health care stops: Therapeutic relationships problems and other reasons for ending youth outpatient treatment. *Journal of Consulting and Clinical Psychology, 70*(2), 439–443.

Gawande, A. (2004). The bell curve: What happens when patients find out how good their doctors really are? *New Yorker.* December 6, 2004.

Gentle Spaces News. (1995). Let there be peace. In J. Canfield, & M. V. Hansen (Eds.), *A 2nd helping of chicken soup for the soul: 101 more stories to open the heart and rekindle the spirit* (pp. 297–298). Deerfield Beach, FL: Health Communications.

Gladwell, M. (2008). *Outliers: The story of success.* New York: Little, Brown.

Gladwell, M. (2005). *Blink: The power of thinking without thinking.* New York: Little, Brown.

Gottman, J. M. (1999). *The marriage clinic.* New York: Norton.

Greenberg, R. P. (1999). Common factors in psychiatric drug therapy. In M. A. Hubble, B. L. Duncan, & S. D. Miller (Eds.), *The heart and soul of change: What works in therapy* (pp. 297–328). Washington, DC: American Psychological Association.

Haas, E., Hill, R. D., Lambert, M. J., & Morrell, B. (2002). Do early responders to psychotherapy maintain treatment gains? *Journal of Clinical Psychology, 58*(9), 1157–1172.

Haley, J. (1973). *Uncommon therapy: The psychiatric techniques of Milton H. Erickson, M.D.* New York: Norton.

Hansen, N., Lambert, M. J., & Forman, E. M. (2002). The psychotherapy dose-response effect and its implication for treatment delivery services. *Clinical Psychology: Science and Practice, 9*(3), 329–343.

Hays, P. A. (2007). *Addressing cultural complexities in practice: Assessment diagnosis and therapy* (2nd ed.). Washington, DC: American Psychological Association.

Hesley, J. W., & Hesley, J. G. (2001). *Rent two films and let's talk in the morning: Using popular movies in psychotherapy* (2nd ed.). New York: Wiley.

Horvath, A. O., & Bedi, R. P. (2002). The alliance. In J. C. Norcross (Ed.), *Psychotherapy relationships that work: Therapist contributions and responsiveness to patient needs* (pp. 37–69). New York: Oxford University Press.

Horvath, A. O., & Greenberg, L. S. (1989). Development and validation of the Working Alliance Inventory. *Journal of Counseling Psychology, 36*(2), 223–233.

Horvath, A. O., & Luborsky, L. (1993). The role of the therapeutic alliance in psychotherapy. *Journal of Consulting and Clinical Psychology, 61*(4), 561–573.

Horvath, A. O., & Symonds, B. D. (1991). Relation between working alliance and outcome in psychotherapy: A meta-analysis. *Journal of Consulting and Clinical Psychology, 38*(2), 139–149.

Howard, K. I., Kopte, S. M., Krause, M. S., & Orlinsky, D. E. (1986). The dose-effect relationship in psychotherapy. *American Psychologist, 41*(2), 159–164.

Howard, K. I., Moras, K., Brill, P. L., Martinovich, Z., & Lutz, W. (1996). Evaluation of psychotherapy: Efficacy, effectiveness, and patient progress. *American Psychologist, 51*(10), 1059–1064.

Howe, M. J. A. (1999). *Genius explained.* New York: Cambridge University Press.

Hwang, J., & Hopkins, K. (2012). Organizational inclusion, commitment, and turnover among child welfare workers: A multilevel mediation analysis. *Administration in Social Work, 36,* 23–39.

Jacobson, N. S., & Truax, P. (1991). Clinical significance: A statistical approach to defining meaningful change in psychotherapy research. *Journal of Consulting and Clinical Psychology, 59*(1), 12–19.

Johansson, F. (2002). *The Medici effect: Breakthrough insights at the intersection of ideas, concepts, and cultures.* Boston, MA: Harvard Business School Press.

Kivlighan, D. (2001). Patterns of working alliance development. *Journal of Consulting and Clinical Psychology, 47,* 362–371.

Kraft, S., Puschner, B., Lambert, M. J., & Kordy, H. (2006). Medical utilization and treatment outcome in mid- and long-term outpatient psychotherapy. *Psychotherapy Research, 16*(2), 241–249.

Lambert, M. J. (2010). *Prevention of treatment failure: The use of measuring, monitoring, and feedback in clinical practice.* Washington, DC: American Psychological Association.

Lambert, M. J., & Bergin, A. E. (1994). The effectiveness of psychotherapy. In A. E. Bergin, & S. L. Garfield (Eds.), *Handbook of psychotherapy and behavior change* (4th ed.) (pp. 143–189). New York: Wiley.

Lambert, M. J., & Burlingame, G. R. (1996). *Outcome Questionnaire 45.2.* Wilmington, DE: American Professional Credentialing Services.

Lambert, M. J., & Burlingame, G. R., Umphress, V., Hansen, N. B., Vermeersch, D. A., Clouse, G. C. et al. (1996). The reliability and validity of the Outcome Questionnaire. *Clinical Psychology, 3*(4), 249–258.

Lambert, M. J., & Finch, A. E. (1999). The Outcome Questionnaire. In M. E. Maruish (Ed.), *The use of psychological testing for treatment planning and outcome assessment* (2nd ed.). Mahwah, NJ: Lawrence Erlbaum.

Lawson, D. (1994). Identifying pretreatment change. *Journal of Counseling and Development, 72*(3), 244–248.

Le Guin, U. K. (1968). *A wizard of Earthsea.* New York: Bantam Books.

Linley, P. A., & Joseph, S. (2004). Positive change following trauma and adversity: A review. *Journal of Traumatic Stress, 17*(1), 11–21.

Lord, B. B. (1990). *Legacies: A Chinese mosaic.* New York: Fawcett Columbine.

Luborsky, L., Barber, J. P., Siqueland, L., Johnson, S., Najavits, L. M., Frank, A. et al. (1996). The revised Helping Alliance Questionnaire (HAq-II): Psychometric properties. *Journal of Psychotherapy: Practice and Research, 5*(3), 260–271.

Luborsky, L., Crits-Christoph, P., McLellan, T., Woody, G., Piper, W., Imber, S. et al. (1986). Do therapists vary much in their success? Findings in four outcome studies. *American Journal of Orthopsychiatry, 56,* 501–512.

Lyubomirsky, S. (2007). *The how of happiness: A scientific approach to getting the life you want.* New York: Penguin.

McCoy, H., & McKay, C. (2006). Preparing social workers to identify and integrate culturally affirming bibliotherapy in treatment. *Social Work Education, 25*(7), 680–693.

McMillen, J. C., Morris, L., & Sherraden, M. (2004). Ending social work's grudge match: Problems versus strengths. *Families in Society, 85*(3), 317–325.

Madsen, W. C. (2007). *Collaborative therapy with multi-stressed families* (2nd ed.). New York: Guilford.

Maslow, A. H. (1943). A theory of human motivation. *Psychological Review, 50*(4), 370–396.

Masten, A. S., Cutuli, J. J., Herbers, J. E., & Reed, M. G. J. (2009). Resilience in development. In C. R. Snyder, & S. J. Lopez (Eds.), *Oxford Handbook of Positive Psychology* (2nd ed.) (pp. 117–131). New York: Oxford University Press.

Miller, S. D., & Duncan, B. L. (2004). *The outcome and session rating scales: Administration and scoring manual.* Chicago, IL: Institute for the Study of Therapeutic Change.

Miller S. D., & Duncan, B. L. (2000). *The Outcome Rating Scale.* Chicago, IL: Author.

Miller, S. D., Duncan, B. L., Brown, J. S., Sparks, J. A., Claud, D. A. (2003). The Outcome Rating Scale: A preliminary study of the reliability, validity, and feasibility of a brief, visual, analog measure. *Journal of Brief Therapy, 2,* 91–100.

Miller, S. D., Duncan, B. L., & Hubble, M. A. (1997). *Escape from Babel: Toward a unifying language for psychotherapy practice.* New York: Norton.

Miller, S. D., Duncan, B. L., Sorrell, R., & Brown, G. S. (2005). The Partners for Change Outcome Management System. *Journal of Clinical Psychology, 61*(2), 199–208.

Miller, S. D., Hubble, M. A., & Duncan, B. L. (2007). Supershrinks: What's the secret of their success? *Psychotherapy Networker, 31,* 27–35, 56–57.

Myers, D., & Deiner, E. (1995). Who is happy? *Psychological Science, 6,* 10–19.

Ness, M. E., & Murphy, J. J. (2001). Pretreatment change reports by clients in a university counseling center: Relationship to inquiry technique, client and situational variables. *Journal of College Counseling, 4*(1), 20–31.

Norcross, J. C. (Ed.). (2011). *Psychotherapy relationships that work: Evidence-based responsiveness* (2nd ed.). New York: Oxford University Press.

O'Hanlon, B., & Bertolino, B. (2012). *The therapist's notebook on positive psychology: Activities, exercises, and handouts.* New York: Routledge/Taylor & Francis.

O'Hanlon, B., & Bertolino, B. (2002). *Even from a broken web: Brief, respectful solution-oriented therapy for sexual abuse and trauma.* New York: Norton.

O'Hanlon, B., & Bertolino, B. (1998). *Even from a broken web: Brief, respectful solution-oriented therapy for sexual abuse and trauma.* New York: Wiley.

O'Hanlon, W. H. (1987). *Taproots: Underlying principles of Milton Erickson's therapy and hypnosis.* New York: Norton.

O'Hanlon, W. H., & Weiner-Davis, M. (2003). *In search of solutions: A new direction in psychotherapy* (2nd ed.). New York: Norton.

Orlinsky, D. E., Grawe, K., & Parks, B. K. (1994). Process and outcome in psychotherapy—noch einmal. In A. E. Bergin, & S. L. Garfield (Eds.), *Handbook of psychotherapy and behavior change* (4th ed.) (pp. 270–378). New York: Wiley.

Orlinsky, D. E., Rønnestad, M. H., & Willutzki, U. (2004). Fifty years of process-outcome research: Continuity and change. In M. J. Lambert (Ed.), *Bergin and Garfield's handbook of psychotherapy and behavior change* (5th ed.) (pp. 307–390). New York: Wiley.

Pascale, R., Sternin, J., & Sternin, M. (2010). *The power of positive deviance: How unlikely innovators resolve the world's toughest problems.* Boston, MA: Harvard Business Press.

Percevic, R., Lambert, M. J., & Kordy, H. (2006). What is the predictive value of responses to psychotherapy for its future course? Empirical explorations and consequences for outcome monitoring. *Psychotherapy Research, 16*(3), 364–273.

Peterson, C. (2006). *A primer in positive psychology.* New York: Oxford University Press.

Prochaska, J. O., & DiClemente, C. C. (2005). The transtheoretical approach. In J. C. Norcross, & M. R. Goldfried (Eds.), *Handbook of psychotherapy integration* (2nd ed.) (pp. 147–171). New York: Oxford University Press.

Prochaska, J. O., DiClemente, C. C., & Norcross, J. C. (1992). In search of how people change: Applications to addictive behaviors. *American Psychologist, 47,* 1102–1114.

Prochaska, J. O., & Norcross, J. C. (2002). *Systems of psychotherapy: A transtheoretical analysis* (5th ed.). Pacific Grove, CA: Brooks-Cole.

Proyouthwork America. (2011). *Youth work practice: A status report on professionalization and expert opinion about the future of the field.* Bonita Springs, FL: Proyouthwork America.

Rapp, C. A., & Goscha, R. J. (2012). *The strengths-model: A recovery-oriented approach to mental health* (3rd ed.). New York: Oxford University Press.

Reese, R. J., Norsworthy, L. A., & Rowlands, S. R. (2009). Does a continuous feedback system improve psychotherapy outcome? *Psychotherapy: Theory, Research, Practice, Training, 46,* 418–431.

Reese, R. J., Usher, E. L., Bowman, D.C., Norsworthy, L. A., Halstead, J. L., Rowlands, S. R. et al. (2009). Using client feedback in psychotherapy training: An analysis of its influence on supervision and counselor self-efficacy. *Training and Education in Professional Psychology, 3*(3), 157–168.

Reiter, B. (2013). Birds on a power line. *Sports Illustrated, 118*(22), 62–69.

Ricks, D. (1974). Supershrink: Methods of a therapist judged successful on the basis of adult outcomes of adolescent patients. In D. Ricks, A. Thomas, & M. Roff (Eds.), *Life history research in psychopathology: Vol. 3* (pp. 275–297). Minneapolis, MN: University of Minnesota.

Robinson, K. (2011). *Out of our minds: Learning to be creative* (2nd ed.). Chichester: Capstone.

Rogers, C. R. (1957). The necessary and sufficient conditions of therapeutic personality change. *Journal of Consulting Psychology, 21,* 95–103.

Rogers, C. R. (1951). *Client-centered therapy: Its current practice, implications, and theory.* Boston, MA: Houghton-Mifflin.

Saleeby, D. (2012). *The strengths-perspective in social work practice* (6th ed). Boston, MA: Pearson.

Sapyta, J., Riemer, M., & Bickman, L. (2005). Feedback to clinicians: Theory, research, and practice. *Journal of Clinical Psychology: In Session, 61*(2), 145–153.

Seita, J., Mitchell, M., & Tobin, C. (1996). *In whose best interest?* Elizabethtown, PA: Continental Press.

Seligman, M. E. P. (2011). *Flourish: A visionary new understanding of happiness and well-being.* New York: Free Press.

Seligman, M. E. P. (2002). *Authentic happiness: Using the new positive psychology to realize your potential for lasting fulfillment.* New York: Free Press.

Seligman, M. E. P. (1991). *Learned optimism: How to change your mind and your life.* New York: Knopf.

Seligman, M. E. P., & Csikszentmihalyi, M. (2000). Positive psychology: An introduction. *American Psychologist, 55*(1), 5–14.

Shaffer, D., Gould, M. S., Brasic, J., Ambosini, P., Fisher, P., Bird, H. et al. (1983). A children's global assessment scale (CGAS). *Archives of General Psychiatry, 40*(11), 1228–1231.

Solomon, G. (2001). *Reel therapy: How movies inspire you to overcome life's problems.* New York: Lebhar-Friedman Books.

Sparks, J. A., & Munro, M. L. (2009). Client-directed wraparound: The client as connector in community collaboration. *Journal of Systemic Therapies, 28*(3), 63–76.

Staudt, M., Howard, M. O., & Drake, B. (2001). The operationalization, implementation, and effectiveness of the strengths-based perspective. *Journal of Social Service Research, 27*(3), 1–21.

Steering Committee. (2001). Empirically supported therapy relationships: Conclusions and recommendations of the Division 29 Task Force. *Psychotherapy, 38*(4), 495–497.

Sue, D. W., Arredondo, P., & McDavis, R. J. (1992). Multicultural counseling competencies and standards: A call to the profession. *Journal of Counseling and Development, 70*(4), 477–486.

Summitt, P. H., & Jenkins, S. (2013). *Sum it up: 1,098 victories, a couple of irrelevant losses, and a life in perspective.* New York: Crown Archetype.

Surowiecki, J. (2004). *The wisdom of crowds.* New York: Anchor Books.

Swift, J. K., Greenberg, R. P., Whipple, J. L., & Kominiak, N. (2012). Practice recommendations for reducing premature termination in therapy. *Professional Psychology: Research and Practice, 43*(4), 379–387.

Syed, M. (2010). *Bounce: Mozart, Federer, Picasso, Beckham, and the science of success.* New York: HarperCollins.

Tedeschi, R. G., Calhoun, L. G., & Cann, A. (2007). Evaluating resource gain: Understanding and misunderstanding posttraumatic growth. *Applied Psychology: An Interactional Review, 56*(3), 396–406

Tilsen, J. (2013). *Therapeutic conversations with queer youth: Transcending homonormativity and constructing preferred identities.* New York: Aronson.

van der Kolk, B. A. (1994). The body keeps score: Memory and the emerging psychobiology of posttraumatic stress. *Harvard Review of Psychiatry, 1,* 253–265.

van der Kolk, B. A., McFarlane, A. C., & Weisaeth, L. (Eds.). (1996). *Traumatic stress: The effects of overwhelming experience on mind, body, and society.* New York: Guilford.

Vilakazi, H. (1993). Rediscovering lost truths. *Reclaiming Children and Youth, 1*(4), 37.

Walfish, S., McAlister, B., O'Donnnell, P., & Lambert, M. J. (2012). An investigation of self-assessment bias in mental health providers. *Psychological Reports, 110*(2), 639–644.

Wampold, B. E. (2001). *The great psychotherapy debate: Models, methods, and findings.* Mahwah, NJ: Lawrence Erlbaum.

Wampold, B. E., & Brown, G. S. (2005). Estimating variability in outcomes attributable to therapists: A naturalistic study of outcomes in managed care. *Journal of Consulting and Clinical Psychology, 73*(5), 914–923.

Warren, J. S., Nelson, P. L., Burlingame, G. M., & Mondragon, S. A. (2012). Predicting patient deterioration in youth mental health services: Community mental health versus managed care settings. *Journal of Clinical Psychology, 68*(1), 24–40.

Warren, J. S., Nelson, P. L., Mondragon, S. A., Baldwin, S. A., & Burlingame, G. A. (2010). Youth psychotherapy change trajectories and outcomes in usual care: Community mental health versus managed care settings. *Journal of Consulting and Clinical Psychology, 78*(2), 144–155.

Waters, D. B., & Lawrence, E. C. (1993). *Competence, courage, and change: An approach to family therapy.* New York: Norton.

Wedding, D., Boyd, M., & Niemiec, R. M. (2005). *Movies and mental illness: Using films to understand psychotherapy.* Cambridge, MA: Hogrefe & Huber Publishing.

Weiner-Davis, M., de Shazer, S., & Gingerich, W. J. (1987). Using pretreatment change to construct a therapeutic solution: An exploratory study. *Journal of Marital and Family Therapy, 13,* 359–363.

Wen, P. (2010). A legacy of unintended side effects. *Boston Globe,* December 12, 2010.

Whipple, J. L., Lambert, M. J., Vermeersch, D. A., Smart, D. W., Nielsen, S. L., & Hawkins, E. J. (2003). Improving the effects of psychotherapy: The use of early identification of treatment and problem-solving strategies in routine practice. *Journal of Counseling Psychology, 50*(1), 59–68.

Whitaker, R. (2010). *Anatomy of an epidemic: Magic bullets, psychiatric drugs, and the astonishing rise of mental illness in America.* New York: Crown.

White, M., & Epston, D. (1990). *Narrative means to therapeutic ends.* New York: Norton.

Whyte, D. (2011). Keynote address: Crossing the unknown sea. 2011 Psychotherapy Networker Symposium. Washington, DC.

Wierzbicki, M., & Pekarik, G. (2002). A meta-analysis of psychotherapy dropout. *Professional Psychology: Research and Practice, 24*(2), 190–195.

Wilson, M. (2009). Supporting the direct-service workforce in behavioral health programs for children and youth in New Hampshire: A report to the New Hampshire Endowment for Health. New England Network for Child, Youth and Family Services. Retrieved from www.nenetwork.org/publications/NH_Behav_Hlth_Workforce.pdf

Wolin, S, J., & Wolin, S. (1993). *The resilient self: How survivors of troubled families rise above adversity.* New York: Villard Books.

Zeig, J. K. (Ed.). (1985a). *Ericksonian psychotherapy: Vol. I: Structures.* New York: Brunner/Mazel.

Zeig, J. K. (Ed.). (1985b). *Ericksonian psychotherapy: Vol. II: Clinical applications.* New York: Brunner/Mazel.

Zeig, J. K. (Ed.). (1982). *Ericksonian approaches to hypnosis and psychotherapy.* New York: Brunner/Mazel.

Index